The Hurlers

The Hurlers

*The First All-Ireland Championship and
the Making of Modern Hurling*

PAUL ROUSE

PENGUIN
IRELAND

PENGUIN IRELAND

UK | USA | Canada | Ireland | Australia
India | New Zealand | South Africa

Penguin Ireland is part of the Penguin Random House group of companies
whose addresses can be found at global.penguinrandomhouse.com

First published 2018
001

Copyright © Paul Rouse, 2018

The moral right of the author has been asserted

Set in 13.5/16 pt Garamond MT Std
Typeset by Jouve (UK), Milton Keynes
Printed and bound in Great Britain by Clays Ltd, Elcograf S.p.A.

A CIP catalogue record for this book is available from the British Library

ISBN: 978–1–844–88439–1

www.greenpenguin.co.uk

Penguin Random House is committed to a
sustainable future for our business, our readers
and our planet. This book is made from Forest
Stewardship Council® certified paper.

'The history of this championship is a most disgraceful one . . .'

Sport, 5 April 1888

Contents

For Cáit, Éilis and Joe

Prologue:
Forty-two Hurlers

Easter Sunday, 1 April 1888

Forty-two men stand in military formation on the roadway outside William Cunningham's hotel in the middle of Birr, a small town in the south of King's County. It is a cold, fine afternoon. At the head of the formation stand three Fenians, members of the Irish Republican Brotherhood: a revolutionary society dedicated to the overthrow of British rule and the establishment of an Irish republic. The one giving the orders is James Lynam, said to be a veteran of the American Civil War; he is now one of the chief Fenian organizers in Galway. The others are Andrew Callanan and Hugh Ryan, who regularly feature in police Special Branch reports of subversive activity across Co. Tipperary. All three were in Hayes' Hotel, in Thurles, five months ago, when one of their colleagues fired a shot in over the head of Michael Cusack, the founder of the Gaelic Athletic Association. They were also involved when the following day's GAA annual convention descended into a brawl between Republicans and priests.

The forty-two men arrayed behind Lynam, Callanan and Ryan are hurlers. They represent the two clubs – Meelick, from East Galway, and Thurles, from Co. Tipperary – that have come to Birr to play in the first-ever All-Ireland hurling final. They stand in parallel lines in front of the hotel. The

I

Thurles men are carrying their hurleys upright against their shoulders like long rifles. Their jerseys are green, with a little galaxy of stars around the centre. The Meelick men are also wearing green jerseys, but with a large white stripe running across the middle; and on their heads are green knitted caps with tassels. The hurlers still have on their everyday boots, though these will later mostly be discarded: many of the players will compete barefooted.

With everyone in position, James Lynam calls them to attention and shouts: 'Right, about.' The hurlers turn as one and march shoulder to shoulder through the streets of Birr. It has quickly become a tradition that, when a big hurling match is played in a town, the parade of hurlers is led by a local band, to draw people to the match and to create a sense of pageant. But not on this day. The Frankford Brass Band, which regularly plays music at the hurling matches in Birr, is out at a huge demonstration at nearby Broughal Castle, where 2,000 people are protesting against the eviction of a farmer, Rody Dooly. The Irish countryside continues to be convulsed by waves of boycotting, evictions and murder. In the heartlands of hurling, this 'Land War' between landlords and their impoverished tenantry is waged fiercely. The Thurles and Meelick teams both include men who will, in the coming years, be evicted from their farms.

To the cheering of the townspeople, the hurlers parade through the streets towards the hurling field, off Railway Road on the edge of town. The field, measuring 100 yards wide by 200 yards long, is level and not too grassy. It has already been used for local championship matches and has drawn general approval from players and spectators.

Around 3,000 people wait in the field for the hurlers. Hawkers sell their wares, and tricks-o'-the-loop do a roaring trade while other men try to entice spectators to gamble on which of three thimbles covers the pea. Among the crowd are off-duty members of a British army regiment, the Scottish Highlanders, who are stationed in nearby Crinkle barracks and who regularly attend hurling matches around Birr. Some of the spectators have travelled with the teams from Thurles and from Meelick; many more have come by train, by horse and cart, by bicycle and on foot from all across North Tipperary, King's County, Queen's County and Galway, even though they are not associated with either team. They have come to the final for the love of hurling and for the day out. Some will enjoy the day too well and end up in court charged with drunkenness.

Waiting in the centre of the field is the referee, Patrick White, a native of Toomevara, Co. Tipperary, who lives and works as a butcher in Birr. White initially declined the job of refereeing on account of his links with Tipperary, but was eventually persuaded that his impartiality was beyond dispute. At 3 p.m. he calls the hurlers to the middle of the field and, for the second time that day, the two teams line up alongside one another. They lower the blades of their hurleys to the ground and set themselves to play. White takes the red leather ball into his hand and throws it in between the hurlers. Amid the jostling shoulders and swinging timber, the first All-Ireland hurling final is under way.[1]

1. 'Splendid and by no means dangerous'

Modern hurling began with an anonymous letter to a newspaper. The man who wrote the letter – published in the *Irish Times* on 21 December 1882 – said that he had played hurling in his youth and he lamented that the game had now disappeared from his life:

> No such glorious game ever was played as real old Irish hurling . . . The game is manly, generous and exhilarating, giving full scope to every energy, and practically devoid of serious danger . . . Hurling requires as much coolness, eye, judgment, muscle as cricket, and all the élan, fire, speed and self-devotion of football . . . Were such a game played in the Phoenix Park, I am certain ten thousand people would assemble to witness such a splendid and by no means dangerous national revival.

And revival it would have to be – because hurling was dead to Dublin. Indeed, there was no hurling club anywhere in Ireland. The game survived on the margins of modern life, played in traditional ways by a handful of rural communities in areas such as North Tipperary and East Galway. Hurling's antiquity had seen it celebrated in Ireland's heroic literature, bardic and legal texts, newspapers and travel journals extending back across a millennium of history. But the glories of hurling appeared almost entirely confined to the past, evoked in songs and poems, echoes of a time when it was the most celebrated sport on the island. The modernization of sport in the second half of the nineteenth century had seen clubs for cricket, rugby, soccer, tennis and many others established across Ireland. It was a phenomenon that had remade the Irish sporting world – and hurling had been left behind. There was no agreed set of rules, no governing body, no structure. And even in those redoubts where the game clung on to older ways, the forces of law, pressure from a Catholic Church determined to exercise much tighter social control, post-Famine emigration, and the gathering swell of British sporting culture placed still greater pressure on hurling.

Now, though, in this letter to the *Irish Times*, a man who signed himself as 'Omega', and who lived at 6 Fairview Avenue on the north side of Dublin city, called for the modernization of this 'true old Irish game'. 'Omega' explained that he was one of just four people in Dublin who knew the game of hurling 'thoroughly', and – as the eldest of the four – he had been deputed to write the letter and test the water. He said that he was 'too insignificant' in himself to make a revival happen – but that if he were to receive even a dozen communications, he would organize a meeting and help to found a hurling club.

I

In the second half of the nineteenth century, newspapers flourished across Ireland. The abolition of stamp duty together with enhanced printing technology made newspapers cheaper. Improved transport and the expansion of towns allowed for more efficient distribution, while rising rates of literacy – by 1881, 75 per cent of the Irish population was literate – offered new potential readers. The consequence was an explosion in the number of newspapers published in Ireland and a transformation in how people communicated with each other. This transformation was fundamental to the making of modern hurling.

The day after 'Omega' published his letter in the *Irish Times*, a second letter appeared in the paper. Its author was Michael Cusack, a schoolteacher and journalist. Cusack had been born into poverty in Co. Clare at the height of the Great Famine of the 1840s, but now ran a school from his Dublin home on Gardiner Place. Cusack's Academy was exceptionally successful in preparing Irish boys for examinations to join the civil service.[1] Since the summer of 1882, Cusack had also been contributing a weekly column called 'Our Boys' to the *Shamrock*, a Dublin-based magazine. In this column, Cusack wrote of mathematics and literature and history; he explained how fireworks could be made and how magic tricks could be done; he entertained and educated and provoked.[2]

Now, in his letter to the newspaper, Cusack spoke of his great pleasure at the proposed revival of hurling. He described it as the 'most magnificent of all games' and wrote: 'I have no doubt the athletes of the coming generations will bless us for the service we have rendered them.' He professed his willingness to help and said that he would gladly be a goalkeeper in any match that might be played.[3] It is all but certain that he was one of the four people in Dublin to whom 'Omega' referred as being thoroughly knowledgeable in the game of hurling.

That it was the *Irish Times* that was the publisher of this correspondence is fascinating in itself. Already in 1882 it was considered a bastion of unionism, and it is something of a puzzle that this paper – rather than, say, the nationalist *Free-man's Journal* – should have been chosen by 'Omega'. In any event, a further letter appeared the following day from a man called Vivian Crowe, who wrote that 'this most ancient Irish game should be revived, and Irishmen should not let all the games of their ancestors die out before new ones less worthy'. He was joined in those sentiments by 'F. F. B.', who wrote that he had often watched the peasants of Connacht play the game on Sunday afternoons and lamented the fact that it was now almost forgotten. He, too, promised his support and said he knew of several others who would join a hurling club.

Three days later, on St Stephen's Day, 'Omega' sought to give substance to the talk of revival that he had started. He wrote to say that he was 'highly honoured' that his proposal had been so enthusiastically received. It was, he said, now time for 'the crucial test'. He had been given the use of a lecture room at the Royal College of Surgeons at 35 York Street, and he was calling a meeting for 2 p.m. on the following Saturday, 30 December 1882. The purpose of the meeting would be to form a hurling club, and 'I particularly ask the favour of the presence of that champion among the athletes, Mr. Michael Cusack. As he is the Alpha, so I am the Omega.'

II

Among the difficulties facing the hurling revivalists was the fact that there was already a game being played in Dublin called 'hurley'. This game had been played at Trinity College since the 1860s at least, and the Dublin University Hurley Club had published its rules in the *Handbook of Cricket in*

Ireland, 1869–1870. The club's members regularly played internal matches such as 'Smokers v Non-Smokers', and 'The First Team v The Philosophical Society'. Throughout the 1870s – as part of the general expansion in organized sport in Ireland – hurley spread beyond the confines of the university. It became important in the sporting life of various prestigious schools in Dublin, including High School, Rathmines School and King's Hospital. Rugby clubs such as Lansdowne took on the game and clubs were also formed from workplaces such as the Royal Bank. The Irish Hurley Union was established at Trinity College in 1879, setting out its objective as the establishment of 'a code of rules to be played by all clubs which should join the Union, and to foster the noble and manly game of hurley in this its native country'.[4]

Although hurley was codified in Dublin, the manner in which it was influenced by English hockey was clear. When the rules of hurley were first printed in 1869, they included provisions for offside and for hitting off one side of the stick only. And at that first meeting of the Irish Hurley Union in 1879, 'the secretary was directed to apply to several English hockey clubs for copies of their rules of the game, to aid the Union in forming rules which should meet with the approval of all hurley players'.[5]

'Omega' condemned hurley as 'a melancholy spectacle . . . utterly uninteresting'. The game, he wrote, had 'no pluck, no dash, no physical prowess'. Ultimately, hurley's great defining characteristic was the 'complete apathy' that it inspired.[6] These words were echoed by Michael Cusack, who said that those who played hurley were merely 'civilised eunuchs' and 'grown-up little boys'.[7]

The game of hurling, as envisaged by the men who wished to revive it, would be something quite different. Drawing on the recollections of their youth and on the imagery of hurling that flowed from the stories of Cúchulainn and the myths of Irish history, they imagined a game that would be free and natural and unrestrained. 'Omega' wrote: 'The rules are few and easily learned . . . I long to see the ball flying in the air, stopped by the hurl, and ere it reached the ground, driven back 50 yards, to be stopped again, and this time to be carried on the flat of the hurl by a player rushing towards the opposite goal, dodging his opponents, or tossing the ball over their heads, he slips through them, and again gets at his ball before it touches the earth.'[8]

III

The lecture room at the Royal College of Surgeons was made available by Dr Hugh A. Auchinleck, Professor of Medical Jurisprudence. Dr Auchinleck was an unlikely midwife for what would become a major act of Irish cultural nationalism. He was a regular attendee at state balls and levees given in Dublin Castle by the Lord Lieutenant; an active member of the Church of Ireland, serving as a churchwarden and on school boards; and, later, he would become a prominent Freemason.[9] When the meeting began on Saturday 30 December 1882, there was just a small crowd present, 'the day being exceedingly wet'.[10] Among these was a delegation of hurley players.

On the motion of Michael Cusack, Auchinleck was chosen as chair and 'Omega' was asked to act as secretary. Both agreed – and 'Omega' was now revealed to be Frank A. Potterton, a Co. Down man who was a graduate of Trinity College. He was friendly with Michael Cusack, who had connections in the county: he'd worked in St Colman's College in Newry and had married a Down woman, Margaret Woods.[11]

A committee of eight men – including Auchinleck, Cusack and Potterton – was chosen to draw up a code of rules for a new club and for the game it would play. The hurley delegation promised support for the Dublin Hurling Club on condition that the rules for hurley were to be properly studied and incorporated as far as possible into the rules for hurling. A motion was passed agreeing to this, 'with such alterations as the superiority of the old game [hurling] and machinery render necessary'.[12] A second meeting was held five days later – again in Auchinleck's lecture room – and at this meeting the Dublin Hurling Club was formally established and a set of rules adopted. Auchinleck was elected president, Cusack was chosen as vice-president and Lloyd Christian was installed as secretary.[13] 'No hurling has been played in Dublin . . . within the memory of the oldest inhabitant,' wrote Michael Cusack a few weeks later. This new club now set about changing that.[14]

IV

The next challenge was to secure a suitable venue for play. At a meeting of the Dublin Hurling Club held in Cusack's Academy on Monday 8 January 1883 – and with Michael Cusack in the chair – it was resolved to write to the All-Ireland Polo Club, asking for the use of their grounds, the Nine Acres, in the Phoenix Park. This request was granted, and the club set about holding its first practice match at 2.30 p.m. on the following Saturday, 13 January.[15]

Final preparations for that match were to take place the previous evening at Cusack's Academy – but there was a problem. Frank Potterton had described hurling as a game played with 'a kind of a bat called a "hurl", made of well-seasoned, long-grained ash'. And the ball to be used was to be made of cork that was boiled in milk and gum and then stitched with leather.[16] But it proved extremely difficult to get sticks suitable for hurling in Dublin. Eventually, it was necessary to order specially made hurls from Fitzsimons' Factory in the city – but these did not arrive in time for the scheduled practice match. At the last minute, the match had to be postponed.[17]

It took another two weeks for the hurls to arrive, and the first hurling practice took place at the Polo Grounds on Saturday 27 January 1883. Two teams were picked by Michael Cusack from the 'colts and oldsters' who turned out, and a 'fast hour's play ensued'. The following day's *Irish Times* contained the news that 'all the preliminary difficulties which beset the path of the executive of this club in their efforts to revive this old national game [had] been overcome'.[18] The first public match took place on Saturday 3 February 1883, and there were further matches on each of the remaining Saturdays that month. The rules were amended in the light of experience of actual play and the game of hurling as played by the Dublin Hurling Club began to take a more definite shape, with all members expected to conform to the rules or 'be prevented from playing'.[19] The new rules were distributed to all members and published in the *Irish Sportsman* newspaper.[20] Matches continued on Saturday afternoons through March and into early April. Teams were picked by Michael Cusack and Lloyd Christian, and the games were reported to be very enjoyable to play in and to watch.[21]

And then it all fell apart.

The Dublin Hurling Club committee met on 12 April 1883 and decided unanimously, after extended discussion, to suspend all activities. The suspension hardened into dissolution: the club never met again. The explanation for its sudden demise is not recorded in the minutes, but what is clear is that the club struggled to attract members. At best there were a mere ten playing members who had paid the 5s subscription to join.[22]

This difficulty had not been entirely unforeseen. The founders of the club were starting from scratch, trying to revive a game that had, by their own reckoning, only four adherents in Dublin. And then there was the awkward fact of hurley: a somewhat similar game with an almost identical name and an established presence. In founding the club, several members had spoken of the necessity to cultivate good relations with hurley clubs and had been at pains to stress that they wished to avoid any hostility. Every announcement in the newspapers that a practice match was to be held included an invitation to hurley players to come and play – and a number did. Indeed, initially, several players took part in both hurling and hurley matches on the same weekend, hoping to combine the two games.[23]

But Cusack and Potterton had written dismissively of hurley; and the hurley people must have wondered at the hurlers' true agenda. Perhaps they rethought the wisdom of their insistence that the rules of hurling should closely resemble those of hurley: this could have been a recipe for a takeover. The *Irish Sportsman* was deeply sympathetic to the game of hurley and noted, approvingly, how those who played it had changed 'the swiping game of the savage to a scientific recreation which may be indulged in by anyone without being in constant dread of having one's brains dashed out by an adversary's hurl'.[24] Unable to resist, Michael Cusack responded to this claim by accusing hurley clubs of trying to smother the Dublin Hurling Club before it had arrived beyond a chrysalis state.[25] But the awkward truth was that without the hurley players on board, the hurling revivalists simply did not have the numbers.

And so – in April 1883 – the Dublin Hurling Club collapsed.

V

Michael Cusack's obsession with reviving hurling was, in many respects, the zeal of the convert. It is true that he had played hurling during his childhood in Clare, but throughout the 1870s – and, indeed, right up until the weeks before the Dublin Hurling Club had been founded – Cusack was engrossed in the sports of the British Empire.

Cusack placed sport at the heart of the curriculum at Cusack's Academy, the school he had established in Dublin in 1877. He wrote admiringly of how schools in England provided physical recreation for their students: 'and the result is that when the boy becomes the man and leaves school he has plenty of stamina and vitality in him to battle his way through life'. The fact that many Irish boys would have to emigrate made physical development all the more vital: 'When we consider the fierceness of the fight, in the struggle for existence, which is going on at the present moment, in all parts of the globe, the keenness of the competition for positions in life ... we can hardly fail to appreciate the importance of physical training in the life of man and to fix its proper place in his education.' He believed that not nearly enough was being done for physical education in Ireland, and proclaimed: 'No school or college should be without its gymnasium or its ball-alley and athletic grounds.'[26]

Two years after the establishment of Cusack's Academy, he founded a rugby club with his students and began playing matches against other Dublin clubs.[27] The team played out of the Phoenix Park, and Cusack was club secretary and trainer, as well as playing in the forwards, where he built a reputation as a powerful operator. One journalist observed darkly: 'Everybody knows what Cusack is in a scrummage.'[28] Some of Cusack's students had experience of playing the game; others were country boys whose raw strength was harnessed through a season's coaching. By the end of the 1879–80 season Cusack's team had won six matches and lost four, and in an article printed in R. M. Peter's *Irish Football Annual*, Cusack referred to himself as 'a sterling lover of the game'.[29]

The bright future was soon behind them, however. Most of the school's prominent players had left after success in examinations in November 1880. In January 1881 the *Irish Sportsman* reported that the team was being reorganized.[30] But by the summer of 1881, Cusack had tired of the struggle and the club folded, even though the school continued to thrive. Cusack then threw in his lot with the Phoenix Rugby Club. He was a member of the Phoenix team that played Dublin University at Lansdowne Road on 10 December 1881 in the first-ever match in the Leinster Senior Cup competition.[31] One of his opponents that day was Thomas St George McCarthy – a past pupil of Cusack's Academy and a man who would later attend the founding meeting of the Gaelic Athletic Association. Phoenix lost that cup match, but Cusack played out the 1881–2 season with his new club and a photograph of him posing with his teammates is one of the few that survive. His last known match was in February 1882 – less than a year before he helped found the Dublin Hurling Club.[32]

VI

If Michael Cusack's winter game was rugby, his summer game was cricket. Contrary to the received image of cricket as a game of the English, or its garrison, or of the upper classes, it was played by people from every section of Irish society. It was, in fact, the most popular team game in Ireland in the 1870s.

The first record of Michael Cusack as a cricketer dates to the summer of 1874, when he had gone to work as a teacher in the French College in Blackrock, though it seems likely that he had previously played for other teams in other places. The French College (later known simply as Blackrock College) had about 200 students at the time and there is a record in the accounts of Cusack buying a pair of specialized cricketing trousers.[33] By the time he had reached his mid-thirties, Cusack was able to recall his involvement in 'many a hard-fought match'.

His passion for the game was obvious. In the summer before he and Potterton launched the Dublin hurling revival, he wrote in the *Shamrock* that he believed there was no better game for boys than cricket, and that every town and village in Ireland should have its own cricket field. He noted that there were plenty of good handbooks available which would give basic instruction and that the expense of founding a club in a country area was minimal.[34] That October, in the same paper, Cusack wrote that cricketers could pass away the dark days of winter by dreaming of the wonderful six that they had hit in midsummer, and of feeling pride at having walked to the crease, the forlorn hope of their parish, before saving the day with a memorable performance.[35]

For Cusack, cricket was not merely a game: it was also a matter of character and values. 'To play cricket well you must play with judgement and pluck – both are indispensable. To stand up to your wicket against fast bowling, or to field a hard-hit ball, there is need of genuine courage, not differing much from the quality which impels a student to face a battery. You may be certain that the boy who can play cricket well, will not, in after years, lose his head and get flurried in the face of danger.'[36] Just two months before he helped found the ill-fated Dublin Hurling Club, Michael Cusack was offering readers of the *Shamrock* advice on how to season a cricket bat using linseed oil and how to store it for the winter.[37]

It was the last time that he ever wrote about cricket in his newspaper column. From the beginning of 1883 onwards, the sport he wrote about was hurling and its putative revival.

VII

Why did Michael Cusack so suddenly abandon the sports of the Empire and take up the revival of hurling? The answer lies partly in the politics of Ireland in the 1880s. The tumultuous events of the Land War left the scent of social revolution hanging in the air.

The ownership of the land of Ireland lay in the hands of landlords who were increasingly despised – as a class – by the people who rented it from them. In 1879, against the backdrop of agricultural depression and food shortages all along the west coast, tenants unable to pay rent to a landlord in Co. Mayo faced eviction. A meeting was called in the village of Irishtown, and what emerged from this meeting – in time – was a popular protest movement that ultimately transformed not just Irish politics, but also Irish society. The movement became formally known as the Irish Land League from August 1879 and its immediate strategy was straightforward: tenants were to refuse to pay unjust rents and were also to resist every eviction. There were shootings, some houses were burned down, cattle were maimed and crops dug out; but the greatest weapon was the decision taken to ostracize landlords and those who had anything to do with them – they were to be boycotted. This manifested itself in local campaigns of isolation where workers declined to work for landlords, where local shops and traders declined to do business with landlords, and where people passed on the street and declined even to acknowledge or greet a landlord, his family or his agents.

Charles Stewart Parnell, the leader of the Irish Parliamentary Party and, by the early 1880s, the most important constitutional nationalist in Ireland, had prospered in association with the Land League. His growing power – and shifting political allegiances in Britain – suggested the prospect of Irish legislative independence.

The strains in the union of Great Britain and Ireland were becoming more apparent and, by 1883, it was entirely unclear what would next come to pass. Just a year earlier, the two most important British officials in Ireland had been murdered while strolling through the Phoenix Park. It was a reminder that, as well as constitutional nationalists, there were also radical separatists at work in Ireland. Prime among these were the members of the Irish Republican Brotherhood (IRB), a secret revolutionary organization dedicated to the overthrow of British rule in Ireland.

The desires of Irish separatists stood in opposition to the reality of British power in the country. And wrapped around this political power was the culture of the Empire. Dominant in Ireland in the 1880s was the flourishing British imperial culture, easily visible in music, theatre, books and newspapers. This suggested an Ireland that, in the words of the historian F. S. L. Lyons, 'seemed little more than a province in the empire of Victorian taste'.[38]

The overpowering reach of British culture across the Empire was epitomized by the spread of new forms of sport. In the second half of the nineteenth century, the social and cultural life of Britain was transformed by the establishment of clubs to cater for men and women who wished to play sport. It proved an enduring social phenomenon that redefined how people passed the hours between work and sleep. This phenomenon gathered extraordinary momentum, with many thousands of sports clubs established in a short period of time. Some clubs catered for long-established sports such as cricket and golf; others for newly codified versions of old games, such as rugby and soccer; and still others pursued newly invented ones such as badminton and lawn tennis. These clubs were usually associated with a centralized governing body, which regulated the manner in which a particular sport should be played. In Ireland, the Victorian sporting revolution was viewed as a model that the Irish could adopt for their own cultural–nationalist ends.

The gathering swell of the Gaelic revival in the 1880s in Ireland was a clear reaction against the power and prestige of the British Empire. This revival – from the most modest of beginnings in the 1870s – aimed at promoting the Irish language, Irish literature, Irish industry and a distinctive Irish historical narrative. Crucially, in the late 1870s and the early 1880s, the Gaelic revival was evolving from the preserve of a small vanguard into a more broad-based popular movement.

For Michael Cusack, the key development was the establishment of the Gaelic Union for the Preservation and Cultivation of the Irish Language, an organization that promoted the speaking of Irish and that was determined 'to save the country from the disgrace of letting the national language die'.[39] By the autumn of 1882 Cusack was serving as treasurer of the Gaelic Union and he was a key figure in funding and writing the Union's publication *Irisleabhar na Gaedhilge*. Gaelic Union meetings were usually held in Cusack's school on Gardiner Place – the same room in which meetings of the Dublin Hurling Club were held.[40]

Beyond the revival of the Irish language, reshaped ideas of Irishness clearly changed Cusack's thinking in the early 1880s. We know from his journalism at the time that he was influenced by the publication of cheap editions of books such as P. W. Joyce's *Old Celtic Romances* (1879), which included references to hurling amid the stories of Fionn, Oisín and Diarmuid from Ireland's mythical past. He later described how this literature transformed him and how he now sought to merge this heroic past with the sporting present: 'The full strength of Fionn's national guard in the fourth century was one hundred and five thousand men. When I look at a good hurling match I go back to the past, a film comes over my eyes, and through that film the scene is transformed. The forty-two players become three times one-hundred-and-five-thousand hurlers, sweeping across the country with the speed of a cloud shadow on a March day.'[41]

In the newspaper columns which he wrote in the days when the Dublin Hurling Club was attempting to establish itself, Cusack described hurling as an act of freedom, and as an inheritance from the heroes of Irish history.[42] He called for schools and colleges across Ireland to arrange for an hour's hurling every Tuesday, Thursday and Saturday. He rooted this in practicality as much as in patriotism: 'Young men who seek appointments as outdoor officers of Customs must be thirty-four inches around the chest and at least five feet four inches in height . . . A chest can easily be brought up to the required size by the hurling . . . Hurling is for hard-working students the best possible preserver of health and mental vigour.'[43]

The revival of hurling would now, if Cusack had his way, take its place alongside the revival of the Irish language, literature, industry and history. And, as would soon become apparent, Michael Cusack was a singular individual, as well as a formidable one. The collapse of the Dublin Hurling Club was a setback, but its failure was to prove a liberation to Cusack. Hurling was about to take on a new life.

2. A New Beginning

The summer of 1883 had come and gone before Michael Cusack was ready to move again to revive hurling. In early September, he arranged for a handful of enthusiasts to join him on a Saturday afternoon in the Phoenix Park on ground beside the Wellington monument. He brought with him the hurleys left over from the Dublin Hurling Club's brief adventure. In the beginning there were just four of them – Cusack, L. C. Slevin from Armagh, and Paddy and Tom Molohan from Clare – hitting the ball around. But the hurlers came back every Saturday afternoon for the rest of the autumn of 1883 and slowly their numbers grew. Interested spectators – generally country people living in Dublin – gathered to watch what was happening. 'They were told to fall in and slash away,' Cusack later recalled. He used his column in the *Shamrock* to advertise the fact that hurling was now being played for two hours every Saturday afternoon. Men who worked in the commercial and composing sections of that newspaper were cajoled to come and take part.

Cusack persuaded (or compelled) the students from his school to join in the Saturday hurling. These students came from all across Ireland and were sufficient in number for Cusack to consider them as 'the nucleus of a fairly good club'. By October he was confident enough to establish the Cusack's Academy Hurling Club.[1] The hurlers continued to come to the Phoenix Park every Saturday, now with Cusack's Academy lining up against whatever combination of others appeared for the 3 p.m. start. The logical step was for all the other hurlers to unite as a club. This they did at a meeting in Cusack's Academy on 5 December 1883, when the Metropolitan Hurling Club was formed. It was a significant milestone in the history of Irish sport. Michael Cusack was later to claim that this was the club 'out of which the GAA sprang'.[2]

Some reports survive of the initial matches between the Cusack's Academy hurlers and those of the Metropolitan Hurling Club. One report, written by Cusack, records a 'gloriously enjoyable game' played on 1 December 1883: 'During the third and fourth quarters the hurling became so fast and furious, the goals were so threatened on the one hand and defended on the other, that spectators expected to be called on after each charge to help the disabled to Steevens' Hospital.'[3] Metropolitans continued to play with the students every Saturday in all weathers.[4] By the spring of 1884 there were sometimes fifty hurlers on the field, a scene that was captured by a cartoonist in the London-based *Illustrated Sporting and Dramatic News* in March 1884.

I

Dublin was the epicentre of Cusack's attempt at a hurling revival. But in the stretch of East Galway that bordered the river Shannon, hurling had never died. From Ballinasloe across to Loughrea and down to Portumna and Gort, hurling matches remained a feature of the social life of the people. Press reports of the revival of hurling in Dublin were noted in Galway and a publican in the village of Killimor, Patrick Larkin, invited Metropolitans down to play against his own team, which was reputed to be the best in East Galway. Cusack accepted the challenge and the match was arranged for the Fair Green in the middle of Ballinasloe on Easter Monday, 13 April 1884. Two Ballinasloe businessmen commissioned a special silver trophy for presentation to the winners.[5]

The list of Metropolitans players to travel to Galway was published in the Dublin press during the week before the game. The players were instructed to be at Broadstone station for the 9 a.m. train. They arrived in Ballinasloe shortly after 1 p.m. and were met by cheers from the many locals who had turned out at the station in anticipation of their arrival. Metropolitans were brought to the local Agricultural Hall, where they were given refreshments and a place to change into their hurling clothes. The Killimor team had arrived by jaunting cars and long horse-drawn coaches. The local press had noted that a mere look at them would 'give an assurance that their opponents from the "Big Smoke" would have a hard nut to crack to win the cup'. Their captain, Francis Lynch (a local horse trainer and farmer), met Cusack and the pair agreed a set of rules for the game – twenty-two players a side, and no wrestling allowed. A number of men were also appointed to act as linesmen and goal-umpires.[6]

A huge crowd gathered for the match, not least because advertisements in the Galway papers had heralded the arrival of 'the Dublin champion club'. The Killimor men quickly gained the upper hand and scored a goal. Before they could score a second, Cusack intervened. The play of the Galway men, he said, was 'too rough'; they 'slashed in a reckless and savage manner'.[7] Cusack asked that the field be cleared so that Metropolitans could play an exhibition match in order to demonstrate the rules of the game to the Killimor men. When this exhibition was complete, Killimor came back onto the field and played an exhibition of their own. A *Western*

News journalist claimed that 'to the keenest judge no material difference could be detected in the style of either team'. Despite the wishes of several of his players to play out the match, Cusack refused and declared that Metropolitans would play no more. According to the newspapers, the decision was scorned by spectators in Ballinasloe who believed that Cusack had simply withdrawn so as to avoid seeing his team badly beaten.[8]

As the day's sport on the Fair Green continued with pony races and tug-of-war contests, the Killimor team set off for home. All along the way they were met by bonfires lit in celebration of their perceived victory. By the time they had reached Killimor, the townspeople were out on the streets and bonfires blazed at every corner. A fife-and-drum band paraded the team through the town and speeches were made lauding the hurlers for the honour that they had brought to their home town. Metropolitans returned to Dublin under something of a cloud, but the day was not a complete loss for Michael Cusack. A letter to the *Western News* made a public plea for the nationwide revival of hurling, 'a sport which we all love . . . as a relic of a time that was the golden age of Ireland'.[9]

II

A nationwide revival of hurling would require a network of clubs, and a governing body to establish standardized rules for the game. But in the aftermath of the Killimor challenge match, there was no immediate move to establish a national organization. When that move did eventually come, the circumstances had hardly anything to do with hurling.

The immediate impetus for the establishment of a national

hurling organization was, oddly enough, a crisis in the world of Irish athletics. When he had first come to Dublin to work in 1874, Michael Cusack had immediately involved himself in the Dublin athletics world. An Irish Athletics Championship had been run by the Irish Champion Athletic Club since 1872, and Cusack actually won two weight-throwing championships during the decade. In the wake of that success, he was offered a seat on the council of the Irish Champion Athletic Club. It placed him at the heart of an organization that was at once a bastion of conservatism and a leader in the modernization of sport in Ireland.

Formally organized athletics had become prominent across Ireland from the 1860s onwards. This extended to every county, and almost every significant town had its own athletics meetings. But by 1883, the promise of a vibrant, organized athletics scene had fallen away. The Irish Champion Athletic Club had disbanded, and in the resulting vacuum the sport was dogged by petty internal squabbles and personal disputes. The annual Athletics Championship was on the verge of collapse, and the entire sport suffered for the want of a proper organizational structure.[10] Increasing numbers of Irish athletics clubs – particularly down the east coast from Belfast to Dublin and beyond – were turning to the Amateur Athletic Association of England (AAA) to fill the vacuum in leadership. It was not that they affiliated to that body, rather they chose to adopt its rules when they were organizing athletics meetings.

To Michael Cusack, this appeared to symbolize the absorption of all things Irish into the way of Empire. In terms of the music played and the toasts made and the flags waved, the symbolism at AAA meetings was almost invariably British. Against the backdrop of political and social upheaval – and with the influences of the Gaelic revival becoming more manifest – the growing influence of the AAA became a cause of irritation to Michael Cusack. He abandoned all involvement with such clubs and sporting organizations where the symbolism of the Empire was the orthodoxy.

Apart altogether from this, there were other reasons for Michael Cusack to resist the spread of the English AAA. A weight-thrower himself, he regarded the power events as best suited to the Irish character, but this organization was concerned more with running than with weight-throwing events. Also, while officially recognized athletics meetings were held on Saturdays, the traditional day for sport in rural Ireland was Sunday.[11] This was partly related to work practices, and partly to religion: the Catholic Church was comfortable with Sunday sports, while the Protestant churches generally were not. Sunday athletics meetings were also in direct contravention of the Lord's Day Observance Act. A dispute over an athletics meeting held on a Sunday in Cork provoked a lengthy correspondence in the *Irish Sportsman* during September and October 1878; this culminated in an editorial in which the paper argued: 'Gentlemen should be ashamed of engaging in such displays on Sunday; but we are willing to make allowance for humble men employed in hard labour all week.'[12] Later still, in May 1884, when word reached Dublin that the Riverstown Sports was to be held on a Sunday, the *Irish Sportsman* reminded those who were thinking of competing that 'some time ago many of the leading clubs in Ireland passed a resolution that they would receive no entry from any athlete who took part in any athletic meeting held on the Sabbath'.[13]

If the Saturday/Sunday debate had a class dimension, so did the AAA's insistence on amateurism. This was at odds with traditions in Ireland – both in the cities and in the countryside – of racing for cash prizes.[14] In his *Handbook of Cricket in Ireland,* John Lawrence wrote: 'While we are rejoiced to find that the peasantry of our country are encouraged to go into training and compete for money prizes, we think it is advisable, and indeed necessary, to warn amateurs of the danger they run of losing that title by competing with pedestrians for such prizes, or with any who cannot qualify as gentleman amateurs.'[15] In the early 1880s, the AAA narrowed the definition of 'amateur' to exclude anyone who had ever even competed against a professional; and eventually the rules were expanded to outlaw anyone who so much as received expenses for competing. Remarkably, certain professional athletes who posed as amateurs were pursued for fraud and imprisoned with hard labour for up to six months.[16]

When G. Stenchrid won the 220-yards hurdles and the half-mile at a meeting in Dublin, an objection was lodged that he was not an amateur. On being questioned, Stenchrid said that he was the Duke of Leinster's coachman and had given his home address as Carton Stables. The committee had overlooked the word 'Stables' and thought that they had a nobleman coming to run when they accepted the entry. In light of their error, they overruled the objection; but the message in relation to class was clear.[17] This was acute snobbery dressed up as morality.

Through 1883 and 1884, more and more athletics meetings across Ireland were organized under AAA rules.[18] In 1884 alone, there were sports days held under AAA rules in Belfast, Dublin, Kildare, Louth and Waterford, but also in Irish country towns as far south as Mitchelstown in Co. Cork and as far west as Ballinasloe in Co. Galway. The Irish Athletics Championships for 1884 were also held under AAA rules.[19] Cusack's reaction to these developments was brutal. In early

1883 he wrote: 'In the English parts of Ireland the term "athletics" has often of late been applied to that thing which a number of oldish young persons of a doubtful gender do in fine weather after having undergone several weeks of careful nursing, and when nobody outside their own class is allowed to compete.' He claimed that the competitors manage to achieve feats 'in the costume of a circus clown which one of "our boys" could do without unbuttoning his coat'.[20]

As recently as the summer of 1881, in a series of newspaper articles, Cusack had made an eloquent case for the establishment of a sporting body that would be beyond politics. He had said it saddened him to see the way each successive political crisis in Ireland, by dividing unionist from nationalist, caused the sporting world to suffer. He had described himself as a sportsman who was 'trying to keep the platform of sport clear of the party spirit'. He had said that, in a country like Ireland where political differences were so fundamental, sport was the ideal 'unifying factor'. To that end, he had argued for the merits of drawing in unionist and nationalist, rich and poor, all under the banner of sport.[21] But it had not taken long for this idealistic vision to curdle, and he now railed against any 'English influence' he discerned in Irish sport.

In April 1884, the Caledonian Society in Dublin staged a Caledonian Games which remade the Scottish 'Highland Games' into modern sport. There was weight-throwing and tossing the caber and tug-of-war. There were also bagpipe and Highland dancing competitions in which 'full Highland dress must be worn by the competitors'.[22] Cusack was struck by the possibilities of what the Scots were doing. This, he claimed without evidence or elaboration, was exactly what the Irish had been doing fifty years previously – combining national music and dancing and sport on the same field in celebration. And, he continued, he was encouraged now 'to hope that we shall yet see the good old games revived in every village and town'.[23]

III

During these years, Michael Cusack emerged as a prominent and often divisive presence in Irish life. His behaviour became increasingly outrageous, sometimes almost cartoonish. At his best, he was capable of great generosity and vision. But Cusack's flaws were as generous as his talents. He thrived on confrontation and he now managed to find it wherever he travelled.

He cultivated an image that enabled him to stand out from the crowd. He walked through the city in heavy working boots, a blackthorn stick swinging from his arm, and with a large frieze coat covering his heavy-set, broad-shouldered frame. His full black beard was beginning to streak with grey. Cusack was remarkably conscious of his appearance, which seems to have been not so much a mark of eccentricity as a statement of defiance.[24] He gloried in the idea of his distinctiveness, that he was a singular man of singular beliefs. And this almost invariably saw him engage in insulting those with whom he disagreed.

But alongside the capacity for harsh words and conflict, there thrived a parallel capacity for humour. He had no problem laughing at himself. In responding to suggestions that he was a rash, impulsive man, he wrote that this was far from the case and that he was, in fact, 'as cool as a New England lawyer eating a cucumber at the back of a tombstone during a blizzard'.[25] Cusack was also a man of warmth and decency.

When he learned that his one-time friend J. A. H. Christian, with whom he had had a ferocious public falling-out, was emigrating to America, Cusack wrote a charming account of how their friendship had formed and then soured. He gently jibed at how Christian was the soul of loyalty to England and that he had established a world record in proposing toasts to the Queen. However, he ended the article by warmly acknowledging the athletic ability, courage and absolute integrity of Christian, and wrote: 'May he soon enjoy the happiness and prosperity which the great Republic of the West has bestowed on so many of his fellow-countrymen; and may he realise that, while we may be irreconcilable foes on National grounds, in private life we may wish one another all the blessings attached to the communion of Saints.'

IV

Cusack could be an intemperate man, but he was not blind to his own limitations. He understood that, acting alone, he would never be able to develop a successful athletics movement. His sphere of influence lay within Dublin, and even there he was already a divisive figure. So he turned to his old friend Maurice Davin.

Davin had been born into middle-class comfort on a medium-sized farm at Deerpark, a mile from Carrick-on-Suir in the south of Co. Tipperary. As well as running their farm, the Davin family had been engaged for generations in a river-haulage business. Ships brought their cargoes in from the Irish Sea and up the river Suir as far as Carrick, beyond which they were unable to pass. The Davins then drew the goods onwards in barges pulled by teams of horses to the town of Clonmel, twelve miles further along the river.[26] The work started at 6.00 every morning, with goods being loaded onto the barge. The horses set off from Carrick by 9.00 and it generally took five and a half hours to travel to Clonmel. The return journey – aided by the downstream current – generally took two and a half hours, with the barge propelled along by a man using a pole, in much the same fashion as a Venetian gondolier, while the horses trotted back by road to be watered and stabled. When Maurice's father died before he had turned eighteen, he took over the running of the family farm and the river-haulage business in tandem with his mother, Bridget. He ran both enterprises for the rest of his life.

The river Suir provided the focal point for Davin's earliest sporting activity, and the revival of the Carrick-on-Suir regatta – known locally as 'The Boat Races' – saw him develop a passion for rowing. The Carrick regatta had been revived in the mid-1860s, as had regattas in Clonmel, Waterford and all across the south-east of Ireland. Davin was the star turn at many of these sporting festivals. He won races in singles, in doubles and as stroke with a four-man crew. Not content merely to row boats to victory, from 1868 he raced in boats he built himself, first a two-oared wherry and then a thirty-five-foot four-oared racing gig, the *Cruiskeen Lawn*. Consumed with the idea of perfecting racing boats, he designed and built a whole range of craft from canoes to out-riggers – each endeavour backed by his practical experience of working the river and by the technical knowledge learned from the books which he ordered. In fact, he never lost a race in one of his own boats.

Davin also played cricket – he was reckoned to be a 'fair batsman and . . . a very good slow underarm bowler' – and was devoted to boxing.[27] It was not until he was in his late twenties that he turned to athletics – and quickly determined to abandon every other sport. He was no idealized amateur, content merely to turn up, take off his coat and compete. A notebook that Davin used through the 1870s details the extent of his preparations. He kept a detailed log of the age, weight, height and best performances of his opponents, and refined his own training to meet the challenges they presented. He constructed a mini-gymnasium at his home in Deerpark, where he used dumb-bells and assorted weighted clubs to increase the power in his muscles. He was meticulous in his diet. Every morning he drank pints of water from the clear well at Deerpark. He followed that with a bowl of porridge, a little bread and some beef or mutton. The midday meal was usually beef or mutton again, with a variety of vegetables, and then in the evening he ate toast and porridge. He avoided salty bacon and butter. He lauded the virtues of fresh fish, but abstained from tea and coffee. He neither drank nor smoked, and believed that anyone who smoked cigarettes would never be any good at anything.[28]

The Irish Athletics Championships, staged by the Irish Champion Athletic Club in Dublin, offered Maurice Davin the perfect stage to indulge his new obsession. He became the dominant figure at these events and went on to win ten gold medals in weight-throwing events. In some years he was reckoned to be so untouchable that he was given a walkover. But, at least in the mythology of Irish sporting history, Davin's most spectacular moment on the sports field was during the first-ever international athletics match held anywhere in the world, when Ireland met England in Lansdowne Road in June 1876. He won the shot-put, defeating the fancied English representatives, Stone and Winthrop. But these victories were mere warm-up for a far more enjoyable success. According to legend, midway through the afternoon, during a break in the competition, assorted members of the visiting English team were out in the middle of the grounds, preening and posing as they performed feats of strength for the crowd. Davin watched for a while, then strolled over and proposed that he would single-handedly carry three of the heaviest members of the English team down the field. The challenge was accepted and three men with a combined weight of forty-six stone stepped forward. Davin threw one on his back and another up on each shoulder, and set off in front of the main stand. The Irish crowd rose to acclaim the power and style of their hero. Always the adoring younger brother, Pat Davin observed in his 1938 memoir that, in performing the feat, Maurice 'appeared to be no way overloaded'.[29]

Davin retired for a period in his late thirties, but then was apparently goaded into a comeback by suggestions in the English press that there were no good athletes left in Ireland. On the strength of two weeks' training, he travelled to compete in the 1881 British Championships, the most prestigious athletics event in the world at that time which was organized by the AAA – and he won the hammer and the shot-put.[30]

Davin had long held an interest in the administration of Irish athletics. He had said as much to the *Irish Sportsman*, in an interview at the height of his fame in 1877.[31] In terms of temperament and upbringing, Davin and Cusack had little in common. Where Cusack was volatile and restless, Davin was genial and methodical – and together they were about to turn the Irish sporting world on its head.

V

It was at the Irish Athletics Championships in 1875, held in Lansdowne Road on a suitably 'wild and tempestuous day', that Michael Cusack had first met Maurice Davin.[32] Over the years that followed they met at this championship, where both won medals, and other athletics events in Dublin. An exchange of letters between Cusack (who initiated the correspondence) and Davin in the summer of 1884 led, ultimately, to a plan to establish a new sporting association. On 11 October 1884 the pair went public when Cusack published his epistle – 'A Word about Irish Athletics' – in the nationalist *United Ireland* newspaper. Cusack wrote that neglecting 'the pastimes' of the Irish people was 'a sure sign of national decay and of approaching dissolution, smoking and card-playing'. He also railed against the Englishness of Irish sport and declared: 'We tell the Irish people to take the management of their games into their own hands, to encourage and to promote in every way every form of athletics which is peculiarly Irish, and to remove with one sweep everything foreign and iniquitous in the present system.'[33]

In the following edition of the paper, Maurice Davin offered unequivocal support and called for the establishment of an association to draw up proper rules for athletics, hurling and 'Irish football'.[34] Cusack and Davin then combined to issue a circular announcing that a meeting was being called for Hayes' Hotel in Thurles, Co. Tipperary, on 1 November 1884. The purpose of the meeting was 'to take steps for the formation of a Gaelic Association for the preservation and cultivation of our national pastimes and for providing rational amusements for the Irish people during their leisure hours'.[35]

VI

The Thurles meeting was fixed for 2 p.m., but – establishing a precedent that was to become one of the new association's hallmarks – it was 3 p.m. before proceedings got under way, in the billiards room of the hotel. The delay most likely was related to the poor attendance: reports of the meeting say that between seven and thirteen people turned up.[36] Michael Cusack later claimed that he received more than sixty letters and telegrams in support of his endeavour. Given Cusack's propensity for exaggeration, this is a claim which might be treated with scepticism were it not for the fact that he read every one of the missives out to those present.

At Cusack's instigation, Maurice Davin took the chair. He said that they were there because the rules that governed Irish athletics were English ones and, although good in their own way, they were unsuitable for Irish pastimes. He announced that they intended to draft rules for the guidance of amusements and recreations for the ordinary people of Ireland who now seemed born into 'no other inheritance than an everlasting round of labour'.[37]

The 'athletics' that Maurice Davin alluded to in his opening remarks were running and jumping events. Establishing an association to govern athletics in Ireland was in itself an onerous task – at least five previous attempts had failed.[38] Now, Cusack and Davin were joining the ambition to take control of Irish athletics with a proposal to revive hurling and to write rules for a game of 'Irish' football. If the revival of hurling was clearly included because of Cusack's growing obsession with the game, the inclusion of football was motivated by Davin. Various types of football had existed in Ireland – just as they had in Britain, across Europe, and in other regions – for centuries. This folk football had evolved into soccer and rugby in England in the middle of the nineteenth century, and Cusack and Davin now set about constructing their own football game under new rules. Davin stated his desire to make rules for a 'fine manly game', but one that was not as 'brutal and demoralising' as rugby.[39] He had already written that he regarded 'Irish football' as 'a great game' when played under proper rules. He had seen such games played when he was a younger man and he wished to see it remade under new rules that would render it less dangerous.[40]

The remaining business of the founding meeting was conducted in a straightforward way. Maurice Davin was elected as the first president of the organization. Michael Cusack and two other journalists who attended the meeting – John Wyse Power and John McKay – were appointed as honorary secretaries. That group of joint secretaries was called on to draft the laws for the new organization, which was initially called 'The Gaelic Association for the Preservation and Cultivation of National Pastimes'. Almost immediately, the simpler rubric 'Gaelic Athletic Association', or GAA, was adopted.

It was decided to invite Archbishop Thomas Croke of Cashel (considered the most nationalist member of the Catholic hierarchy), Charles Stewart Parnell (the leader of the Irish Parliamentary Party) and Michael Davitt (the founder of the Land League) to act as patrons of the new association. All three quickly agreed. Hurling had, until now, lived outside the modern world of sport in Ireland, but that had now changed. What happened next transformed the game, and assured it of a future. Many years later, in his dying days, when he cast an eye back on his motivation for founding the GAA, Michael Cusack offered a succinct summary: 'I resolved to bring back the hurling.'[41] This wasn't all that motivated him – but it proved to be his crowning glory.

3. The Making of a Modern Game

The GAA, Michael Cusack admitted later, was born 'quietly' and 'unostentatiously'.[1] The list of names of those who promised support was impressive, but those promises would likely come to nothing without evidence of real progress. The association's ambitions were remarkable. Starting from scratch, it proposed to set itself up as a rival to a well-established athletics organization; to codify and promulgate rules for the new game of Gaelic football; and to revive hurling.

I

The second meeting of the GAA was held in the Victoria Hotel in Cork on Saturday 27 December 1884. (It had been announced that the first hurling match to be organized by the association would be played in tandem with that meeting; that never took place, perhaps because of the decision that the association had better draw up its rules before proceeding with matches).[2] Maurice Davin, as president, was asked to head a committee, which included the secretaries (Cusack, McKay and Wyse Power), to draft the rules for athletics, hurling and Gaelic football. In the event, it appears that Davin went about drafting them largely on his own, a job he was well placed to do. A detailed notebook that he kept during the 1870s and 1880s contains notes and newspaper cuttings on the rules and organization of English athletics, as well as notes on the rules and terminology for soccer. At the third GAA meeting – held in Thurles on 17 January 1885 – Davin presented a set of rules that were unanimously adopted. They were published in *United Ireland* on 7 February 1885, and in early May they were reprinted and sold in pamphlet form at the cost of 6d.[3]

The rules for athletics were relatively straightforward and largely followed established practices in running events, while introducing special provisions for traditional Irish weight-throwing and jumping events. In general, the GAA's ambition for athletics, according to Michael Cusack, lay not in the desire to promote a few dozen elite athletes in an annual show, but to bring the people together to compete on Sunday evenings and on holy days.[4] For his part, Maurice Davin was committed to the GAA drawing a line between 'amateurs and those who compete for cash prizes', and this should mean that 'international athletics meetings between Ireland and England could continue'. The challenge for the GAA would be to marry Cusack's populist and nationalist ambitions with Davin's desire to preserve a relationship that would allow its top athletes to compete in and against Britain.

Producing rules for football was problematic. Ultimately, the game of 'Irish' football invented by Davin was supposed to stand in opposition to rugby and soccer. In practice, the game that Davin invented drew from the laws which had already been devised to regulate football in England. This meant, for example, that when a ball was kicked out over the sideline by one team, a throw-in was awarded to the opposition. But Davin also drew from the traditions of the Irish countryside, and so the rules permitted wrestling off the ball. The rules were somewhat vague, and for several years, Gaelic football would remain a game very much in the making.

II

What would Maurice Davin do with hurling? Fragmentary records of this sport in Ireland extended back to the Middle Ages. The hurling matches of the eighteenth century were reported in the newspapers – or described in songs and poetry – in ways that offered no clear guidance as to the rules of the game. There were more detailed accounts from the nineteenth century, but the manner of play varied from area to area. The antiquity of hurling was acknowledged by all, but this was an antiquity that was painted in broad strokes – the finer details, so essential to the rules of modernizing sport, were notably absent.

As it turned out, the great challenge for Davin was not how he would remake the past; rather, it was how he would respond to the demands of the present. In this, there was a careful balance to be struck. In the first instance, there was a need to respect local traditions in the areas where hurling was still being played. For this reason, Cusack initially claimed that the GAA's first rules would be 'adopted rather for the guidance of those who have never seen hurling, than for general use'. But Davin was having none of that – he had not drafted rules to see them roundly ignored – and the GAA decided that Davin's rules 'should be strongly recommended with the view to securing uniformity in the manner of play all over the country'.[5] In practice, the rules were sufficiently broad to allow for a degree of local interpretation. They numbered just twelve in total and laid out the fundamental principles of the game.

Hurling pitches were to be at least two hundred yards long and one hundred and fifty yards wide 'when convenient'; otherwise pitches were to be 'as near that size as can be got'. The sideline could run no closer than five yards from any fence. The goalposts were to be twenty feet apart, with a crossbar ten feet from the ground. The only way a team could score was to shoot the ball into the goal. The number of players on each team was to be at least fourteen and not greater than twenty-one, and matches were to last for eighty minutes, with the teams changing ends at half-time.

Each team would provide an umpire who would follow the play around the field. In the event of disagreement between the umpires, a referee would have the final say. Play would start with both teams lining up side by side in the middle of the field and the ball would be thrown in by the referee, either along the ground or up over their heads. In the event of the ball going out over the sideline, it could be thrown back into play by the referee or umpires; if it rebounded into play off a barrier or a spectator, the game would continue as previously. A ball struck behind the goals by an attacker gave the defending team a free puck-out. A ball struck behind his own goal-line by a defender allowed the attacking team a free puck at goal from twenty yards out.

Any player who tripped or pushed from behind was to have a free puck awarded against him and was to be sent from the field. The same penalty was to apply against any hurler who intentionally struck an opponent. Players were not allowed to have nails or iron tips on their boots; rather, strips of leather were to be fastened on the soles to prevent slipping. The playing gear was to consist of knee breeches and stockings. It was soon added to the rules that the ball should ideally be a light one, about four inches in diameter, made of cork and woollen thread, and covered with leather. And players could use whatever style of hurley they wished.

III

The tentative nature of the rules demonstrated the scale of the challenge facing the GAA. There was no guarantee that its rules would be accepted in existing hurling areas, nor that the game produced would inspire sportsmen across Ireland to take up hurling. It was one thing to write rules on a page; it was entirely another to put them into practice. The big question remained: what would a modern hurling match look like? It took a while for that question to be answered, because the first matches played under GAA rules were football ones. A large crowd turned out in Callan, Co. Kilkenny, to see the local team play against a team from Kilkenny city on 15 February 1885. The match ended in a scoreless draw.[6]

No representative of any area where hurling continued to be played had attended the founding meeting of the GAA. Further, there was no formal club structure that would facilitate the promulgation of uniform rules. Despite these disadvantages, the GAA's hurling rules – published in *United Ireland* on 10 February 1885 and promoted through newspaper columns – caught on with remarkable speed. Through February and early March 1885, hurlers in Tipperary, Galway, Cork and Dublin came together and experimented with the new rules by playing matches among themselves. Although it is impossible to be certain, it appears that the first competitive hurling matches played under GAA rules took place on Sunday 22 March 1885. A team from the Meelick area (playing as 'The Shannon District') competed against a team from Lusmagh, directly across the river Shannon in King's County. The game was played on a field near Lusmagh, and 'although the teams hailed from different counties, the utmost good humour prevailed'.

On that same day, a match was played between Nenagh and Silvermines in Tipperary. The two teams togged out in the Nenagh National Literary Institute before parading through the town behind the Nenagh Brass Band to the field, which was most likely the grounds of the Nenagh Cricket Club. A huge banner across the entrance to the field read 'God Save Ireland'. The pitch was marked out by green and white flags, and over 2,000 people ringed the field. It was felt that many of the crowd had come in the hope of seeing a revival of faction-fighting, but Michael Cusack wrote that the game had actually been a skilful, disciplined affair.[7] The *Nenagh Guardian*, in the briefest of reports, noted that the match had ended in a draw, although Silvermines had been the stronger team.[8] During 1885 these teams of players began to formalize themselves into clubs and moved to affiliate with the association.

The earliest reports of hurling matches do not offer precise descriptions of what the game looked like. What is certain is that goals were a rarity: it was commonplace for a match to end scoreless. And Cusack's dream – 'I long to see the ball flying in the air, stopped by the hurl, and ere it reached the ground, driven back 50 yards, to be stopped again, and this time to be carried on the flat of the hurl by a player rushing towards the opposite goal' – was surely not matched by the reality. The games were generally played out by men driving the ball along the ground rather than in the air. Often this involved many (or most) of the hurlers moving around the field together as a large body – known as a *scriob* – while the weaker players hung around the fringes waiting for the ball to come loose. These fringe players were known as whips.

The critical fact, though, is that the first steps had been taken by the GAA in the making of a modern game. There was much about the game that remained a mystery, much that would need to be ironed out as particular circumstances demanded; but the revival of hurling had moved to another level.

IV

Throughout 1885, as the first hurling matches were played under GAA auspices, the association was entangled in a battle for control of athletics in Ireland. For two decades, formal athletics in Ireland had developed in a range of different ways. Almost every town of note had its own annual sports day, in which athletics played a central part. Occasionally, in towns such as Enniscorthy in Co. Wexford, these sports days helped promote the development of athletics clubs which organized activities across the whole year. But most of the significant Irish athletics clubs were based in the cities. These clubs, though generally not formally affiliated to the AAA, increasingly followed that association's rules. The question was: what would they do next? Although the involvement of an old athlete as well regarded as Maurice Davin must have lent credibility to the GAA, there were two significant difficulties perceived by existing clubs which led to them not merely rejecting the GAA, but moving to form their own governing body. This rival body – the Irish Amateur Athletic Association (IAAA) – was founded in February 1885 and drew extensively on the rules of the AAA, with which it expressed kinship, particularly in relation to its strictures on amateurism.

Michael Cusack, who had been friendly with the leaders of several of the Irish athletics clubs, described the new IAAA as a 'ranting, impotent West British abortion'. He derided the men who ran it as 'Orange Catholics', and accused one of its leading members of possessing the 'characteristically idiotic insolence of his class'.[9] And when John Dunbar, the secretary of the IAAA, wrote a conciliatory letter to Cusack, Cusack replied in an open letter: 'Dear Sir, I received your letter this morning and burned it.'[10] Both organizations banned from their own sports meetings athletes who took part in events run by the other.

The row was an extraordinary blessing to the GAA, affording it a level of publicity and status which it could scarcely have dreamed of following the damp squib of its inaugural meeting. It also allowed the GAA to place a simple equation before the Irish people. On the one hand, it could point to the patronage it received from Archbishop Croke, Michael Davitt and Charles Stewart Parnell, and present itself as nationalist and patriotic. On the other hand, it could paint the IAAA as pro-British and elitist. As Cusack neatly put it, Irishmen could now 'choose between Irish and foreign laws'.[11]

In June 1885, the two associations went head to head with rival athletics meetings in nearby fields in Tralee, Co. Kerry.[12] A massive organizational and propaganda drive by the GAA saw it attract more than ten thousand people to its sports meeting, while just a few hundred attended that of its opponents.

As the summer rolled on, the scale of the GAA's success

became clear, a success which owed as much to appearance as it did to substance. The GAA did not found athletics clubs all over Ireland in order to hold athletics meetings under its rules. Instead, it got numerous existing meetings to stand under the GAA's umbrella. Fifteen major sports days were run under the association's rules in towns across Ireland in the early part of August alone, and a total of around one hundred and fifty meetings over the course of the year.[13] By the time it held what it billed as its first national championships in Tramore, Co. Waterford, in October, the GAA was the dominant force in Irish athletics.

V

The row between the GAA and the IAAA somewhat obscured the remarkable surge of interest in hurling across Ireland during 1885. This interest swelled from the few remaining traditional hurling heartlands out into areas where the game had been unknown for generations. It was charted by Michael Cusack in the weekly column he had secured in the popular nationalist newspaper, *United Ireland*. Cusack later wrote that getting that column was proof that 'our dream was not all a dream', but something genuinely possible.[14] Cusack used his column to promote hurling at every opportunity. This was crucial when it came to developing a game unfamiliar to many parts of Ireland. Building on the credibility that came from its success in athletics, the GAA was now able to place the idea of hurling at the very centre of the Irish sporting world.

Every scrap of information about hurling was moulded by Cusack to present the image of momentum. Week after week his column lauded Metropolitans for their work in the Phoenix Park, where every weekend they organized games in which he himself played. Also in Dublin, the Faugh-a-Ballagh club – its name forged from a battle cry – was formed when a group of countrymen living and working in the city got together at Easter 1885 under a tree in the Phoenix Park.[15] From there Cusack looked west to the Galway–Clare border and hailed the formation of hurling clubs in Gort and Tubber, which played a match against each other in May 1885. He turned south to Cork and reported that the hurling clubs there were drawing swarms of spectators to Cork Park – a municipal recreational space where the GAA played many of its early matches – every summer Sunday, with three games often being played at the same time.[16] And looking north, he wrote that there was hurling in a field off the Falls Road in Belfast, and then at a sports day in Desertmartin, Co. Derry, in July 1885.[17]

Cusack swept across the countryside like an evangelist. He went to matches everywhere and brought descriptions of those matches to his readers. He mapped out his vision of hurling by describing the rules, the pattern of play, the technical details of the game.[18] If he was disappointed by the earthbound nature of the game, he did not show it: his columns revelled in the primal battle of wills for control of the ball, the sense of 'men lovingly at war'. He wrote of a match in Tralee in July 1885: 'When two hurlers came to very close quarters they sometimes caught each other and wrestled in capital style. After the fall they took to the timber and joined their respective sides in the most good-humoured manner.'[19] He described the place where the battle for the ball took place as the 'seat of war', and stressed time and again that shouldering (or jostling, as it was known in many country areas) was perfectly legal.[20] He wanted hurling to be honest and hard and full of passion.

Cusack drew from literature, from science, from art and from music in his columns: 'The mighty spirit of Tolstoi was not more refreshed by his first sight of the mountains after his journey over the vast plains of Russia, than is the soul of a true-born hurler at the sight of a good hurling match.'[21] He wrote about hurling as if it was more than mere sport, asserting that 'no imagination ever conceived a loftier ideal of courage and chivalry'.[22] And what was a good hurling match? According to Cusack, it was 'like a city on fire, where the crackling of burning timber and the hissing of the flames swell into the roar of conflagration'.[23] As the months of 1885 rolled on, that fire was slowly spreading across the country.

VI

Turning age-old local pastimes into a modern national sport involved distilling tradition and a certain element of compromise. Unsurprisingly, there were men who were unwilling to meet the GAA on that journey, at least initially.

Take, for example, the hurlers of Killimor, Co. Galway, who had met Metropolitans in that match in Ballinasloe in April 1884, before the establishment of the GAA. In the aftermath of the association's publication of its rules of play, a meeting of the Killimor hurlers was held on 22 February 1885 in the home of Francis Lynch, a horse trainer and farmer who (along with a local publican, Patrick Larkin) ran the team. The report of the meeting in the *Western News* made it plain that the Killimor men would not abandon the traditional game of hurling as played in East Galway in favour of the GAA's rules. Instead, they formally published their own 'Killimor Rules'.[24] These included the stipulations that teams should be comprised of thirty men and that any player 'who is under the influence of drink, who loses temper, or strikes any of his opponents intentionally' could be ordered off the field. The goals used in East Galway were much wider than those used by the GAA and sidelines were not considered necessary. The Killimor meeting also made clear, however, that they were not issuing a complete rejection of the GAA. Instead, they simply decided to continue playing under their own local rules until a general meeting of the GAA could be held in November 1885 to redraft its rules for hurling.[25]

There was a certain disdain around Killimor when some other teams formed into clubs and embraced the new GAA rules.[26] This view was distilled in a letter sent to the *Western News* in October. The writer, 'An Old Hurler', claimed that 'the game played by the GAA is not considered by the Killimor, Meelick, Lusmagh or Mullagh clubs as hurling, but "hurley", an importation, and a slight improvement on those effeminate games, croquet and lawn tennis'.[27] The 'Old Hurler' concluded by defending the traditional hurling rules of East Galway, saying that 'nothing vicious or unchristian is tolerated amongst them'. During 1885 Killimor continued to resist playing by GAA rules, preferring to retain what they termed 'the real old Irish style' of play.[28] In reality, there appears to be no evidence that the Killimor rules, or the traditions of aggression and violence in East Galway hurling, made it in any respect more or less 'effeminate' than GAA hurling. Rather, 'effeminacy' was an all-purpose insult to be thrown as deemed necessary.

Traditional ways of play carried on, too, in Co. Donegal and North Co. Antrim. In both of these areas, traditions of stick-and-ball play were as deep as in Tipperary or Galway, although the games were called various things other than hurling: shinny, commons, *camán*. The GAA did not make immediate inroads into these communities; indeed, the first hurling match played under association rules in North Antrim was not organized until the early years of the next century. And in Donegal, reports of traditional hurling matches survive from as late as 1906; in that year teams of farmworkers played cross-country hurling against each other in the Glengesh Pass, linking the villages of Glencolmcille and Ardara between the mountains of Glengesh and Mulmosog.[29]

Elsewhere, traditional forms of hurling were coming under severe pressure. In Galway, clubs such as Meelick – Killimor's neighbouring club and regular opponents – were willing to play under GAA rules on one Sunday and by traditional rules on another, depending on what suited.[30] As hurling clubs in various parts of Galway were formed and affiliated to the GAA, a seemingly unavoidable logic attached itself to the momentum of the GAA's progression.

In late August 1885, Craughwell, a newly formed club in Galway, won a tournament played under GAA rules in Athenry and were being referred to in the press as the hurlers 'who are now considered the best in the game in south Galway'.[31] This could not be let pass. Killimor had a view of themselves as the finest hurlers in the country, let alone in Galway. They challenged Craughwell to a match to be played in Loughrea on Sunday 27 September 1885, without specifying which rules the game should be played under; Craughwell agreed, on condition that the match be played to GAA rules. In keeping with the old tradition of playing for a wager, the stake to be put forward by each team was agreed at £6. The match was due to start at 3 p.m., but by 4 p.m. there was still no sign of the Killimor men. To entertain the crowd, the Craughwell players played a match amongst themselves.

The reason for Killimor's absence was straightforward. The Killimor captain, Francis Lynch, had written to the captain of the Craughwell team, P. Cawley, requesting a meeting to agree the rules for the match. He asked that Cawley reply by return of post. Cawley did indeed reply, saying that he would be in Loughrea on Sunday to meet Killimor's challenge, but for some reason, that letter did not reach Killimor in time. The hurlers, thinking there was to be no match, decided not to travel to Loughrea. Later, the Killimor men apologized in the press for any inconvenience caused to the Craughwell club, who, for their part, claimed the stake money.[32]

Even as it became obvious that the hurling world was changing around them, Killimor remained outside the GAA. They continued to follow their old ways of issuing challenges to other clubs. In early 1886, they directed a challenge to play a match against any club from outside Galway for the Championship of Ireland. The stakes were to be £20 a side.[33]

Before Killimor were able to get their Championship of Ireland under way, however, Michael Cusack pulled the rug out from under their feet.

VII

In the autumn of 1885, Cusack had been considering ways to hold a major hurling match in Dublin. He was proud of the progress being made in Dublin, particularly by the Metropolitans club, but he had also arrived at the view that hurling as played in the countryside was of a superior standard and that bringing it to Dublin would help in spreading the game's development in the city. In October 1885 Cusack wrote in *United Ireland* of his plan to bring two teams of seasoned hurlers to Dublin – one from Tipperary, the other from Galway. The Nenagh club, led by Frank Maloney, began preparations to bring a representative team from the clubs across North Tipperary by holding a tournament from which the best players from the area would be chosen. Cusack then called on the men of Galway to send up a team of first-class hurlers to Dublin to play a challenge against them.[34] By the end of December, he had his answer. Twelve hurling clubs from South Galway came together to play a series of matches in the town of Gort and, afterwards, they sent word to Cusack that they had a team ready to meet the North Tipperary challenge in late January or early February 1885.[35] The team was led by Daniel F. Burke, an old friend of Cusack from his time teaching around Gort in the late 1860s and early 1870s.[36]

Cusack arranged for the game to be played in the Phoenix Park on Tuesday 16 February 1886. The match was played there only because Cusack was unable to secure the use of Lansdowne Road or any other enclosed ground in the city; it is not clear why a Tuesday was the chosen day. In the week of the match, newspapers billed the game as the 'Championship of Ireland'.[37]

The North Tipperary team had arrived by train to Broadstone station at 5 p.m. on the evening before the game. They went first to their lodgings on Marlborough Street, and then to Dan Lowrey's Star of Erin theatre on Dame Street. At 9.30 p.m. Cusack called for them at the theatre and brought them back to Broadstone station to meet the Galway men, who were arriving on the 10 p.m. train. The two teams exchanged cordial greetings and mutual admiration, before a disagreement arose over the ball to be used in the match. The Galway men viewed the ball used by the Tipperary men as being too big and too soft. They retired to the Clarence Hotel where they were staying. On the morning of the match, they made a ball that was smaller and harder, and headed to the Phoenix Park.[38]

The press reported that despite the damp, cold weather, a very big crowd turned out, with 'every class being represented', and that 'quite a large number of vehicles fringed the ground'. The North Tipperary men wore green-and-orange striped jerseys, stockings and caps; the South Galway players wore white jerseys, corduroy knicks, grey stockings and green caps. The jerseys for the Galway team had been knitted for them by nuns in Gort at their knitting factory, while their knicks had been sewn by a local tailor, Packie Shaughnessy.[39] It was decided that the Tipperary ball would be used for the first half and the Galway one for the second. When the two teams lined up in the middle of the field, they made an arch in the air with their hurleys and let out a huge cheer.

The clash of styles immediately became apparent. The Tipperary men sought to move the ball first time by hitting it on the ground or in the air. The Galway team preferred to dribble the ball forward on the ground in front of them. It was also clear that the Tipperary team was stronger and, for almost all of the first half, they pinned the Galway men close to their own goal without managing to score. Midway through the second half, Martin Gleeson finally scored for North Tipperary, securing victory. The Tipperary goalkeeper on the day was Pat Gleeson from Gow, and he was reported to have roared at his teammates: 'For God's sake, will ye let the ball come this way. I'm dying with the cowld.'[40]

Cusack was evidently relieved that the match had passed without a fight or a serious injury. He wrote that the rules of the GAA had been 'observed with a scrupulousness which was almost religious' and that the GAA had 'passed triumphantly through the most critical ordeal of its existence'. The journalist for the Dublin weekly sports newspaper *Sport*, which up until that day had largely ignored the GAA, was not nearly as effusive. He praised the fine physiques of both sets of players, but viewed the general standard of play as 'crude and primitive' and lamented that there was 'a regrettable absence of science' in the match.[41]

Cusack responded to these barbs with a typical rhetorical flourish and dismissed the naysayers as 'haters and traducers of our race'. He was buoyant at the success of the match and wrote that the championship of Ireland now rested with the North Tipperary team: any club that wished to wrest it from them should send a challenge to Frank Maloney, Castle Hotel, Nenagh, Co. Tipperary.

For the team from South Galway there was nothing but recriminations. There had been local dissatisfaction at the team selected to travel to Dublin, and in the days before the match several key players had withdrawn. Local tradition in Gort has it that those hurlers who had travelled now preferred not to take the train home and face their public. Others offer a more mundane explanation: many of the players had missed the train because they had been taken by horse and car to the wrong station.[42]

4. The Triumph of Hurling

The progress of hurling during 1885 was rooted in the places where the game had survived, or had only recently been lost. But what happened next went beyond those places. The year 1886 was when the rebirth of hurling gathered a relentless, unshakeable momentum. It was not the case that hurling now swept the land and was played or acknowledged in every community. Indeed, there were large swathes of the country where hurling remained something unseen. Nonetheless, the spread of the game during 1886 was confirmation that the revival of hurling was now a thing of substance.

I

In the week after the North Tipperary–South Galway match, Metropolitans put down permanent goalposts in the Phoenix Park and established a dedicated hurling pitch. The hurlers now had a place to play in Dublin and hundreds of people came out on the city's trams to watch them. Some of these bystanders joined the club, and the number of people playing hurling in Dublin began to grow.

Around the country, new networks of play were established. In April 1886, a team from Killaloe in Co. Clare crossed the river Shannon into Tipperary and played a match against the Shamrock hurling club from Limerick.[1] Shortly afterwards, Nenagh went west to Portumna and played a match against

Meelick in front of 6,000 spectators. Clubs in towns and villages such as Templemore, Feakle and Ogonnelloe rented fields and began to issue challenges to rivals.[2]

For the old-style hurlers from Killimor, it had now become apparent that there was little choice but to join the GAA. On 17 April 1886 the *Western News* reported that the Killimor club had held its first practice match under GAA hurling rules, 'the club having recently affiliated'.[3] For Michael Cusack, the rise of the GAA was unstoppable and the entry into the association of wayward clubs and players was simply a matter of time, part of what he now called the 'inevitable process of absorption'.[4]

On Easter Sunday 1886, Thurles was chosen as the venue for a 'Monster Tournament' of hurling and football matches played between clubs from Dublin and Tipperary. A special excursion train brought one thousand 'Dublin Gaels' to Thurles. As well as hurlers and footballers from five different clubs, the train carried two brass bands and hundreds of supporters. The tournament took place on the edge of the town in a field where Daniel O'Connell had staged a vast meeting in 1843 in support of Irish independence. It was a most appropriate venue. As one of the local organizers in Thurles, James Butler, later explained, the tournament took place against the backdrop of a wild, political fervour: 'The time was one of intense political excitement. Irish hearts beat high, Irishmen were about to see the fruition of their hopes. Gladstone had introduced his Home Rule Bill seventeen days before in the House of Commons.'[5]

But Irish nationalist hopes were to be dashed. Unionists and Tories were joined in opposition to the Home Rule Bill by members of Gladstone's own Liberal Party, and the bill was defeated, in June 1886, by 343 votes to 311. Defeat led ultimately to a General Election in which the Liberal Party lost power. Home Rule would be off the agenda for as long as the Tories held power in the House of Commons.

By contrast, the Thurles tournament of Easter Sunday 1886 was, wrote Michael Cusack, 'the greatest victory yet achieved by the Gaelic Athletic Association'.[6] A huge crowd turned out to see the games. It says much for the nature of hurling at the time that five of the matches ended in scoreless draws; in the sixth, the local Holycross team defeated Metropolitans by one goal to nil. In time, the lack of scoring would have to be addressed in the rules.

II

It was one thing to convince the small number of existing hurling areas – or even areas with a lost tradition in the game – to adopt and promote the GAA rules for hurling. The greater challenge was how to promote the game in the areas where it simply did not have any presence, real or remembered – as was the case in most of the country. Using newspapers to advise clubs how to start hurling, how to arrange practice sessions and how best to lay out their teams was useful, but only went so far.[7] Inducements were offered: a Wexford MP promised to put up a cup to encourage hurling locally, and Michael Cusack promised a challenge cup worth 25 guineas to be played for by clubs north and west of the river Shannon. Neither cup seems ever to have been produced or played for.[8]

Of far greater value was the work of hurlers in spreading their own game. Metropolitans were among the most important evangelists. One of their players, Paddy Molohan, moved to Co. Kildare for work. There, he set up the Monasterevan Brewery and Distillery Club, which began playing hurling in its chosen colours of blue and straw.[9] Patrick Kiernan, who played for Metropolitans in the Thurles match on Easter Sunday 1886, set about establishing hurling in Blackrock College when he went to work there in the autumn of 1887. Kiernan appears to have been supported by the dean of the college, Fr Brennan, and the belief was that the example set by Blackrock would inspire other Catholic colleges to adopt hurling.[10]

The Dublin clubs also began to travel outside the city to play exhibition matches. When hurlers from Faugh-a-Ballaghs, Metropolitans and Dunleary travelled by train to Dundalk, the game was abandoned after ten minutes, with the crowd rushing onto the field in ignorance of the rules. Time and persistence brought better fortune. In early 1887 a hurling club was established in Dundalk and another team of hurlers from various Dublin clubs went up and played a match. P. P. Sutton, from Metropolitans, noted that the faults of the Dundalk men were the same as those of inexperienced hurlers everywhere: stopping the ball with their feet and then scraping it forward along the ground, instead of hitting it a hard, quick blow. He offered a coaching lesson: 'Get a few balls and puck them about indiscriminately. Strike both left and right as hard and as fast as possible, and let no-one stop the ball with his feet.'[11]

Faugh-a-Ballaghs – considered second only to Metropolitans in the hierarchy of Dublin hurling clubs – committed to travelling to play the Waterside club in Derry. The Faughs' club minute book noted that 'though it is very hard to get a team to go such a distance, they could not see such a rising energetic club from the north disappointed, and as the Derry boys say the games are not very well known up there, we shall have much pleasure in instructing them'.[12]

III

Irish emigrant communities now also began to promote the GAA's rules for hurling. The Irish had played hurling across three continents long before the founding of the association. This was a fragmented history: the playing of the game invariably depended on the presence in a foreign city of a critical mass of emigrants from an area of Ireland where hurling was played. In the 1750s, people had paid to see hurling matches in London. The game had also been played in Paris and New York in the eighteenth century, and in various North American cities (such as San Francisco and Toronto) in the 1850s and 1860s, as well as New Zealand in the 1870s.

In two foreign places, the game had taken on a modern aspect before the GAA was even founded. The first of these was Melbourne, and its surrounding towns in the Australian state of Victoria. During the late 1870s, Irish emigrants looked at the explosion of Australian Rules football, rugby and cricket clubs, and adapted their traditional game of hurling to this new sporting model. Through 1877 and 1878 clubs were formed, a league was organized, and rules for the game laid down.[13] Between 1877 and 1884 some twenty teams, appearing and disappearing again, played hurling matches around Melbourne at one point or another – with some players using hurleys imported from Ireland. The presence of numerous emigrants from North Tipperary was crucial here. They were instrumental in the establishment of the Victorian Hurling Association in 1878, and although the organization collapsed soon after its formation (it may not even have lasted a season), hurling continued to be played in Melbourne by Irishmen and their sons.[14] The foundation of the GAA brought a new impetus to hurling in Australia almost immediately, and its rules were published in full in the Melbourne *Advocate* in March 1885.[15] When Patrick Long from Tuam, Co. Galway, established a hurling club in Sydney in May 1885, Australian newspapers reported that he used the code of rules prepared by the GAA. Hurling clubs were also established in Brisbane and in the New South Wales towns of Lismore and Coraki later in 1885.[16]

The second city where the GAA's rules for hurling were taken on was Boston, where a match under association rules was played in 1886. The game was already being played in the city, at least from the early 1880s when the Boston and South Boston hurling clubs played for stakes of up to $300, with the Boyle O'Reilly Cup, worth $250, presented to the winner.[17] The trophy was named for John Boyle O'Reilly, a Fenian who had been transported to Australia and sentenced to twenty years' penal servitude. He escaped to Boston, where he became editor of the *Pilot* newspaper and published volumes of poetry during the 1870s. Like Michael Cusack, Boyle O'Reilly read of hurling in modern editions of ancient texts. He wrote that hurling had been opposed by the English, 'whose object has ever been to unman and degrade Irishmen until ignorance of conflict, even in sport, had robbed them of self-confidence and fitted them for the position of hopeless subjection designed for them'.[18] Reports of hurling matches in his paper make clear that, in Boston, there was no written code of rules; rather, matches were arranged between teams who agreed the rules of the contest before play.[19] The result was a certain disharmony: the 1885 hurling contest for the

Boyle O'Reilly Cup ended in the district court.[20] The adoption of the GAA rules saw hurling now played on Boston Common, and in the following years GAA rules were also used in Canada and Argentina.[21]

But did influence flow in the other direction? Had the new GAA rules for hurling been shaped by the game as played in Australia and America? And, more to the point, was the very project of the GAA an imitation of what Irish emigrants were attempting in foreign cities? It seems inconceivable that Michael Cusack and Maurice Davin were unaware that in some emigrant communities hurling was still being played. Equally, it is possible that they had heard of the brief existence of the Victoria Hurling Association and that Maurice Davin was aware of the rules which it used when he wrote the new rules for hurling in early 1885. Yet none of these facts were referred to by Cusack and Davin either at the time the GAA was being founded or later, when they reminisced about their deeds. In none of the tens of thousands of words written in the newspapers before or after the founding of the GAA was reference made to the existence of hurling clubs in emigrant communities as an influence on the revival of the sport.

IV

The rise of hurling, dramatic though it was, could not match that of Gaelic football. The bottom line was that more clubs played football than played hurling. This was the cause of bitter lament for some writers of letters to newspapers. One correspondent wrote: 'Having seen what a noble, what a magnificent game is hurling, is it not a matter for sincere regret that hurling clubs are not more numerous throughout Ireland at the present time, and that football seems to be taking the lead.'[22]

There was no getting away from the fact that it was easier to spread Gaelic football than it was to spread hurling. P. P. Sutton observed: 'The revival of hurling is heavily handicapped in comparison with that of football. The implements for playing it are far more expensive and more difficult to procure, while the practice necessary to attain any degree of proficiency with the *camán* [hurley] is vastly greater than that required for football. As regards football, all that is required to play it is a ten- or twelve-shilling ball, and without more ado a whole parish may indulge in the game to their hearts' content.'[23] Gaelic football also had the advantage that its early rules were markedly similar to those of rugby and it was able to convince rugby players and, indeed, entire rugby clubs to join the GAA.

Cusack made clear in his early columns in *United Ireland* that his love for hurling was unsurpassed, but he was also clear that the GAA would make room for all 'national sports', even if they were not all 'old ones'. He opened the GAA up to handball and to road-bowling, a sport which he considered ideal for hot weather, the equivalent to tennis for the English. When the Dalkey GAA club in Dublin established a rowing section, he said that this was a great idea for association clubs based beside rivers, lakes and the sea. He welcomed the establishment of the Limerick Gaelic Bicycle Club and reported that GAA events often featured horse-racing, as well as donkey- and jennet-racing. The early association also ran Grand Bands contests across a wide range of musical tastes, often in conjunction with its sports; it was a broad sporting 'church' which drew people in through its doors by any means available.[24] While Gaelic football quickly became – and would remain – the most popular of the GAA's games, hurling benefited from being associated with football, athletics and other pursuits during these crucial early years. Hurlers complained that their matches were often merely tacked onto the end of vast football tournaments and athletics meetings, but at least hurling was on the bill. And the sheer breadth of pursuits catered for by the GAA created an impetus and an energy that benefited them all.

V

The speed with which GAA tournaments spread through 1886 and 1887 cannot be explained by mere love of sport. This was, instead, an extraordinary cultural phenomenon. From the very beginning the association offered Irish people a day out with a difference – a unique cocktail of sport and drink and music and pageantry, which mixed the local with the national.

On any given Sunday, towns across Ireland filled with locals and visitors. Archbishop Croke endorsed the Sunday matches, saying that they did not lead to desecration of the Sabbath as GAA players were 'never unmindful of the obligations of hearing mass'.[25] Some must have taken mass at a very early hour in order to jump on the special excursion trains that began to criss-cross the country, bringing teams to grand tournaments. It was a boon for the railway companies, who offered special deals for match-day outings, and for travel agents such as Thomas Cook, who filled trains with teams and brass bands and supporters. Journeys were shortened by songs and recitations, by playing cards and dancing jigs.[26]

Bands and their music became central to GAA tournaments. Patriotic songs such as 'God Save Ireland', 'The Wearing of the Green' and 'O'Donnell Aboo' were supplemented by popular music-hall tunes of the age and even operatic pieces. Whether originating at a train station or from some makeshift dressing room in a town or village, the GAA parade immediately established itself as a colourful, militant, raucous Pied Piper, drawing spectators towards the field of play. The parades wound along roads and streets, the players marching in military formation behind at least one band and their club banners. In Carrick-on-Suir, Co. Tipperary, the hurlers opened their playing season by marching through the town with their hurleys on their shoulders.[27] Later, more than seventy-five men on horseback wearing GAA uniforms, what police called a 'Gaelic Cavalry', galloped through the same town.[28] When the Kanturk Brass Band led players down Main Street in Charleville, Co. Cork, and out to a field on the edge of town, it was a clarion call: 'Over the hedges and across the fields from all directions, the people poured.'[29]

It is impossible to accurately gauge the numbers of people who did actually pour in, given the tendency of newspapers to exaggerate crowds. Nonetheless, regular reference is made to 3,000 or 5,000 and even up to 15,000 people attending matches in 1886 and 1887. The Thurles tournament of 1886 had been important to the early development of hurling, and the tournament held in the town the following year offered an opportunity to assess the growth of the GAA. The headlines in the press said it all.

Two Monster Gaelic Meetings at Thurles

———

Upwards of Twenty Thousand Spectators

———

Two Hundred and Ninety-Four Players

———

A Stone-Blind Man 'Looking' at the Hurling

As Michael Cusack reported: 'From the streets and lanes of Thurles and surrounding towns, in carriage and cart, by road and rail, on foot and horseback, on crutches and in arms, streams of human life flowed for several hours on to the hurling fields.'[30]

VI

And it was not just men who turned up. Clubs such as Dauntless in Kingstown, Co. Dublin, offered free admission to women.[31] It was de rigueur in newspaper reports of the time to note the presence of women in every sporting crowd, and hurling was no exception. According to Cusack, women turned up at matches dressed in their 'gala attire . . . to flash looks and smiles of approval on their rustic knights'. He went to a hurling tournament in Carrick-on-Suir and noted that many of the 7,000 crowd were women: 'Their presence had a perceptible influence on the players, especially the Tipperary contingents, souls so tender-hearted and so susceptible to female charms.'[32] For Cusack, it was not just the number of women present that mattered, more the type. He wrote of a match in Louth where 'females were there in great force – not the wasp-waisted, artificial-chested young ladies of the promenade, but the fine, free-and-easy, full-hearted, picture-of-health-like daughters, mothers, sisters and aunts'.[33]

It was in the scenery, rather than on the playing field, that women were expected to feature. The notion was still current that excessive sporting activity might diminish a woman's capacity to procreate. The general tendency of the Victorian sporting world was to patronize and parody the sporting female, as evidenced in a newspaper column suggesting that 'when a woman throws a brickbat, the great problem seems to be not how to hit the target, but how she can avoid knocking her brains out with her elbow'.[34] The *Nenagh Guardian* asked its readers what the best sort of wife for an athlete might be. Its answer: 'A dumb belle.'[35]

A report from Co. Kildare noted the 'comical aspect' of one match: 'No less than sixty hurlers took the field and one gentleman, apparently of Ethiopian extraction, came in for a large share of notice – particularly from the fair sex – presumably because he was different from all the others, although he wielded his camán like a true son of St. Patrick.'[36] Michael Cusack, though given to questioning the masculinity of men he disagreed with, never lapsed into this kind of sneering or innuendo when writing about women. He repeatedly praised women and lamented the manner in which they were treated by Irish society. He wrote: 'To shut every woman in a dwelling-house and make of her an animated broom and dust-pan is to abuse a great many women and ruin a great many houses.'[37] Cusack was a long-time supporter of the need to develop industry for women, yet he was also typical of his age in that he saw the role of women in sport as auxiliary and decorative. At a match in Tipperary, he wrote, so taken was one woman 'with the dexterity and skill of the play, that she expressed her regret [women] were not eligible for election as members of the GAA, because, she said, if they could not kick football itself, they could decorate the jerseys for the boys'. When Cusack called for the establishment of embroidery clubs, he was supported by a letter writer who argued that the GAA should set up a special 'GAA Young Women's Industrial Department', allowing women to exhibit their fancy handiwork on the sidelines at matches.[38]

VII

The sidelines at matches were also populated by men betting on the outcome. At Cork Park gaming tables were a regular feature, leading to complaints that 'the rattle of the dice and the roll of the roulette constituted a disagreeably inappropriate accompaniment to the manly games in progress within ear-shot'.[39] Michael Cusack railed against gambling at GAA matches, believing it the greatest enemy of the association. Betting, he wrote, was a 'degrading vice. It has reduced millionaires to beggary; it has ruined thousands, body and mind; and it has peopled the felons' cell and the suicides' grave, many a time and oft.' The scale of gambling is impossible to quantify, but there was enough for Cusack to worry about the capacity of bookmakers – 'the man with the glazed hat, who stands on an upturned soapbox' – to lead the innocent down dangerous paths.[40]

Con artists and hucksters were also to be found on the sidelines. At matches in King's County, there were repeated references to 'tricks-o'-the-loop' and other gambling games in which men tried to lure spectators into betting away their hard-earned cash. A local newspaper noted that they invariably enjoyed huge success: 'Many of the rustics made grievously bad calculations, and judging by the lugubrious expression which pervaded many of their countenances as they retired, there is every reason to believe that a goodly number, to quote the words of one young fellow, got "dropped on".'[41]

VIII

The judgement of those who were conned was most likely clouded by drink. The GAA offered publicans and drinkers the ideal vehicle with which to sidestep the licensing laws. Except in the cities of Dublin, Belfast, Cork, Limerick and Waterford, where pubs were allowed to open between 2 p.m. and 7 p.m. on Sundays, the law mandated complete Sunday closing following the Sale of Liquors on Sunday Act (Ireland), 1878. This was the latest in a series of laws that gave extensive powers to the police in Ireland to regulate the opening hours of pubs and to suppress the operations of shebeens and other illegal traders in alcohol. It had a significant loophole, however, in that anyone who journeyed more than three miles from their home was considered a bona-fide traveller and was entitled to be served in a pub. This – coupled with an uneven approach to the use of the enforcement powers conferred on police and magistrates – essentially ensured that anybody who wished to drink alcohol on a Sunday in Ireland could easily do so. Indeed, when a GAA tournament was staged in a town, the numbers who arrived made the idea of Sunday closing an irrelevancy.[42] And, as was routinely demonstrated, local people appear to have found no difficulty in persuading publicans to sell them drink, whether they had travelled the requisite three miles or not. Sunday after Sunday, the licensing laws of Ireland were as honoured in the breach as they were in the observance.[43]

In the 1880s leading GAA figures such as Cusack and Croke repeatedly sought to praise GAA players and spectators for the manner in which they abstained from alcohol. There was more than a hint of wishful thinking to this. In reality, the GAA was awash with drink. Perhaps the clearest evidence of the scale of the drinking at GAA games was the number of different rules passed at local and national level by the association, calling for drunkenness at matches to be quashed.[44] Drinking was, from the beginning, a central element of the day's entertainment. Alcohol was sold on the sideline (under licence) at some GAA events, drawing occasional complaints that it was overpriced;[45] and pubs in the vicinity of pitches were thronged on match days.

For the hurlers, post-match drinking sessions were part of the day's ritual. Hurlers taking the train home from various parts of Ireland were reported as being 'well fortified for the journey', as 'the wants of the inner man had been fully attended to'.[46] When it came to drinking, hurlers were encouraged to support their own. After Jim Costelloe of the Davitt hurlers bought a pub in Fairview in Dublin, a player from the rival Metropolitans club considered that drinking in Costelloe's was now almost a matter of patriotism: 'It is the proper thing for Gaels to support as much as possible those who have been doing their best since the foundation of the GAA to further the cause of our national pastimes.'[47] Various other prominent Dublin hurlers and footballers bought or leased pubs during the 1880s, and when another bought a tobacco

and cigar divan opposite the Queen Theatre on Great Bruns-
wick Street, Gaels were called upon to 'patronise him liberally
when wanting a supply of the fragrant weed'.[48]

The good news was that drinking, as well as smoking, was
not merely patriotic, but actually good for you. Columns in
the Irish sporting press regularly extolled the dietary value of
alcohol. Temperance campaigners were condemned as 'modern fanatics' and dark warnings were issued on the nature of
a world without drink: 'The people who used it least are sav-
ages, Hindoos and Turks . . . And every nation that has done
any good in the world, without exception, have brought up
their splendid races on a diet in which alcohol has formed a
constant and essential part.'[49] To preserve Ireland from such
fanaticism, publicans had established the Society for the Pre-
vention of Intemperance. They need not have worried about
many of the hurlers, who drank before and even during
matches. When Roscomroe beat Frankford in a match in
King's County, the players were so thrilled with the victory
that they spent the afternoon drinking despite the fact that
they were due to play Dunkerrin and Moneygall later in the
day. In part, of course, this provided the ideal excuse for sub-
sequent failure, as a famous local ballad in Roscomroe
concluded: ' "Twas the liquor that defeated us!'[50]

5. The Fall of Michael Cusack

The advance of hurling through 1886 was testimony to the vision of Michael Cusack and the pragmatism of Maurice Davin. Hurling had been redesigned to fit with the new ways in which sport was being organized in the Victorian world and was now beginning to flourish under the auspices of the GAA. It should have been Cusack's finest hour, but this was not to be. In a dramatic turn of events, he was removed from his position as secretary of the GAA. Under his secretaryship, the GAA had (in his own words) 'spread like a prairie fire'. How was it that Cusack could be dismissed from leading the thriving association that he himself had founded?

I

Michael Cusack has been painted as the victim of a Fenian coup. This version of events imagines that the Irish Republican Brotherhood had used Cusack as a stooge in founding the GAA. Later, having tired of him and his volatility in the summer of 1886, the Fenians ruthlessly removed him.[1] There is some logic to this interpretation. At least two of the men who attended the first meeting of the GAA in Hayes' Hotel on 1 November 1884 were active in the IRB, and Fenians were involved in setting up GAA clubs in towns and villages in the months that followed. The extent to which the IRB was involved in the GAA was detailed at considerable length in a series of secret reports that were sent to Dublin Castle from police districts all over Ireland.

The British government had established a Crime Branch Special division within the Royal Irish Constabulary to enhance its surveillance of the IRB. The detectives of the special branch relied heavily on secret informers. Within months of the founding of the GAA, informers were being paid to infiltrate its ranks. These reports made clear the view that the GAA was far more than a sporting organization, even if the evidence produced by spies and informers was sometimes a little fanciful. Throughout the 1880s, special branch detectives regularly shadowed GAA leaders as they went about their business. Detailed portraits were written of these men and their habits. Michael Deering, a leading IRB man and Cork GAA official, was the clerk of a brewery, and his ruddy complexion was the result of 'intemperate habits'.[2] P. J. Kelly was a farmer who was prominent in IRB and GAA circles in Galway; he had dark grey eyes, a crooked nose and whiskers, and walked with a stoop.[3]

Some of these Fenians were certainly involved in ousting Michael Cusack from his position as secretary. But the reasons for his removal were sporting and personal, not political.

II

The almost immediate success of the GAA had fuelled Michael Cusack's sense of mission. With his school also thriving and his newspaper columns giving him further prominence, Cusack was a man in full bloom. But he was also singularly unable to avoid confrontation. Differences of opinion over sporting matters developed quickly into personal quarrels. By 1886 Cusack seemed incapable of diplomacy and was devoid of perspective in personal exchanges. This brought about a series of disputes that culminated in his removal from the GAA.

Cusack's problems in 1886 had their origins in Cork in the autumn of 1885, and related to Gaelic football. The earliest games of football played under GAA rules had been notably similar to rugby, with players prone to carrying the ball under their arm rather than striking it forward with foot or fist.[4] The rules of the game were vague and were the focus of dissatisfaction in certain quarters – most notably in Cork.

In October 1885, football clubs in Cork city held a meeting and adopted a code of rules which, it was intended, would be submitted to the GAA for consideration at its first annual convention. Receiving a copy of the rules, Michael Cusack condemned them as 'rugby undisguised'.[5] Maurice Davin was equally unimpressed and the Cork rules were dismissed out of hand.[6] The Cork city clubs were undaunted and duly established their own association, the Munster National Football League, with J. F. Murphy, a vice-president of the GAA, as its president. That league had framed its rules, as its secretary later explained, because GAA rules were suitable for country clubs, but not for players who worked in the city behind counters: 'If the city men went to work in the city with a black eye they would be sent playing football the other six days of the week.'[7]

Cusack immediately dubbed the new association 'The Murphy National English Football League'. The GAA reacted to the threat from Cork by unanimously agreeing at a general meeting that J. F. Murphy should be expelled from the association.[8] It was further agreed that affiliated GAA clubs should be told not to play matches against any other club that was not playing under GAA rules. When the clubs in Cork held a meeting to protest against the expulsion of J. F. Murphy, Cusack took the train to the city to defend the decision. He adopted a reasonably conciliatory tone at the meeting, but he was appalled at the notion of one set of football rules being suited to 'vulgar rustics' while another was used by the residents of towns and cities.[9]

The Munster National Football League quickly disappeared, but the true importance of the Cork meeting lies in how it was reported in the *Freeman's Journal*. Cusack had long had a poor opinion of the *Freeman's Journal* and of its sister paper, the weekly *Sport*. He believed (with some justification) that the papers had never given the GAA adequate coverage. The editor of *Sport*, P. B. Kirwan, was also the representative of the English Amateur Athletic Association in Ireland.[10] Cusack regularly launched scandalous public attacks against the two papers and their staff.

Cusack was enraged by the (relatively innocuous) report that appeared in the *Freeman's Journal* regarding the football dispute in Cork. He turned to Frank Maloney and the North Tipperary branch, and arranged for them to pass a motion condemning the *Freeman's Journal* for its persistent hostility to the GAA. The owner of the newspaper, E. D. Gray, an Irish Parliamentary Party MP, published the North Tipperary motion and replied that neither he nor his papers had ever been hostile to the GAA. However, in a clear allusion to Cusack, he continued: 'I found one of its officials almost intolerable, which is quite another thing.'

This row would have had no consequences for Cusack if Archbishop Croke, still a patron of the GAA, had not intervened. One of the charges which Cusack had made was that the *Freeman's Journal* had 'delayed and cut down' its report of a speech which Croke had made in Waterford in which he lauded the work of the GAA. The problem for Cusack was that Croke had privately raised Cusack's allegations of bias with Gray and had come away satisfied that they were not correct. The archbishop had also clearly reached the view that Cusack's confrontational approach to running the GAA needed to be challenged. On 19 March 1886, Croke wrote publicly that Cusack's claims were 'utterly and absolutely without foundation', and asked that an end be put to this 'irritating and useless controversy'.

Backed into a corner, Cusack acted with courage – and with stunning ill judgement. He wrote privately to Archbishop Croke and claimed that the reality was that the GAA had been treated 'vilely' by the *Freeman's Journal*. He promised that, with God's help, he would face down both Croke and E. D. Gray. Croke immediately quoted Cusack's threat in a public letter, which he ended with a threat of his own: that he would resign as patron of the GAA 'if Mr. Michael Cusack is allowed to play the dictator in its counsels, to run a reckless tilt with impunity and without rebuke against me and everybody else who happens not to agree with him, and to keep the Irish athletic world in perpetual feud and hot water'.[11]

GAA clubs across the country immediately passed motions condemning Cusack's 'insult' to Croke. The Lee football club lamented 'the unfortunate knack possessed by Mr. Cusack in a superlative degree of offending and insulting those with whom he comes in contact'. The Dungarvan club went further and condemned Cusack's 'power for evil', and even the North Tipperary branch condemned his 'insolent letter'. The general feeling was that Cusack would have to be removed as secretary, and an extraordinary general meeting of the association was duly called by the president, Maurice Davin.[12]

III

On Tuesday 6 April 1886, representatives of more than forty GAA clubs met at 2 p.m. in Hayes' Hotel in Thurles to consider Cusack's position as secretary. Cusack produced a bravura performance in making a full apology. The letter, he said, had been written in a fit of 'extreme irritation' at the *Freeman's Journal*. 'In view of the work we have been doing for the last eighteen months . . . I ask you to believe, as an Irishman born of the people, working and living and thinking for Ireland from the time I was able to hold up my head, I never dreamt of insulting the Archbishop.'

A large section of the meeting was not satisfied, believing, as one delegate put it, that Cusack 'was most indiscreet, and too impulsive, and that his actions would bring discredit to the association'. Cusack replied that he agreed his letter had been ill advised, but that he thought that his demeanour since then in abstaining from appearing in print showed his '*bona fide* desire to keep quiet'. Cusack's supporters moved that his apology should be sufficient to keep him his position, but others were determined that he be removed. The matter was put to a vote and Cusack survived by thirty-eight votes to fourteen. The fact that Davin had deemed the apology to be sufficient was crucial. He had himself received a private letter from Archbishop Croke saying that everyone knew that Cusack did not weigh his words sufficiently before expressing them, but he felt that no offence had been intended. It was also decided that Cusack was not to write a letter to the press without it being countersigned by one of his co-secretaries or by Davin.[13]

IV

Michael Cusack returned to Dublin, continued to write his newspaper columns, continued to promote hurling, continued to travel the country attending matches and tournaments. He clearly made a genuine effort to temper his behaviour and managed to avoid large-scale confrontations. But only for a time. By June 1886 his columns in *United Ireland* again strayed into criticism of his colleagues in the GAA.

More importantly, even his supporters within the GAA were growing increasingly irritated at Cusack's shortcomings as an administrator. Almost from the outset, he appears to have neglected the basic day-to-day running of the association. He rarely answered letters, did not forward affiliation fees to the treasurer, and ignored numerous requests from fellow officials in respect of basic organizational matters. The explanation for this neglect is surely bound up with the variety of other commitments that Cusack had at the time – his school, his journalism, and a young family that now extended to six children. Also, his talents clearly did not lie in the grind of routine administrative duties that are so central to the operation of a modern sporting organization.

A special meeting of the GAA was called for Sunday 4 July 1886 in Hayes' Hotel in Thurles to consider Cusack's position. On the day before the meeting, Cusack wrote in his column in the paper of 'rumours that one of the honorary secretaries has not been working in harmony with his colleagues'.[14] Maurice Davin could not be present, and the meeting was chaired by Frank Maloney, Cusack's old friend from Nenagh.

The meeting became a litany of Cusack's failings. His fellow secretary, John Wyse Power, submitted a letter that claimed 'mismanagement' and 'unaccountable neglect' by Cusack, and noted: 'Unless I submit to being a catspaw of Mr. Cusack I must endure endless annoyance.' He noted the progress made in framing rules, but concluded that 'the best rules will be useless unless they are properly administered'. To this end, Wyse Power submitted to the meeting what he considered to be 'a fair sample' of the complaints against Cusack from around the country, and declared the GAA to be 'wandering in confusion'. Cusack later derided Wyse Power's statement as being worthy only of 'a half-ecclesiastical student'.[15] However, the third secretary of the GAA, John McKay, a man who had done much to smooth over disputes created by Cusack in the past, confirmed the scale of Cusack's neglect of his administrative duties. McKay said that he had personally written dozens of letters to Cusack without ever receiving a reply. He said that Cusack had arrogated to himself the working of the association and never consulted with anyone else. He concluded that no secretary of any association or body had ever been as remiss, and that Cusack compounded this by insulting anyone who disagreed with his position on any point, small or large.[16]

Cusack's defence effectively confirmed the charges against him. He reached into his pocket and produced a bundle of cheques and postal orders which he threw out on the table in front of him. He had done no administrative work in the past three months, he said, because his hands had been tied by his colleagues who would not allow him to write a letter unless it was countersigned. Cusack's position worsened when the meeting was read a letter from the GAA treasurer, John Clancy, referring to Cusack's failure to provide accounts as he had been required by motion to do and describing Cusack's 'wanton insults'. Clancy concluded by saying that he feared for the success of the GAA if Cusack were 'permitted any longer to continue indiscriminately to insult and traduce his brother members'.

The meeting then considered a threat which Cusack was supposed to have made to a member of the Cork GAA. Cusack denied out of hand making the threat, but was called 'a damned liar' by J. K. Bracken, a Tipperary delegate and Fenian who had attended the founding meeting. At this point Cusack gathered his papers and left. As he went he called out: 'Brave Tipperary!'

As the meeting progressed without him, some of Cusack's long-time allies in Dublin hurling offered something of a defence. A representative of the Faugh-a-Ballagh club, George Washington, complained that not enough information on the charges against Cusack had been provided to clubs in advance of the meeting. However, Washington accepted that Cusack was 'guilty of all the charges brought against him'. He argued against expelling Cusack only because the opponents of the GAA would consider the organization unable to govern itself. A motion was put forward that Cusack be allowed stay on as secretary, on the condition that he be required to respond to all letters within three days of receiving them. But too much damage had been done. When an amendment was put that Cusack be requested to resign his position, it was carried by forty-seven votes to thirteen. The result was declared to the sound of applause in the room.[17]

V

Michael Cusack did not go quietly. In his column in *United Ireland* on the following Saturday he wrote a deadpan, one-paragraph account of the meeting, which ended with the line: 'A resolution was passed calling on Mr. Cusack to resign because he had not replied to letters addressed to him.' Above the column, he still referred to himself as a secretary of the GAA and beneath the column he wrote a letter to the editor of *United Ireland* which underlined his commitment to the association and included the pithy line: 'Perhaps I have not discharged my duties to everyone's satisfaction, but I will not give up.' He made a loose appeal for support and said he looked forward to the annual convention in November to tidy up the year's business.[18]

The following week he sat for a photograph with the Metropolitan hurlers. In his column in *United Ireland*, he continued to give a glowing description of the extent to which hurling and football matches and tournaments were taking place across the countryside in that summer of 1886. The strategy was a straightforward one: Cusack was taking the approach of ignoring the vote removing him from office in the GAA.

The 31 July 1886 edition of *United Ireland* carried a letter from the executive of the GAA: 'Mr. Cusack insists that he shall be an officer of the Gaelic Athletic Association; that body insists that it does not want him as an officer.' The letter called for Cusack's column to be dropped from the paper. It was. An editorial note lamented the 'domestic quarrels' of the GAA and announced that the limited space in the paper would be used for other purposes.[19]

Michael Cusack never again returned to high office within the GAA. When he finished working as secretary, *Sport* reported, Cusack 'locked up all communications, including post office and postal orders for affiliation fees', and declined to hand them over.[20] There was no suggestion that he had used the money for his own ends, and Cusack himself later said: 'It was well known that the orders had not been cashed.'[21] He was disgusted at being removed from office and at being replaced by men whom he now considered to be his sworn enemies. It was a squalid end to what should have been a glorious summer.

VI

Although Michael Cusack was not the victim of an IRB coup, the Fenians were ideally placed to benefit from the space which was now created in the leadership of the GAA. For the IRB, the attractions of seizing control were obvious. The prospect of staging an armed revolution to overthrow British rule in Ireland was remote. A radical splinter group had embarked on a dynamiting campaign which resulted in explosions in London in early 1885 in the Tower of London, in Westminster Hall and at the House of Commons, and there had been other less spectacular revolutionary acts over the years, but all of these served mainly to highlight the sense that the IRB existed on the margins of political life. In this context it is not a surprise that some IRB men saw in the GAA the opportunity to move into the mainstream.

In September 1886, the president of the Supreme Council of the IRB, John O'Leary, was invited to join Croke, Davitt and Parnell as the fourth patron of the GAA. It was a symbolic acknowledgement of the importance of the role that Republicans had played within the GAA. Then, at the GAA's second annual convention in Thurles on 15 November 1886, the IRB claimed almost every position of importance in the GAA. The four vice-presidents – J. K. Bracken, J. E. Kennedy, Pat Hoctor and Frank Maloney – were all Fenians. Ditto all four secretaries: John Wyse Power, Tim O'Riordan, J. B. O'Reilly and James Butler. And, finally, another IRB man, Patrick Hassett from Ahane in Co. Limerick, was appointed the new treasurer.[22] The only remaining official of importance who was not a Fenian was the re-elected president, Maurice Davin.

The success of the IRB in securing so many positions within the leadership of the GAA suggests a bloodless coup. But it was a more complicated victory than that. For a start, a simple question hung in the air: what exactly did it mean to be a Fenian? Membership of the IRB did not necessarily make you a revolutionary. There were many people who saw the organization as a vehicle for social outings and cultural prestige.

At least three of the IRB men in key GAA positions – Frank Maloney, J. K. Bracken and J. E. Kennedy – appeared to be in thrall to sport at least as much as they were to Republicanism. Kennedy had been the one who brought hurleys to Dublin in 1883 to help with the formation of the Metropolitan club, and had later played in goal for that team.

It is also true that the reason why various IRB men were able to assume positions of importance within the GAA was because they were supported by a wide range of non-Fenians. It was Maurice Davin who proposed J. E. Kennedy for the position of vice-president. And Davin – who was in no shape or form an adherent of the IRB – supported the elevation of

John O'Leary as patron of the GAA by saying that the GAA (with O'Leary joining Croke, Parnell and Davitt as patrons) now had a four-leafed shamrock and that O'Leary would have a very prominent position in the association.[23] This was a clear acknowledgement of the broad alliances that existed in Irish politics in the 1880s, with the representatives of church, land, parliamentary politics and revolutionary separatism more closely linked than ever before. It would be wrong to overstate the extent to which the various nationalist traditions in Ireland were truly united in the 1880s, but there can be no escaping the fact that the events of that decade had radicalized many moderates.

In 1886 the political situation revolved around two basic issues. Firstly, the defeat of the Home Rule Bill had led to a summer of murderous rioting and mob violence. Secondly, the launch of a 'Plan of Campaign' by William O'Brien and three other Irish Parliamentary Party MPs in October 1886 brought a new dimension to land agitation. The 'Plan' came in the wake of a new agricultural crisis and increased evictions across rural Ireland. It was published in *United Ireland* on 23 October 1886 and offered a clear path of resistance against landlords. It advised that tenants who had sought and been refused reductions in their rents should offer a rent that they considered to be fair. If this was refused by the landlord – or by his agents – the tenants would pay the proposed rent into an 'estate fund' that would be used to support any tenant who might be evicted. It was not as dramatic as the Land War of 1879 to 1882, but it was potent nonetheless.

VII

The second annual convention of the GAA, which had brought the election of so many IRB men to positions of consequence within it, was not a Fenian political caucus. It was first and foremost a gathering that made some important sporting decisions. Prominent among these was the decision to establish national championships in hurling, football and handball. It has been argued to the point of cliché that the GAA thrived because of its success in channelling local rivalries between parishes. This is true, but it is also the case that the GAA thrived because it understood almost immediately the value of national competition, of providing a sporting challenge that would transcend parish boundaries and local rivalries to encompass the entire island. The informal growth of challenge matches between clubs from separate counties through 1886 had brought a new dynamic to the association. This was apparent to everyone connected to the GAA as early as the Thurles tournament of Easter 1886, and it was underlined in many other places. There was, for example, the hugely successful tournament played in 1886 between teams from Wicklow and Wexford at Parnell's lands in Avondale in the south of Wicklow.

And then there was the extraordinary success of a tournament between teams from Cork and Tipperary in August 1886. On a warm summer's day, five Tipperary teams took the train south for a series of matches against the best Cork clubs, drawing a crowd of more than 20,000 to Cork Park. It was a remarkable occasion, full of pageantry and music. The Cork teams were declared to be generally victorious but even the local papers felt obliged to note how the partisan behaviour of the home-town referees and the continuous interference of home supporters hurt the chances of the Tipp men.[24]

These matches were to the fore of the minds of the new executive as they set about revising the constitution of the GAA in the autumn of 1886. The new constitution contained a series of innovations, at the heart of which was a proposal to establish All-Ireland hurling and football championships. The proposal was greeted with unanimous approval when it was put to the second annual convention of the GAA in the Thurles Young Men's Society Hall on Monday 15 November 1886. The rules for the proposed hurling championship, read out by John Wyse Power, were as follows:

1. The championship was open to all affiliated clubs of the GAA.
2. All entries were to be made before 1 January 1887 and the entrance fee per team was 2s.6d.
3. Clubs in each county would first play off a championship between themselves on a knockout basis, and these internal county championships were to be played off between 1 February and 17 March. For this reason County Committees would now be established.
4. The winning club in each county would then proceed to play off against the winning teams from the other counties, with the All-Ireland final to be played by the end of the first week in May.
5. The format for the championship was open-draw throughout, with no provincial divisions.
6. No player was to play for more than one club.
7. The winning club in the final would receive a cup and a set of medals, while the losing team would receive a set of silver crosses.[25]

VIII

As well as its obvious sporting purpose, it was also considered that the All-Ireland championship would be useful in encouraging clubs to affiliate to the GAA – and paying much-needed dues. There were a number of clubs who regularly played hurling and football matches under GAA rules, but who were not affiliated to the association.[26]

This situation needed to be resolved and a model already existed: the English FA Cup. The FA Cup had transformed the fortunes of the Football Association, which had been founded in London in 1863 but had initially made little impact. Developing a nationwide knockout competition open to every club in the country changed that. Through the 1870s and the early 1880s, the growth of the FA Cup brought a dramatic increase in the number of clubs affiliating to the Football Association. The men at the top of the GAA might have been reluctant to acknowledge a debt to the English FA, but it seems plausible that they looked at the prosperity which a knockout cup competition had created and imagined a parallel path for the GAA.

The decision to stage All-Ireland championships was taken in November 1886, and the competitions were to be up and running across Ireland within ten weeks. What actually followed next was not precisely what the GAA dreamed of – but it was utterly compelling.

6. A New Era in Dublin

The establishment of the GAA's All-Ireland championships unleashed a flurry of activity through December 1886 and January 1887. Clubs began to organize County Committees to run their local championships. The county structure was one that had served football, cricket and rugby as those sports spread across England, and now it served the GAA as it sought to develop a framework for its games.

I

By the beginning of February 1887, twelve counties were sufficiently organized to announce that they would be running county championships. Six of them were in Leinster: Dublin, Meath, Wicklow, Wexford, Louth and Kilkenny. Five were in Munster: Cork, Tipperary, Clare, Waterford and Limerick. Galway was the sole Connacht county to enter the championship, while no county in Ulster was sufficiently organized to compete.

It was expected that all the counties would stage championships in both football and hurling. In the end, though, draws for hurling championships were made in just six of the twelve: Clare, Tipperary, Cork, Kilkenny, Limerick and Dublin. The manner in which the championships were run varied from county to county. But in each and every county, controversy was everywhere to be seen.

II

Thurles may have been the formal birthplace of the GAA, but the idea of the association was forged on the grass of the Phoenix Park in Dublin. It was there that Michael Cusack had launched the revival of hurling even before he founded the GAA, and it was also there that he had returned when he sought to stage that spectacular inter-county match in February 1886 between teams from North Tipperary and South Galway. For all that Dublin was central to the development of the GAA, the association was markedly different in character there than it was in any other part of the country.

At its annual convention in November 1886, the GAA had stipulated that each club should be based on the boundaries of Catholic parishes. Although the rule was interpreted liberally in rural areas, where many parishes were more than happy to take in outside players if it meant a better chance of success, it had absolutely no meaning in Dublin, where it was never implemented. Instead, clubs in Dublin were formed around businesses (e.g. the Freeman's Journal Hurling Club), around trades (the Grocers' Assistants Gaelic Athletic Club), around institutions (Erin's Hope was based in a teacher-training college), and around localities that were not defined by parish boundaries (such as Dunleary and Golden Ball, a small village in the foothills of the Dublin mountains). Many were based around groups of friends banding together; this gave them a transience which accounts for the extraordinary number of clubs in the history of Dublin GAA that bloomed and then died.[1]

Dublin was also different in the extent to which other team sports had already established a significant level of organization in the city. From Michael Cusack downwards, numerous men who became active in Dublin GAA circles had already been involved in athletics, hurley, rugby or cricket clubs in the city. The GAA in Dublin adopted many of the non-sporting recreations that existing sports organizations wrapped around the playing of games, and moulded them into a shape that suited its purpose. GAA clubs fostered a social life that was a whirl of annual balls, of smoking concerts, of literary and book clubs, and of rail excursions across the country. When they held sports meetings in the city, the Dublin GAA married all the things that were part of country sports – hurling, football, athletics and tug-of-war – but also included sideshows such as steam roundabouts, swings, velocipedes and shooting galleries.[2]

For all that the Dublin GAA professed to be a reaction against the elitism of other sporting organizations, a lot of what it did was influenced by what its rivals said and thought. The hurlers of Dublin were particularly sensitive to the repeated claim that Gaelic games were crude, undisciplined and unscientific – the clear message being that games such as rugby and cricket were markedly more sophisticated. Perhaps it is because of this that reports on early hurling matches in Dublin make repeated reference to the stylish, scientific and organized nature of the play. Much emphasis was placed on the supposedly more sophisticated tactics adopted by teams of hurlers in Dublin (in contrast with the anarchic approach of rural hurlers) and on the fact that so few players received injuries.

Following the establishment of an All-Ireland championship, the leading clubs of the city came together on the night of 12 December 1886 in the rooms of the Regular Carpenters' Society, at 75 Aungier Street. The meeting was chaired by John Wyse Power, who had been at the founding meeting of the GAA.[3] The establishment of a Dublin county championship was the principal business of the night, and a special committee was established to ensure its smooth running.

Ultimately, fifteen teams entered the football championship, and four entered the hurling: Metropolitans, Faugh-a-Ballaghs, Feagh McHughs and Michael Davitts. The entry for the hurling was disappointing, as there were more than four clubs playing the game in Dublin at the time. The Freeman's Journal Hurling Club, Crodhas and Eblanas played regular matches in the Phoenix Park, but did not enter the championship.[4] There was press criticism of clubs such as Kickhams for not entering hurling teams: 'Of course every club cannot win, but it is better to have tried and lost than not to have tried at all. Another thing, if all the clubs that believed they were not likely to win would do the same the entries would be very few.'

A great exception was Feagh McHughs, whose entry drew high praise: 'We did not expect [them] to enter for hurling, as we have heard very little about them in this line, but their action in doing so shows them to be plucky fellows.'[5] Feagh McHughs was based in the village of Blackrock, on the southern shore of Dublin bay. It was primarily a Gaelic football club, backboned by students of Blackrock College, and it would go on to win the Dublin football championship in 1888. Its hurling team was captained by Tom Keating from Tipperary. Keating remained the driving force behind hurling in Blackrock before he emigrated to America in 1891, and the club collapsed shortly afterwards.[6]

Another club that participated in both codes was Faugh-a-Ballaghs.[7] As well as being one of the strongest Gaelic football clubs in the city, they had attracted into their ranks many experienced hurlers who had moved to Dublin from Tipperary.[8] After its formation in 1885, the club had taken rooms on Duke Street and went about establishing a written set of rules distributed among members who paid an annual subscription. Faugh-a-Ballaghs became a hub of social activity, with Gaelic games at its core.[9] During 1886 the hurlers regularly played practice matches in the Phoenix Park – sometimes with up to fifty players on the field. A singular feature of some of these matches was the tradition of calling a break in the play in order to run sprint races.[10] The number of players the club attracted created difficulties of its own: the club's minute books reveal disputes over the selection of teams, both in terms of who was selected and how they were selected.[11]

The third club to enter the Dublin championship was Michael Davitts, captained by the Fairview-based publican Jim Costelloe. Davitts drew their players from among the young countrymen who worked in Dublin's pubs and grocery shops. They were one of the first clubs to affiliate to the GAA in Dublin and, having first specialized in football, were now considered a serious hurling outfit.[12]

Overshadowing all the other clubs, though, were Metropolitans. By 1887 Cusack had retired from playing, but he was still president of the club. Metropolitans were overwhelming favourites to win the Dublin hurling championship. Indeed, they were also considered serious contenders to win the All-Ireland championship.

Since the founding of the GAA, Metropolitans had been defeated only once in their numerous journeys to play country teams. Even this defeat – by Holycross in Thurles on Easter Sunday in 1886 – had been avenged by the end of that summer. They had also gained a certain celebrity in the city.

When they played practice matches in the Phoenix Park, hundreds of spectators regularly gathered. A photograph of the team, along with the cups and medals which were the spoils of their successes, hung in the front window of Lawrence's photographic studio on O'Connell Street. Most of their players had moved to the city from ten counties across Munster, Leinster and Ulster. This was typical of the Dublin clubs, but there was something that marked Metropolitans apart: what the *Irish Sportsman* called 'the appearance of Catholics and Protestants hurling shoulder-to-shoulder'.[13] The nationalist rhetoric of the GAA and the early divides in the Irish sporting world ensured that Protestant representation in the early GAA was minimal, but Metropolitans were an exception. Michael Cusack had proudly proclaimed: 'The members of the Metropolitan Hurling Club do not belong to any one class, or creed, or country.'[14] Most importantly of all, they were presented in the newspapers as fine, stylish hurlers, with J. J. Kenny as captain and P. P. Sutton as vice-captain.

Metropolitans' preparation for the championship in the early weeks of 1887 was disrupted by snow and by the loss of several key players who had left Dublin.[15] Their weekend training sessions became lacklustre and it was remarked in the press that too many of their players 'are far too gentle and play too much in the kid-gloved fashion'. More to the point, it was considered that 'a few of their best players are too much disposed to keep at *camán*'s length from an opponent'.[16] Metropolitans were advised that to win the championship they would have to rediscover the ferocity that had marked their best play through 1886.

III

The draw for the Dublin hurling championship was made on Sunday 22 January 1887. Michael Davitts were drawn to play Feagh McHughs, leaving Metropolitans to play against Faugh-a-Ballaghs. However, there was no prospect of the matches being played over the following weekends. The hurlers had nowhere to play. The Phoenix Park had become the venue for hurling in Dublin, but it was not considered suitable for the championship as there was no enclosed ground which would allow the County Committee to charge supporters an admittance fee. Lansdowne Road, where international rugby was played, was considered, but eventually dismissed because of its dilapidated condition. On the day the GAA had been founded, Lansdowne Road had been condemned in *Sport* as a 'ramshackle, tumbledown, malodorous old rookery', with a stand that had been ruined by fire; and things had evidently not improved dramatically in the meantime.[17] A subcommittee of the Dublin County Committee was established to try to find a suitable ground for championship matches, and a plea for help was made in the press.[18]

It had consistently grieved Michael Cusack that the Office of Public Works had not provided a railed-off piece of land in the Phoenix Park for the GAA, such as existed for cricket and polo. It was, he believed, evidence of how the state favoured 'knots of well-to-do people' who lived in 'charmed circles'. He believed that the public areas of the city should be reclaimed by ordinary working people as a place to play their games 'for the benefit of the children of the poor who are being slowly poisoned in their homes'. To this end, he also called for the building of a gymnasium and public swimming baths in St Stephen's Green, and he called on the clubs of the GAA to claim ownership of the Phoenix Park.[19]

Some heeded his word. The Eblana hurling club played near the Wellington monument, Kickhams played on the Fifteen Acres, Grocers' Assistants took use of the polo grounds, and Faugh-a-Ballaghs and Metropolitans played on the Civil Service cricket ground – although it is not known whether this was with or without the permission of the Civil Service Cricket Club. The problem for all these clubs was that these provisional arrangements undercut any prospect of developing dedicated facilities. Feagh McHughs got use of a field near Blackrock, and Dunlearyites got grounds at Tivoli Terrace in Kingstown, but these were short-term leases with no security of tenure. Indeed, Dunlearyites were soon evicted by their landlord without notice in the month that the championship draw was being made.[20]

It was not until the first week of March 1887 that the Dublin County Committee secured suitable grounds for the playing of their championship. Lord Ffrench, a Catholic and a Home Rule supporter, offered the use of a pitch at his demesne at Elm Park in Merrion (the site of the current Elm Park golf club). It was a convenient location, situated close to Sydney Parade train station and to the Donnybrook and Blackrock tramlines.[21] The Dublin County Committee thanked Lord Ffrench for his 'extreme kindness and generosity' in giving use of the grounds and remarked that Ireland would be a far more peaceful place if a few more of Lord Ffrench's class showed the same regard for the masses.[22]

The rules of hurling had been revised at the end of 1886, and the most important change was intended to address the lack of scoring. Now, for the first time, points could be scored as well as goals. This required changing the goal-posts. Two extra posts were now to be erected outside the old hockey-style goals at a distance of a further twenty-one feet on each side. A ball struck outside the goals but inside the outer posts was now worth one point. A team would also be awarded a point if an opposing defender struck a ball out over his own end-line – this was called a 'forfeit point'. Scoring a goal was still the most important aim, however, and points would come into consideration only if an equal number of goals (or no goals at all) were scored.

The admission fee for championship matches was set at 6d. Getting people to pay that would now be the next challenge. GAA supporters had already shown a talent for avoiding paying in to matches. In Tralee the local committee had been forced to erect wooden screens to block the view of those who did not wish to pay in, while in Limerick 'well-dressed people' were spotted climbing walls instead of paying through the gate.[23] As the championship was the only source of income for the new Dublin County Committee, it sought to attract as many people as possible to Elm Park, including spectators from far beyond the narrow confines of Dublin GAA members. In this, it would be assisted by the press. In the weeks preceding the first championship matches, two new GAA-linked national newspapers would be launched, and the two national weekly sporting papers would dramatically expand their GAA coverage.

IV

The man behind one of the new papers was none other than Michael Cusack. In tandem with a Scottish businessman living in Dublin, Morrison Millar, Cusack started the *Celtic Times* with limited finance, only the faintest idea of how to manage a weekly paper, and no time to devote to writing 'except that which people ordinarily require for amusement or rest'.[24] He was still running his school and was writing a weekly educational column for the *Shamrock*. Nonetheless, on New Year's Day 1887, the *Celtic Times* was launched onto the Irish newspaper market.

The paper's front-page motto laid out its cultural–nationalist agenda: 'Let native industries, literature, arts and pastimes flourish.' There was a page on chess (claimed by Cusack as an old Irish pastime); there were favourable accounts of a whole variety of Irish industries; articles on trade unionism and socialism; notes on veterinary and agricultural matters; serious polemics on the importance of education, of literature and of public libraries; campaigns in support of Irish dancing and Irish music; promotion of the Irish language; and essays and poetry in Irish and English.[25] There was also significant space devoted to women and, in particular, to women's industry. Not all of this material was necessarily emancipationist – Cusack, for example, wrote an article called 'A Plea for Homely Girls', which stated that 'a homely girl, if she realises that she isn't pretty, is generally good, generous, and if she gets married she makes a good wife'.[26] At the core of the paper was Cusack's obsession with the GAA and, in particular, with hurling. Throughout the 1887 hurling championship Cusack wrote charming, illuminating, occasionally vicious, reports of matches all across the country. He was, in short, a wonderful witness to history.

As if to acknowledge the influence which the *Celtic Times* would allow Cusack, the men who replaced him at the head of the GAA decided to establish their own newspaper, which they called the *Gael*. Cusack offered his own jaundiced take on the move: 'A body professing to be the Executive of the Gaelic Athletic Association, met at Nenagh on Monday, the 27th of December [1886], and called on itself to establish a paper to report its proceedings and protect its interests.'[27]

The *Gael* styled itself as the official organ of the GAA. The paper was run by Pat Hoctor, a member of the IRB, and a vice-president of the GAA. The literary editor was the veteran Fenian John O'Leary. Indeed, it was the literary content of the *Gael* that was its most striking aspect, publishing original works from W. B. Yeats and Douglas Hyde, among others.[28] Many of these verses and literary works were published later as the *Poems and Ballads of Young Ireland* (1888) and included Hyde's 'The Marching Song of the Gaelic Athletes'. On top of that, the *Gael* offered a trenchant defence of everything that the new IRB-controlled executive of the GAA was doing and spelled out what opposition to the executive really meant: 'On the one side is independence; on the other, treachery.'[29]

Cusack's reaction to this paper was to deny that it was the official organ of the GAA; it was, instead, the 'organ of idiocy and illiteracy; the organ of a spurious patriotism; and the organ of all that is mean and contemptible. Away with the filthy thing!'[30] To condemn the *Gael*, the people who ran it and the GAA in 1887, he coined a new term of abuse. To Cusack, they were 'baffety'. For those readers who did not understand what 'baffety' was, he explained that it was 'a coarse yellow shoddy cloth of English manufacture, the dust of which, if inhaled when the rag is torn, permanently injures those who inhale it'. Baffety, he further explained, had 'grabbed the Gaelic Athletic Association and wrapped it up in its yellow folds'.[31] For Irish speakers he offered the following: 'The Irish for baffety is *cac air aghaidh*.' And he then kindly translated *cac air aghaidh* back into English: '*Cac* is dirt of the vilest description; *air* is equivalent to on; and *aghaidh* means face.' To Cusack, the usurpers were shitfaces.[32]

The paper war between the *Celtic Times* and the *Gael* started just as the national sporting press began to cover the GAA in a meaningful way. By 1887 Ireland had two dedicated weekly sporting papers. The *Irish Sportsman and Farmer* was dominated by hunting and other horse-related activities, while also carrying reports on the corn and cattle markets of Britain and Ireland. *Sport* was the Saturday publication of the *Freeman's Journal*, the best-selling Irish daily newspaper. While Michael Cusack had been secretary of the GAA, neither of these papers had given any real coverage to the GAA. Instead, they had filled their pages with news of stag hunts and coursing meetings, horse-racing and cricket, tennis and rugby. In the days after the founding of the GAA, Michael Cusack had bitterly condemned the *Freeman's Journal* for what he considered to be their failure to give due support to the new organization. The poor relationship between Cusack and the *Journal* most likely lay at the heart of *Sport*'s failure to cover GAA matters.

For its part, the *Irish Sportsman* had good cause to oppose anything which Michael Cusack engaged in. Remarkably, for a man who was so liberal with his published assaults on others, Cusack had actually taken a libel case against the owners of the *Irish Sportsman* in June 1885 for a rather mild poem that was slightly derisive about his role as a sportsman and educator. Cusack had won, and received £12 in damages.[33] The journalists on the paper were also devout supporters of the IAAA and had been utterly opposed to the GAA. It says much for their editorial priorities that they had managed to write a sporting review of 1885 without once mentioning the GAA.[34]

After July 1886, when Cusack was removed as secretary, both newspapers saw the chance to move in. In September 1886 *Sport* announced: 'We have made arrangements with a gentleman well-versed in Gaelic football and hurling to supply us with reports and gossip during the coming season.'[35] That gentleman was P. P. Sutton, the highly regarded vice-captain of the Metropolitan hurlers, who now took up service as the country's first full-time GAA reporter.

With *Sport* offering regular coverage of the GAA, the *Irish Sportsman* had little choice but to match its rival, and sniffily announced that it would now cover the GAA out of a sense of duty to Irish athletics. It explained that it had initially opposed the association because of Cusack, because it was breaking the Sabbath, because of its political nature and because of its promotion of factionalism. The *Irish Sportsman* now completely reversed its policy and began covering the GAA, saying that it had come to realize that only the priests could stop hurlers and footballers fighting, that educated opinion was now in favour of sport being played on Sundays and that it was now clear that the GAA had only introduced politics into sport in order to gain support.[36] In a remarkable volte-face, the *Irish Sportsman* described the GAA as 'the greatest national democratic movement of the age.'[37]

V

The first match in the Dublin hurling championship was set for Sunday 27 March 1887, with Metropolitans pitted against Faugh-a-Ballaghs. If Metropolitans were considered favourites for the championship, Faugh-a-Ballaghs were seen as the only team likely to defeat them. GAA clubs across the city provided a dozen stewards each for the occasion, and several thousand people travelled out to Elm Park for the match.[38] As they waited they were entertained by three brass bands, and by the time the game was due to start they were 'at a fever heat' despite the wind-blown April showers.

Through the cheering crowd, the teams marched side by side from the players' tent on the edge of the ground with their hurleys on their shoulders. Metropolitans were wearing their primrose-and-green jerseys and blue caps, while Faugh-a-Ballaghs wore black and amber. The Faughs' new captain, Tom Power, won the toss and elected to play with the wind and the slope in the first half. By half-time, no goals had been scored, and Metropolitans led having scored just one point, while Faughs had failed to score at all. Early in the second half, Faugh-a-Ballaghs made a series of attacks which saw them push into a one-point lead. A shock defeat for Metropolitans was now on the cards, but led by Kenny and Sutton they landed a quick point to draw level, before an intricate passing move saw them score a decisive goal. In the closing quarter Metropolitans added two further goals and a couple of points to win comfortably. It was considered the best game of hurling ever seen in the city.[39]

Michael Cusack was thrilled by the victory – and especially by the style displayed by Metropolitans: 'The ball was steered like forked lightning whenever an opening was discovered. We have never seen finer hurling. Over and over again the ball was passed through the air from side to side several times without once allowing it to touch the ground.' In his newspaper, he made no pretence to impartiality: 'Keep together, Mets, and go on making history!'[40] The only sour note was struck by P. P. Sutton, who lamented in *Sport* that so many patrons had managed to get in without paying.[41]

VI

Faugh-a-Ballaghs soon afterwards lost in the Dublin football championship – which they had been considered favourites to win. The secretary had no doubt it was their dual commitment that had cost them: 'It is doubtful whether any club is able under these circumstances to carry off a championship, so expert have many clubs become who devote themselves to one or the other form of athletics.' And, like every other club, Faughs lamented the loss of players who might have been able to bring them success, 'some having succumbed to the never failing seductions of the fair sex, and others unfortunately obliged to seek a livelihood in the great free land of America'.[42]

The play in the Dublin championship never again reached the heights of that first Sunday's hurling. As spring rolled on into early summer, the Elm Park pitch deteriorated, with the playing of weekly football matches as well as hurling: 'There were holes, here and there throughout the field, so large that they might be taken for entrances to some subterranean cavern.'[43] Michael Davitts beat Feagh McHughs easily in the second semi-final, and the Dublin hurling final was fixed for Sunday 17 April 1887 at 12 noon, following the football final. Led by Jim Costelloe, Davitts made it a well-contested match, without ever looking like winners. There was a sense of the inevitable about Metropolitans' victory as they prevailed by four goals and twelve points to one goal and six points.

Having secured victory in Dublin, P. P. Sutton began

dreaming of All-Ireland glory for Metropolitans: 'One thing is certain – they will compare favourably in the science of the games with those of any other county, and though they may not win the [All-Ireland] championship, they will come out of it with honours.'[44] Other members of his team had different things on their mind. After they were presented with their Dublin championship medals, several complained that they were of a very poor quality. A more substantial criticism came from L. C. Slevin, who had hurled with Michael Cusack in the Phoenix Park before the GAA had been founded. He wrote to the press to criticize the Dublin County Committee for its failure to promote hurling by not arranging a second-tier championship for weaker clubs.[45]

In any case, hurling in Dublin continued to grow through 1887. New clubs were formed in various parts of the city. These included Rapparees hurling club from the Lower Bridge Street area, the Celtic hurling club from around Cork Street, Erin's Hope from the Marlborough Street teacher training college, and Brian Boru's from Clontarf. Hurling continued to be overshadowed by football, but it now had a foothold in the city. And, for their part, Metropolitans could look forward to representing Dublin in the All-Ireland championship. Now they waited to see who they would play next.

7. The Home of Hurling?

As early as 1886, newspapermen began to refer to Tipperary as 'the home of hurling'.[1] As much as it may have galled the rest of the country's hurlers, there was a certain justice to this. In those first years of the GAA, there were more hurling matches played in Tipperary than in any other county; and in February 1887, Michael Cusack remarked: 'The championship of Tipperary is almost as good as the championship of Ireland.'[2] The idea of their own pre-eminence was a burden carried lightly by the people of Tipperary: it was seen by them as a simple matter of fact.

I

Writing about North Tipperary, Michael Cusack conjured a sort of Gaelic idyll: 'The inhabitants of this romantic locality live within the mountainous barriers and strongholds which nature, itself, has reared to preserve their liberties and their national pastimes. These are barriers and strongholds, beyond which degenerating and demoralising games and customs have never penetrated, and the glorious game of hurling, so much cherished, so much loved in North Tipperary, holds deserved supremacy over all other games.'[3] It was here, he wrote, that his dreamed-of classless sports organization already existed: 'The doctor and officer and priest mixed promiscuously with hardy sons of toil and the blackened sons of

Vulcan.'[4] Tipperary was the benchmark by which every other county would be judged. Reporting from a match in Avondale, Co. Wicklow, Cusack wrote: 'I could scarcely bring myself to believe that I was not in the heart of Gallant Tipperary, so enthusiastic were the crowds, so charming were the girls, and so thoroughly Gaelic did everything look.'[5]

This elevation of Tipperary was as rooted in the past as it was in the present. There was evidence of centuries of hurling in the county, including the discovery of ancient bog-preserved hurling balls made of hair.[6] More than 300 years of poetry, legal statutes, memoirs, travel journals and newspaper articles recorded the presence of hurling in Tipperary's fields and village greens. In the eighteenth century the game enjoyed the patronage of the landed gentry, who kept teams that played each other for large wagers. The social and political ruptures of the nineteenth century had reshaped social life in Tipperary, but hurling had survived in places such as Clonoulty and Moycarkey up until the establishment of the GAA.[7] Michael Cusack was able to employ this apparently unbroken tradition of hurling towards his vision of what the GAA should be.

II

Despite Cusack's vision of Tipperary as a Gaelic redoubt, it was, in reality, a strikingly diverse county. It was home to substantial landowners who developed their own sporting lifestyle that revolved around hunting, shooting, fishing and tennis parties. Many other sports of Empire also thrived. Rugby clubs were well established across the county by the 1880s and cricket was the most popular game, played by all sections of the community.[8]

After 1884, the relationship that developed between the GAA and sports such as cricket and rugby was a complex one. The *Tipperary Advocate*, based in Nenagh, wrote that the GAA was, in part, designed to 'banish the namby-pamby croquet, lawn tennis, etc., as effectively as St. Patrick banished the more vicious serpents from our isle. We have not the slightest objection to effeminate dandies and romantic ladies to amuse themselves at the exciting games quoted, but they are far, very far, beneath the brawn and sinew of the hearty sons of Tipperary.'[9]

The problem for such rhetoricians was that the games of Empire thrived in Tipperary long after the founding of the GAA. And they thrived, on occasion, with the help of the GAA. After Clanwilliam won the Munster Senior Rugby Cup with victory over Garryowen in March 1887, among those whom the club thanked were the GAA members who had left nothing undone 'to help their rugby friends make their match a complete success'.[10] A member of the Clanwilliam club was St George McCarthy, who had played rugby with Michael Cusack in Dublin and had also attended the first meeting of the GAA in Thurles in 1884, though he did not subsequently involve himself with the organization. Even the language of such sports entered the GAA, with Tipperary footballers reported in the press as shouting such encouraging words as 'Bravo, Conway' and 'Darling to your left foot, Carty', to each other.[11] For their part, local landlords also supported GAA clubs. When Silvermines played Tulla from Clare in October 1886 they did so in a field provided by Lord Dunalley.[12]

For all that some landlords had good relations with their tenants, many more did not. Agrarian secret societies thrived in Tipperary and were associated with considerable violence, including murder, assault, the maiming of animals and the burning of houses. This was conflict born of poverty and competition for land. Tipperary had an abundance of agricultural resources, but the pressure on those resources was such that many families – generally landless ones, or those with tenancy of just a few acres – lived in a state of considerable distress. Land agitation in Tipperary was widespread in the 1880s and police reported that in 1882 alone there were almost 1,000 separate incidents of agrarian outrage.[13] Throughout the 1880s the assault on landlordism in Tipperary was a prominent feature of life in the county.

Following the launch of the Plan of Campaign, the RIC were again drawn to support evictions of tenants across Tipperary. This led the leading local cleric (and GAA patron), Archbishop Croke, to write that Irish people should stop paying their taxes, because they were being used 'to purchase bludgeons for policemen to be used in smashing the skulls of our people; and generally for the support of foreign garrison, or native slaves, who hate and despise everything Irish, and every genuine Irishman'.[14]

III

Along with land agitation, Tipperary had a living history of revolution against British rule. It was here that the Young Irelanders led by Charles Gavan Duffy and William Smith O'Brien had attempted insurrection in 1848, just as the Fenians did in 1867. Even after these failed rebellions, Fenian candidates who contested elections between 1868 and 1880 did better in Tipperary than in any other Irish county. Partly, this was because of high-profile candidates and because several of the leaders of the IRB were Tipperary men. Most

notable amongst these was Charles Kickham, from Mullinahone in the south of the county, who was the head of the
Supreme Council of the IRB until his death in 1882.[15] Later,
one of the first acts of the County Committee of the GAA in
Tipperary was to campaign for the erection of a monument
in honour of Kickham.[16]

Michael Cusack had his own ideas for a fitting memorial.
Like so many Fenians, Kickham had been a writer as well as
a revolutionary. He wrote the most famous novel published
in Victorian Ireland: *Knocknagow, or the homes of Tipperary*.[17]
First published in 1873, *Knocknagow* is a sentimental, evocative portrait of life in rural Ireland. Its central character, Mat
the Thrasher, is a hurler; he also competes in a weight-
throwing contest against Captain French, the son of a local
landlord. In that contest, Mat is staring defeat in the face, but
as he grips the hammer for his decisive throw, he exclaims:
'For the credit of the little village!'[18]

The presence in the book of hurling gave Michael Cusack
licence to bind the words of Kickham into his project.
Cusack wrote that those who wanted to know what the GAA
was all about should 'go and look up Tipperary and hear the
big drums of *Knocknagow*'.[19] Time and again, he referred to
Knocknagow in his match reports, praising a new generation
of hurlers by associating them with the world of Kickham.
'Every parish should have its Mat the Thrasher; at every fire-
side in Tipperary should be found a *camán*.'[20]

IV

The people of Tipperary immediately embraced the GAA. On
top of that, the games were adopted by Catholic clergymen.

Some simply threw in the ball in symbolic fashion to start matches.[21] Others had a more central role: they became club officials and placed hurling at the centre of parish life. The local curate in Dunkerrin, Fr John Maguire, was a well-known lover of hurling who celebrated a hurling match between two Tipperary teams by killing a pig and boiling six stone of bacon for the occasion.[22]

Although the clergy were involved in clubs and attended matches, it was primarily individuals such as Frank Maloney, from Nenagh, who drove the revival of hurling in Tipperary.[23] Like many other sports lovers in the county in the 1880s, Maloney was initially a cricketer. In fact, he was honorary secretary of the Nenagh Cricket Club in 1884 when the GAA was founded.[24] He immediately began chairing a subcommittee of that club which was appointed for 'the revival of national pastimes'. Within a month of the founding of the GAA, the Nenagh Cricket Club began planning to hold a hurling match. By March the subcommittee had evolved into the Nenagh Hurling Club and, on that Sunday in March 1885 when the first hurling matches were played under GAA rules, Nenagh played a team from nearby Silvermines, with Maloney as referee.[25]

Throughout 1885, Frank Maloney's efforts were crucial to the formal organization of hurling across the northern part of Tipperary. He had begun corresponding with Michael Cusack in late 1884, and it was to Maloney that Cusack had turned when he wanted to stage his great hurling spectacle in Dublin in early 1886 by inviting a team from North Tipperary to play one from East Galway in the Phoenix Park. Maloney had arranged the trial matches for players from all the various villages and parishes around Nenagh to choose the North Tipperary team. He used the momentum generated by their victory to establish a sort of umbrella organization for clubs in the areas – the North Tipperary Branch, GAA. In the latter part of that year and into 1887, Maloney arranged a competition between all the clubs of the area; the prize was the silver cup that had been won by the North Tipperary all-star team in Dublin in February 1886. It says much for Maloney's ability that he was scarcely twenty years old at the time.

V

Cusack, always at pains to romanticize Tipperary hurling, wrote: 'We have seen teams of Tipperary hurlers with their blood boiling for hours, and we have not detected the slightest symptom of the revival of faction fighting, or any fighting at all. They want hurling, not fighting.'[26] The reality was that there was fighting everywhere. In his column in *Sport*, P. P. Sutton became increasingly obsessive in his criticism of rough play during 1887. At the start of the hurling championship, Sutton had appealed to all clubs to ensure that matches would be played 'in a friendly spirit, with mutual toleration, and without the introduction of rough or vicious play, which serves no purpose whatever and only brings ridicule on those who indulge in it'.[27] He was proud that the Dublin hurling championship had passed off without violence, but he also believed that the rules of hurling were more faithfully observed in Dublin than in other counties, not least in Tipperary. He was exasperated by the 'rough, vicious and semi-barbaric play' of various rural teams: 'Butting with the head, kneeing in the stomach, giving the elbow in the ribs under the cover of hipping, tripping, and a few other minor forms of what we must call "deceitful play".' And that was not even to mention the crimes committed with the hurley.[28]

Local observers in Tipperary lent credibility to Sutton's claims. Canon Philip Fogarty noted that matches involving teams from the county had occasionally been abandoned 'lest humanity too far forget itself'.[29] When Hollyford met Cappamore, 'play had scarcely commenced when a *camán* was smashed in smithereens. This was an accurate prognostic of what was to come.'[30] On New Year's Day 1887, the *Tipperary Advocate* listed serious incidents in a match on Christmas Day at Rossaguile, and in matches in Nenagh and Tyone on St Stephen's Day. According to the paper, all the incidents were the product of rough play and would have been avoided if 'the shoulder jostling was left out of the fair hurling of the ball'.[31] Elsewhere in the county, there were reports of 'disgraceful scenes' in Clonmel when a team from Carrick travelled over for a match which devolved into a fracas, then into a brawl and, finally, into a bout of stone-throwing. The police were called, arrests were made and several players received fines. It seems to have provoked no small amount of bitterness among the Carrick men that not one Clonmel man was arrested or fined.[32]

Responsibility for keeping violence at bay fell to the referee. It was no easy task. The rules of hurling were still being refined and were, in many instances, no more than vague guidelines. More than that, the whole concept of refereeing was a new phenomenon in hurling.[33] Even as the first championship was getting under way, a system was still being worked out. A referee was to be assisted in his duties by two field umpires, one of whom was appointed by each team. In seeking a decision, the captain of a team was supposed to appeal to the umpire from his club, who would then appeal to the referee, who would convey his decision to the players. This system of decision-making by committee led to matches frequently being stopped as participants gathered around the referee awaiting his decision.[34] Inevitably, umpires sought to use their position 'to try and gain, fairly or foully, all the advantages they possibly can for their side'.[35] Players were given to disregarding the referee's authority or using 'classical language' to abuse him.[36] Teams who felt particularly aggrieved were known to leave the field in protest.

VI

The situation was not helped by the confusion caused by crowds spilling onto the pitch. A supporter of the Mooncoin hurlers in Kilkenny was reported for flourishing an umbrella while he badgered a referee.[37] Supporters of the Templemore club pulled up the goalposts when a match was headed in a direction of which they did not approve.[38] The stewards supposedly responsible for keeping order could also become caught up in events. At the Wicklow championships in Parnell's lands at Avondale there were 'stewards and spectators freely using ash saplings on one another's heads in a manner worthy of the halcyon days of faction fighting'.[39]

Amid the general mayhem, the referee was expected to rule the game by shouting instructions. This was obviously open to malice and mischief. Members of the crowd and other players were known to shout: 'Take up the ball', or 'Time is up', as the game was in full flow. Only in 1888 was it recommended that referees be provided with a whistle.[40] But a more fundamental problem was getting suitable men to referee matches. P. P. Sutton regularly railed against those who were chosen, believing many to be lacking in authority and impartiality: 'In appointing referees their fitness for the position is very often totally disregarded and we have seen men acting as such who knew as much about the duties of a referee, or of the rules of football or hurling, as the man in the moon.'[41]

The result was still more violence. As T. F. O'Sullivan, the first historian of the GAA, recalled: 'The referee enjoyed no particular immunity from rough handling. His person was by no means sacrosanct.'[42] In Dublin, despite Sutton's pleas, a referee was 'severely beaten' by a player at a match in Clonskeagh.[43] Referees were verbally abused before and after games on a routine basis. One referee recalled being 'subjected to the most vile abuse from the very moment the match commenced'.[44] Threats to referees were not without reward. A report on a match in the first Louth football championship records the crowd being 'convulsed with amazement' at the decision of the referee to award victory to Point Road, Dundalk, over a team from Monasterboice. All present were clear that Monasterboice were comfortable winners, but the referee confided that 'if he hadn't made the Dundalk men victorious, there would be no use in him going home'.[45]

In Tipperary, at least one referee was determined not to be intimidated: John Cullinane – an IRB man and land agitator – carried a blackthorn stick whenever he officiated.[46] With the Tipperary championship about to begin, the fear was that even a blackthorn stick would be of scant use: P. P. Sutton had noted that 'teams will be more anxious for victory in the championship ties than in ordinary matches, and this anxiety might operate injuriously against good fellowship'.[47] For all the pious words, the reality was that it was precisely the prospect of *bad* fellowship which was central to the appeal of hurling in Tipperary.

VII

In line with the decision taken at the 1886 GAA annual convention, the clubs of Tipperary came together to form a County Committee to run a local championship. Or, more properly, some of the clubs of the county came together at a meeting in the Nenagh Literary Institute on Monday 27 December 1886. The choice of Nenagh – the largest town in the north of the county – as the venue for the meeting was an eloquent statement by the members of the North Tipperary Branch, GAA of their determination to control the new County Committee. The key executive positions were filled by Frank Maloney and E. M. Walsh from Nenagh; J. K. Bracken, a stonemason from Templemore; and Pat Hoctor, a commercial traveller for a wine merchant, originally from Islandbawn in Tipperary. Hoctor and Bracken were both vice-presidents of the GAA and leading IRB men.[48] Maloney, too, had been drawn into the IRB through his friendship with Bracken – a friendship so close that he asked Bracken to be his best man when he married Marianne Gleeson in the spring of 1887. In truth, Maloney seems never to have truly engaged with the IRB – at least not to nearly the same point as Bracken, who was regarded by the police who shadowed him as a firm advocate of physical-force Republicanism.[49]

There was some grumbling at the choice of the Nenagh venue by clubs from South and Mid-Tipperary before the meeting was even held, and few clubs from those areas attended. But the presence of Bracken and Hoctor ensured that the Nenagh meeting would be sanctioned by the Central Executive of the GAA. The meeting duly designated itself as the Tipperary County Committee and set about arranging the county championship. A closing date was set of 6 January for all teams who wished to enter. There were more than one hundred and thirty clubs active in Tipperary at this point – by far the largest number in any county in Ireland.[50] Nonetheless, just nine entered the hurling championship, while only ten entered the football championship.

The small number of entrants can be explained by a range of factors. These included the dispute that emerged over the County Committee being based in the north of the county and the short time initially allowed for clubs to send in their entries and affiliation fees. On top of that, the lopsided scores carried in the local papers emphasized the difference between clubs of several years' standing and others that had only just been formed. The newer clubs seem to have taken the view that they were on a hiding to nothing when trying to compete with more seasoned opponents.

A further reason was the entry of North Tipperary Branch, GAA as a single entity. The number of clubs who came together under this banner totalled more than thirty by early 1887, and might have been as high as fifty. Such had been the success of the Silver Cup competition run between clubs under the North Tipperary banner that some 15,000 people turned out to a field given by Thomas Ryan at Riverston Mills, near Nenagh, to see Silvermines defeat Holycross in the final in early 1887.[51] All bar two of the clubs that had entered the competition joined as one to play in the Tipperary Championship as 'North Tipperary'. One of the exceptions was the Carrigatoher team, which had lost the Silver Cup semi-final in disputed circumstances. They resolved to enter the county championship under their own steam. And, almost inevitably, when the draw for the first round of the championship was made, North Tipperary were drawn to meet them.[52]

On the Sunday before the first-round match was played, the best hurlers from the clubs of North Tipperary played a scratch match at Nenagh to select the team to play Carriga-toher. How could this possibly square with the idea of one-parish, one-club as laid down at the 1886 GAA annual convention? The general rule passed at that convention actually read: 'That clubs may be formed in every parish and that only one club can be in any parish without the consent of the County Committee.' There was nothing in the letter of the law to stop a team being formed from multiple parishes. Nonetheless, there was criticism of the entry of the North Tipperary team in letters to the press.[53] For all the talk of *Knocknagow* and the credit of the little village, expediency in pursuit of success was the order of the day.

North Tipperary was by no means alone in this. By August 1887, Michael Cusack was describing the GAA's rule on the relationship between parishes and clubs as a 'fruitful source of annoyance. No one seems to know what constitutes a parish. Endless objections are lodged. Each club accuses the other of having men from outside parishes on its team. Strong measures will have to be taken regarding this parish rule ... There is scarcely a match played between country teams in which disputes do not arise regarding their composition.'[54] For all the rhetoric of parish honour and glory, many clubs were more than willing to poach the hurlers of other clubs in other areas if it helped them to win a match.

Against this backdrop, on Sunday 6 February 1887 the North Tipperary team took to Thomas Ryan's field at River-ston Mills, in the green-and-amber jerseys which they had worn to such success against East Galway in the Phoenix Park. The Carrigatoher men, undaunted to find themselves up against a regional all-star team, drew first blood with a goal after fifteen minutes. North Tipps managed two points just before half-time. Early in the second half, John Walsh scored a goal for North Tipps. It was the crucial moment of the match for, although Carrigatoher managed to score another point of their own, North Tipperary held on to win by one goal and two points to one goal and one point.[55]

VIII

The Thurles club, founded in early 1885, was brilliantly organized. It was believed to be the first club in Ireland to establish an underage team, and it also ran a second team which was called the 'Sarsfields'.[56] Its officials, most of whom were leading IRB men, included Andrew Callanan, a publican of medium build who, the police recorded, sported a dark complexion, a grey beard and grey eyes; Hugh Ryan, another publican of commanding appearance, who was more than six feet tall, stout, with brown eyes; and James Butler, a travelling agent for a brewer, who was small and fat, with a lame right leg, and limped around Thurles wearing a blue serge suit and a brown hat.[57]

Although the officials of the club were generally small businessmen or travelling salesmen, the hurlers were largely drawn from the farms that bordered the town. These included eight Mahers from the Killinan end of Thurles: Long Dinny Maher and his brother Ned; Red Dinny Maher and his brother Black Jack; Matty Maher and his brothers Tom and Andy; and, finally, Matty 'the Mason' Maher. Another brother of Long Dinny, Jim Maher, was already in Dublin, serving his time in the licensed trade, and playing hurling for Faughs, with whom he later won a Dublin championship medal.[58]

The first-round match between Thurles and Two-Mile Borris in Holycross was deemed to be a classic. Michael Cusack travelled down by train from Dublin and wrote a joyous celebration of the game: 'The players swept along with the speed and dash of the Fianna of ancient Ireland. No shoes were worn by either side! Dozens were knocked out! 'Tis easily seen why Kickham never described the match in "Knocknagow", for no imagination, not even that of the genius of Mullinahone, could picture what Tipperary hurling is like.'[59]

The Tipperary County Committee opened a fund to cover the costs which the county's champions would incur when competing in the All-Ireland series. Each club in the county was asked to contribute 15s to the expense fund.[60] The foresight involved in opening the fund was admirable – but events were soon to make collecting for it an impossibility.

IX

When the draw was made for the second round of the championship, North Tipperary were pitted against Moycarkey. At a meeting of the Tipperary County Committee at the end of February, the match was fixed for Sunday 27 March. Through the month of March, anticipation of the fixture generated a fervour that reached beyond Tipperary and out into hurling areas of surrounding counties.[61] A certain tension existed between the teams. The North Tipperary team drew heavily from Nenagh, and when Moycarkey had played Nenagh in a scoreless draw at the Thurles tournament in the spring of 1886, newspaper reports euphemistically referred to it being 'very stubbornly contested'.[62] The Nenagh men were in no doubt that they were not the cause of such trouble as had occurred. Their captain was reported to have remarked after the match that he would 'defy even the Angel Gabriel not to lose his temper with Moycarkey'.[63]

Moycarkey was a rural parish which encompassed the village of Horse and Jockey, near Thurles town. At the meeting in early 1885 when the local hurlers agreed to form a club and to affiliate to the GAA, the best hurler in the parish, Tom O'Grady, proposed that a letter be sent to the press. It read: 'We hail with delight the revival of our ancient games, and we wish to place on record that our parish has never abandoned the national pastimes.'[64] Hurling seems to have drawn on every section of the parish. The president of the club was Major John O'Kelly, a retired British army officer who lived at Regaile House. When they held a tournament in July 1886, they did so in a field 'kindly given for the occasion by a Protestant lady'.[65] Most of the hurlers who played for the team worked on the land and their captain, Tom O'Grady, was the closest thing that hurling in the 1880s had to a superstar – *Sport* remarked that he was the '*beau ideal* of a captain' and that his 'name has become a household word in Gaelic circles'.[66] Confronted with O'Grady, P. P. Sutton adopted a condescending tone: 'The surprise of the evening was the eloquent speech which Tom O'Grady made . . . It is only men like him, practical and earnest, who can properly understand the Gaelic ideal.'[67]

Moycarkey's most notable scalp was that of the Cork Nationals (later known as Blackrock) down in Cork in August 1886. Like their second-round opponents, North Tipperary, Moycarkey had been undefeated since the foundation of the GAA. The showdown was held at a 'wild and picturesque' field in the wooded hills at Loughaun, midway between Templemore and Nenagh. There were between 7,000 and

10,000 spectators. Michael Cusack was among them, having travelled down on the train to Templemore the previous night. The reason for the journey was straightforward: 'It is the general opinion that whichever of these two teams wins the tie will also win the Hurling championship of Ireland.'[68] The Moycarkey men made a dramatic entry to the ground. The sight of Tom O'Grady walking in with his hurley shouldered and with his mostly barefooted team marching behind him brought a tremendous roar from the crowd.

In the first half Moycarkey played with the strong wind, and at half-time the teams were level at five points apiece. With the wind at their backs for the second half, North Tipperary were seen as more likely winners. This estimation did not reckon with the spirit of Moycarkey. Early in the second half, the Moycarkey players gathered together in their own half, gained possession of the ball and drove in a phalanx all the way up the field in what P. P. Sutton wrote was 'as fierce a rush as had ever been seen on a hurling field', culminating in a goal.[69] Michael Cusack described what happened next: 'Hats were thrown in the air; men were carried on other men's shoulders; even Major O'Kelly, himself, who witnessed exciting scenes in the Crimean War and the Indian Mutiny, was carried away by the enthusiasm and was guilty of the rash act of throwing his hat high in the air; and to conclude this strange, eventful incident Mrs Grundy was carried off the field in a fit.'[70]

North Tipperary responded immediately. Taking a leaf from the Moycarkey book, they too gathered close together – as if they were a rugby team forming a maul – and set off down the field. Close to the end-line, one of their players shot for goal. The ball went into the goal: North Tipperary had equalized. Again, there were scenes of pandemonium. The

Moycarkey men immediately objected to the goal. Their goal-keeper claimed that he would have stopped the ball were it not for the fact that the goal umpire (a North Tipperary man) had been in the way. Cusack wrote that he believed the ball had actually touched the umpire, who was standing in front of the goalposts, on the way through the goal. For his part, the goal umpire admitted that he was in front of the goal-posts. A long dispute ensued, with claim and counterclaim. It was pointed out that the rules of hurling made provision for a goal umpire to stand at each end of the field, but did not specify where exactly he should place himself. The rules also stated that if the ball struck the referee or an umpire, it should be considered to be still in play. The question now arose: did the rule apply to goal umpires, who might reasonably be expected to stand behind the posts? After lengthy deliber-ation, the referee announced: 'I suppose I must give them the goal.'[71]

With that, the Moycarkey men walked off the field and would not return, saying they were being unfairly treated. As the dispute continued, the Moycarkey men also pointed out that while theirs was a parish team, the North Tipperary team was drawn from numerous parishes. (The *Celtic Times* put the number of clubs who formed the 'North Tipperary' team at five; *Sport* put it at twenty-five; and, later, the Moy-carkey men claimed it to be fifty-six; the precise number remains unclear, though it appears to have been at least thirty clubs.) As players and supporters left Loughaun, it was unclear what exactly would happen next. Michael Cusack offered a solution: 'I think the fairest way to settle the dis-pute would be to have the match played over again.'[72]

X

The disputed match was discussed by the Central Executive of the GAA at their quarterly meeting at Cruise's Hotel in Limerick Junction on Easter Monday, 11 April 1887. At the suggestion of the referee, Denis Talbot, who wired in his views, the decision taken by the executive was that the match should be replayed at Borrisoleigh on Sunday 24 April 1887.[73] On the morning of the re-fixture, P. P. Sutton again took the train down from Dublin. Once more a huge crowd turned out to see the match. The Moycarkey men took the field and were ready to play. The North Tipperary men never showed up, however. No explanation was proffered. Instead, a telegram was sent by the county secretary, E. M. Walsh from Nenagh, to say that the match would not be played on that day. The Moycarkey men were left to play a scratch match among themselves and with some local hurlers in order to entertain the thousands who had turned up.[74]

Finally, after further deliberations, the match was fixed for a third time – again in Borrisoleigh – on Sunday 15 May 1887. A week before the game, Moycarkey announced that they could not attend. They had already given their word that they would play a challenge match against the vaunted Mooncoin hurlers from Kilkenny as the centrepiece of a tournament in Clonmel, and they were not prepared to break their promise. They duly played and defeated Mooncoin, before a huge crowd.[75] Two months had now passed since the dispute began and, as time dragged on, a certain bitterness crept in. Letters to the press sneered that Frank Maloney had traversed the whole of North Tipperary to find a team to give battle against Moycarkey, but hadn't managed it.[76] The

Silvermines Club – some of whose players had turned out for North Tipperary – sent a letter to Moycarkey challenging them to a match. Tom O'Grady replied that he did not see how a single North Tipperary club could expect to beat Moycarkey on their own, when they had been unable to do so with the pick of fifty-six clubs.[77] He refused the challenge and asked once again to play North Tipperary.

The Central Executive of the GAA again considered the matter. The issue of 'parish teams' was causing a great deal of friction across the country. Effectively acknowledging that the original rule on the subject had been poorly worded, the executive had clarified at its quarterly meeting in April 1887 that members of all affiliated clubs must reside within the confines of the club's parish.[78] The logical implication of the new rule should have been that North Tipperary – an amalgamation of clubs from a number of different parishes – should no longer be considered eligible. Applying the logic of the rule to North Tipperary was no straightforward task, however, not least because they had been allowed to enter and play in the Tipperary championship before the new rule came into effect. The dispute lingered on.

And on top of all that, the Central Executive had already become the focal point for extraordinary division within the GAA.

XI

By the early summer of 1887, when the North Tipperary controversy was raging, control of the Central Executive of the GAA had fallen entirely into the hands of Fenians. Maurice Davin, as president, had been isolated to the point where he was no longer involved in any decision-making capacity. Clubs without strong IRB links began to suffer at the hands of Fenians in positions of power in the association at county and national level. Moycarkey, which was not aligned with the IRB, was to be a prominent casualty.

The Fenian coup had been a while in the making. Davin had been unable to attend a meeting of the GAA executive at Wynn's Hotel in Dublin on 27 February, so the chair was taken by J. K. Bracken. All eleven people present at the meeting were members of the IRB. This was the meeting at which the IRB moved to take the GAA into its grip. The members of the executive ignored the new constitution of the association, which said that no new rule could be introduced except at a general meeting of its clubs and with three quarters of all delegates in support.

Firstly, they appointed all members of the Central Executive as *ex officio* members of every GAA County Committee in the country, with full voting rights. Secondly, they decided that no GAA match or sports day could be organized by any club in Ireland without the sanction of a County Committee. Thirdly, it was ordered that every club that wished to hold an event had to forward a copy of the programme and a list of club officials to one of the secretaries of the association. Fourthly, all members of the police were banned from membership of the GAA and from competing at GAA athletics meetings.[79] The executive added these new rules to the existing constitution, altered several of the old rules, printed up new copies and distributed them across the country.

Maurice Davin was outraged. He later said that, while he would support some of the new rules, it was 'to the violation of the constitution by the Executive that I object'.[80] He waited until the next meeting of the executive was called for

Limerick Junction on Easter Monday, 11 April 1887, to make his protest. He chaired that meeting and informed the others present – all of whom were IRB men – that they had had no power to make their new rules and that they were creating dissension and factions within the association. The other members of the executive refused to budge. On 18 April Davin wrote: 'As I find I cannot agree with the other members of the Executive in the present system of managing the Association, I have decided to resign the Presidency.' At a meeting of the executive on 28 May, again held in Limerick, Davin's resignation was accepted and the IRB assumed complete control of the executive.[81] At this point, the IRB members on the GAA Central Executive did not move to fill Davin's position as president, although the constitution appeared to permit them to do so. The reason for this is not entirely clear – perhaps they thought it wise simply to wait until the annual convention later in the year, as the immediate installation of one of their own to the presidency would draw greater scrutiny to their actions.

As we shall see, the effects of the Fenian takeover would be felt at a number of points in the running of various county hurling championships and of the All-Ireland championship. In Tipperary, the consequences first became evident when, at a meeting in June 1887, the Central Executive decided that North Tipperary were a legal team and that they should be allowed to continue to compete in the championship. It is not clear how they arrived at this decision, which seemed to run contrary to the new rule on eligibility; it offered no public explanation. Perhaps the view was taken that North Tipperary, having entered the championship at a time when the letter of the law did not forbid multi-parish clubs, should not be expelled by virtue of a rule established subsequently. But it is difficult to imagine such reasoning carrying the day if it were not for the influence of the network of IRB men who connected the Central Executive with the North Tipperary branch. North Tipperary were represented on the executive by the powerful figure of Pat Hoctor, a vice-president of the GAA and an ardent Fenian. When one member of the executive proposed that North Tipperary be thrown out of the championship at its June meeting, it was Pat Hoctor – chairing the meeting – who launched a staunch defence of their position. He was supported in this by Anthony Mackey from Castleconnell in Limerick, himself a dedicated IRB man.[82]

It was also now left to the Tipperary County Committee to continue with arrangements for their hurling championship, which had been left in abeyance as the dispute between Moycarkey and North Tipperary lingered on.[83] It was still unclear what those arrangements would be when Michael Cusack went down to report on a tournament near Cashel in mid-July. There, among the spectators, he met Major O'Kelly, who was viewing the matches from his 'commodious family trap'. He also met Tom O'Grady, who told Cusack that he was anxious for the dispute to be brought to a close and that he was perfectly satisfied that North Tipperary would be more than able representatives of the county in the All-Ireland championship – but only if they were able to beat Moycarkey.[84]

By then, the Tipperary County Committee, dominated as it was by Fenians based in the north of the county, had given up any pretence of being a representative body. Clubs from other parts of the county were left with a total of just three delegates holding committee places. The manner in which the County Committee had run the championships to suit the clubs in their own area had meant that by May 1887 even those three southern delegates had resigned in disgust. Letters from South Tipperary GAA players referred to 'the evil that can be worked by a packed and unprincipled county board'.[85]

The make-up of the County Committee became a source of controversy in the football championship, too. Fethard had been due to play Templemore in the Tipperary football final, but only received notice of the game at 6 p.m. on the day beforehand. They professed themselves to be 'justly and naturally indignant' at being expected to gather a team at such short notice.[86] They did not travel. The County Committee – chaired by J. K. Bracken, who was also the mainstay of the Templemore club – duly awarded the Tipperary championship to Templemore. Fethard were indignant at the decision and protested at the way Templemore were being treated as a 'pet team'.[87] With North Tipperary men in control of the County Committee, and the Central Executive of the GAA unwilling or unable to act, there was no genuine avenue of appeal for those who felt aggrieved.

As for Moycarkey, it seems that no formal decision was ever made that they were out of the championship. The North Tipperary team were simply pushed through to the semi-final stage and Moycarkey were discarded.

XII

By the beginning of July 1887, Thurles had beaten Borrisoleigh in the county semi-final in Littleton by a single point and were waiting for their opponents in the final. The remaining semi-final and the final were fixed for the same afternoon, Sunday 24 July 1887, at a field near Borrisoleigh. If the County Committee had otherwise appeared biased in favour of North Tipperary, this decision – which would force North Tipps to play a semi-final and, if victorious, a final against a rested Thurles on the same day – did Frank Maloney's men no favours. Were the officials induced to complacency by North Tipps' unbeaten record since the founding of the GAA? That may have been a factor, but after all the delays there was also serious time pressure. The Tipperary champions were due to play against the Dublin champions on Saturday 30 July. If they had not played the two matches off on the same day, Tipperary would have lost its representation in the inter-county championship.

North Tipperary's semi-final opponents were Holycross. Remarkably, Holycross had only entered the draw at the semi-final stage: the County Committee had decided in March to reopen entry into the championship, and Holycross had availed of the opportunity.

Neither North Tipps nor Holycross managed to score a goal or a point. All that divided the teams in the end was a forfeit point which was awarded to North Tipperary after a Holycross player had knocked the ball behind his own goal. It was the grimmest of victories.

Almost immediately, the North Tipperary team was sent back out onto the field to play Thurles. It was too big a challenge. The teams were level at half-time, but in the second half Thurles were dominant, winning by three points and three forfeit points to no score. The *Tipperary Advocate* had no doubt that it was the lack of a break that cost North Tipperary victory, writing that 'the hurlers themselves are not responsible for their defeat, but the gentlemen who sent them into a second contest . . . with an interval of just a few minutes' rest'.[88]

XIII

In the aftermath of its defeat, North Tipperary disbanded as a team and the various clubs that had contributed players entered all future championships under their own steam. Michael Cusack could not disguise his glee at the Thurles success. The victory, he wrote, was popular for many reasons, not least because of the 'stupid attempt' to depose Thurles as the capital town of the GAA and replace it with Nenagh.[89]

For his part, P. P. Sutton was simply outraged by what had happened in Tipperary. In his newspaper column in *Sport*, he asked: 'If the championship is supposed to be over, then what became of Moycarkey? They have not been beaten, nor have they forfeited their right in any way.' Sutton concluded: 'No team can call themselves the hurling champions of Tipperary until Tom O'Grady's champions are disposed of by fair play.'[90] In a magnanimous speech later in the year, Tom O'Grady was more tempered. He looked back across the disputes of the summer and said that he 'exonerated completely the bone and sinew of the northern part of the county, and said that all the trouble was brought about by a couple of gentlemen who wanted to ride to distinction on the back of the North Tipps'.[91]

8. Aristocrats and Beginners

When the All-Ireland championship was being planned in late 1886, it was intended that each of the county championships would be finished by St Patrick's Day 1887. The inter-county championships would then be played off on successive weekends, with the All-Ireland final to be played by the end of the first week in May.

Almost immediately, this timetable was shredded. Dublin, with only four entrants, finished a month late. Tipperary needed until the end of July. No county managed to finish its championship on time. The Central Executive of the GAA had no option but to overhaul the arrangements for the inter-county championship. In their attempts to do this, they created new problems for themselves. The championship began to unravel.

I

The root of the problem lay, again, with the momentous meeting of the GAA's Central Executive on 20 February 1887. The inexperience of the GAA's administrators manifested itself in an absurdly ill-conceived championship structure. The Central Executive had been informed that twelve counties – Dublin, Tipperary, Cork, Kilkenny, Waterford, Louth, Limerick, Meath, Wexford, Galway, Wicklow and Clare – had committed to running local championships. Perhaps it was the desire to create the impression of momentum – or a naive faith in the ability of the newly formed County Committees to conduct tournaments – but the Central Executive decided there and then to make the draw for the inter-county matches. That was not their only mistake. Although in most counties the local championships had yet to start, the Central Executive took the view that entering the inter-county championship meant providing *both* hurling and football champions as representatives. It was a view rooted not so much in optimism as in wilful blindness. While it was reasonable to expect all twelve counties to supply football champions, it should have been obvious that hurling was a different proposition. In several of the counties – Wicklow, Wexford and Meath – there was no hurling being played, still less the prospect of staging a championship. Michael Cusack sneered at the draw: 'The element of stupid design rather than that of chance runs through the arrangement.'[1]

At its meeting on 29 May 1887 – by which time Davin had resigned as GAA president – the Central Executive recognized the unfinished state of the championship in various counties and produced an amended timetable, but it clung to the idea that counties would play each other in football and hurling matches on the same day. The full draw was: Wicklow vs Clare in Athlone on Tuesday 19 July; Louth vs Waterford in Dublin on Thursday 21 July; Galway vs Wexford in Dublin on Sunday 24 July; Kilkenny vs Cork in Dungarvan on Sunday 24 July; Meath vs Limerick in Maryborough on Monday 25 July; Tipperary vs Dublin in Mountrath on Saturday 30 July.[2] No arrangements were made as to how the championship would be structured thereafter.

II

The schedule for the inter-county matches quickly ran into resistance. Wicklow County Committee bluntly refused to travel for their proposed first-round match against Clare in Athlone, stating: 'We are of opinion that it would be most unreasonable to expect any team from this county to go to Athlone to play against Clare.'[3] But this was posturing. Wicklow had run no hurling championship and had been unable to finish the football championship due to an internal dispute – it was said that the county secretary made no more fixtures after his own club was defeated.[4] Accordingly, Wicklow did not feature in the All-Ireland championship, and the champions of Clare got a bye.

Neither Louth nor Waterford had played a hurling championship, and so the scheduled first-round hurling match between their respective champions did not take place. Meath also failed to produce a hurling team to represent it, so the Limerick champions were given a bye.

So it was that the first-ever All-Ireland inter-county hurling championship match would be contested by Galway and Wexford. The manner in which the men of Meelick, representing Galway, and the men of Castlebridge, representing Wexford, came to be in Elm Park on that landmark Sunday afternoon in July 1887 for the first match in the All-Ireland hurling championship was nothing short of bizarre.

III

There was a certain madness associated with the GAA in Galway. When, for example, the people of Moylough decided to found a GAA club in 1887, they celebrated by holding a day of donkey races. The early races were held in fields near the village, but the last one was held down through the main street. It ended in hilarity as the competing donkeys made not for the finish line, but for the public house where their owners most usually strayed. By lovely irony, the prize-giving ceremony for all the races was held that evening in the Temperance Hall.[5] In other areas, the madness was more violent. In Athenry in March 1887 a faction fight developed between members of two rival GAA clubs seeking to establish themselves in the town, and a number of arrests were made.[6]

When a convention was called in February 1887 to establish a Galway County Committee, Michael Cusack took the train down from Dublin to Athenry. Having booked in to the Railway Hotel, he headed straight to the home of P. C. Kelly. Kelly was the head of the Athenry hurling club, and was an ardent Fenian who had been elected to the Central Executive of the GAA at the annual convention of November 1886. It was Kelly who was organizing the following day's convention. Cusack spent Saturday night in his kitchen, drinking whiskey and singing songs. He reported that the following day's convention was 'the most thoroughly Gaelic meeting I have ever seen'. All bar three of the delegates spoke Irish and all could understand it. He wrote that the men who attended were 'Nature's Gentlemen', men whose 'manners came from their hearts, and not from ninepence worth of etiquette, which may be picked up in a second-hand book-shop.

They reminded one of the time when the "Wild Geese" at the Court of Europe were regarded as the first gentlemen in Europe. They showed no trace of the sullenness and suspicion and fear and dread and crouching ruffianism which our English friends put on the stage to show what manner of men we are.'[7]

The new County Committee was formed in a time and place where hurling was flourishing. Although old clubs such as Killimor had been slow to affiliate to the GAA, the association was now thriving, especially in the east and south of the county. Hurling tournaments were organized on a regular basis in the county and matches between its most celebrated teams drew huge crowds. In March 1887, at Clarinbridge, fourteen clubs played a tournament in front of an estimated ten thousand people. Five more clubs were present but did not get matches due to darkness setting in. The number of hurlers and the spirited quality of the play was enough to bring P. P. Sutton to speculate that 'the winner of the Galway championship should show up well in the All-Ireland championship'.[8]

IV

Local folklore suggests the championship was, indeed, a fine one. The hurlers of Meelick and Killimor came together for the Galway championship, it is said, and were far too strong for all-comers and duly beat Kilbeacanty in the semi-final, before beating Ardrahan in the final by three goals and six points to two goals and three points. It was said that these victories won for the Meelick and Killimor men the right to represent Galway in the All-Ireland hurling championship.

This account – which appeared in the *Evening Herald* newspaper in 1965 – is a more detailed version of a story that was told around East Galway about Meelick's victory in the first-ever Galway senior hurling championship.[9]

It is true, certainly, that a team playing under the banner of Meelick, and made up of hurlers from Meelick, Killimor, Eyrecourt and Mullagh, did represent Galway in the All-Ireland championship. It seems, however, that this 'Meelick' team did so without ever winning the Galway championship, because there is no contemporaneous record of one having been played. Despite the great number of clubs in Galway and the existence of a County Committee, no reports of any championship matches played there exist in the local or national press. Challenge matches involving Galway teams were regularly reported – but no championship match. A strange silence seems to have surrounded the non-event that was the Galway championship, though Cusack made an oblique reference in one of his columns to the fact that Meelick were not the champions of the county.[10] We don't know why the County Committee failed to stage a Galway championship – or whether they even tried.

We don't know, either, how Meelick were chosen to represent Galway in the All-Ireland championship, though this is rather less mysterious, given the exalted position of hurling in both Meelick and Killimor. Hurling had been played in East Galway's Shannon basin long before the founding of the GAA. Meelick was a small rural parish situated on the river Shannon, with a village that had developed around an old crossing-point on the river. The crossing-point had attracted a range of different settlements over the centuries. At various times, it had an Anglo-Norman castle, a medieval friary, and a seventeenth-century fort.[11] The closest towns in

Galway to Meelick were Eyrecourt and Killimor. Both were small market towns, which depended on surrounding farm-land for prosperity.

It was Killimor who had defeated Michael Cusack's Metro-politans on the Fair Green at Ballinasloe in April 1884. By early 1887 the hurlers of Killimor and Meelick were coming together regularly to play practice matches. They had started this as early as April 1886, when they had joined forces at a callows along the river Shannon to play together and were watched by a large crowd.[12] Hurlers from the two clubs also travelled together to play matches in Athlone. A look at the two panels of hurlers listed in the newspapers after matches suggests that players moved easily between teams. Both Meelick and Killimor won that day in Athlone, but news-papers suggested that the local Athlone hurlers should not be too downcast as 'the united clubs of Meelick and Killimor had proved themselves to be the best in county Galway'.[13] This idea of the pre-eminence of Meelick and Killimor hurl-ers is repeated regularly in newspaper reports of the time. Other clubs are saluted for their skills; but the hurlers of Meelick and Killimor are accorded a status all of their own.

V

Hurling in East Galway – more than in any other area – was led by political activists. In late February 1887, hurlers from Meelick and Killimor – as well as a few from neighbouring Mullagh, Quansboro, Tynagh and Fahy – came together for a match amongst themselves. Two teams were chosen – one under the captaincy of Patrick Larkin, the other under the captaincy of James Lynam – and afterwards it was announced that it had been proposed to amalgamate the Killimor and Meelick clubs under the banner of 'The East Galway – Matt Harris Club' – a title which does not appear again in the press.[14] Larkin, Lynam and Harris were all Fenians. Harris – the local MP – was at one time a member of the Supreme Council of the IRB.[15]

The proposed union between the hurlers of Killimor and Meelick happened just as the area was once again being convulsed by land struggle. There was a long and bloody tradition of land disputes in East Galway. By the 1880s, the most important figure in East Galway was Hubert George de Burgh-Canning, the 2nd Marquess of Clanricarde, who owned up to 56,000 acres there, as well as property in Galway town.[16] Clanricarde was the most notorious landlord in the country, living up to the stereotype of absenteeism to an absurd degree. William O'Brien, MP, described him as 'one of the strangest monsters in recorded history . . . A creature so abnormal that the first duty of a civilized state would have been to put himself and his affairs in sequestration.'[17] A local priest in Galway, Fr Costello, described Clanricarde as 'a miser, a wretch and a tyrant, unworthy almost of human existence'.[18]

Hubert George de Burgh-Canning was born in 1832. His father, the 1st Marquess of Clanricarde, had served in the cabinet and as ambassador to Russia, while his mother was the daughter of George Canning, who briefly served as Prime Minister. Having been educated at Harrow, he joined the diplomatic service in 1852 and served as an attaché in Turin for ten years. He retired in 1863, having inherited the fortune of his uncle, Earl Canning. The death of his elder brother left him heir also to the property and titles of his father. The family had owned land in the West of Ireland from the early thirteenth century,[19] but Clanricarde was a determined absentee: it was said that after the funeral of his father in 1874, he never again visited his Galway estates. He lived in London and from there maintained an unyielding attitude on the payment of rents by his tenants, even during agricultural depressions. Successive petitions from local Catholic and Protestant clergy, and from his tenantry, brought no compromise. During the Land War of 1879–82 his estate had descended into a cycle of evictions, murder, intimidation, boycotting and imprisonment.[20] For example, two men who paid rent on farms which they worked just outside Killimor had dynamite put down their chimneys and their thatched roofs were burned to powder by those who were at war with Clanricarde.[21] Agents who represented the Marquess in Ireland sometimes urged their master to be more conciliatory, but were rebuffed. One was said to have been told: 'If my tenants think they can intimidate me by shooting you, they are very much mistaken.'[22] This was not a purely rhetorical point. Clanricarde's agents were in genuine danger, and one of them, John Henry Blake, was murdered near Loughrea in the summer of 1882.[23]

When various tenants began to withhold their rents in 1885, the Clanricarde estate around Woodford in East Galway became seriously disturbed. In the summer of 1886, some five hundred policemen and bailiffs moved to evict tenants. The tenants barricaded their houses, felled trees, tore up roads and pulled down bridges. They fought the bailiffs using swarms of bees, lime, boiling water, boat-hooks, sticks and stones. In the end, four tenants were evicted and twenty-one local men were sentenced to prison terms ranging from twelve to eighteen months.[24]

The evictions at Woodford attracted international attention. When foreign journalists came to East Galway, they

stayed in the Killimor public house of Patrick Larkin.[25] Larkin was a central figure in local hurling, having been pivotal
to the establishment of a hurling club in the town. His son,
Pat, played in goal for the team. He was also one of the leading Fenians in the area. If names are anything to go by, Pat
Larkin's children give some insight into his politics: he had
sons called Emmet, Parnell and Theobald Wolfe Tone.[26]

The national Fenian leadership regarded involvement
with land agitation with a certain philosophical disdain,
believing that it was deflecting attention from the primary
ambition of fomenting political revolution. The leading
Fenians in East Galway did not subscribe to this philosophy,
however. Larkin also served as secretary of the Irish National
League in Killimor, and was imprisoned on several occasions for his involvement in the land struggle.[27]

The Galway County Committee had eleven known Fenians controlling it.[28] Michael Cusack's old friend P. C. Kelly
told a meeting in Menlough: 'You should all join the Gaelic
Athletic Association. If you are practised in the hurling
field, in the football field, at the chessboard, it will be little
trouble to you when the time comes for the freedom of your
country to handle a rifle.'[29] Newspapers reported that up to
twenty police officers regularly attended hurling matches.[30]
Police reported that those matches saw Fenian leaders gather
together, 'clearly for no good purpose'.[31] They described
East Galway as the 'headquarters of agitation' in Ireland and
as being filled with 'a disloyal and lawless spirit'. One report
concluded: 'Men of dangerous character reside there.'[32]

One of those was the man who was later to take charge of
Meelick: James Lynam. He was a friend of Pat Larkin and a
large tenant farmer who lived near Eyrecourt. Lynam had
been born in Rahan, King's County, and had emigrated to

America, where he had fought in the American Civil War and been wounded in the leg.[33] Backed, possibly, by his pension from that war, he and his brother Peter had secured large farms on the Clanricarde estate.[34] In the 1880s Lynam became one of the most important IRB men in Connacht and was the leader of the land agitation that developed around Meelick and Eyrecourt. He was a famed orator who spoke with passion and fluency at meetings across East Galway. He said that he viewed the battle between landlords and tenants in Ireland as one between 'the oppressor and the oppressed', in which he hoped the oppressed would ultimately succeed. He organized a campaign among the tenants on the Clanricarde estate, he said, because he wished that 'the tyrant's clutch would be loosened from their throats'.[35]

By contrast, for some tenants around East Galway, their relationship with their landlord was rooted not in struggle, but in compromise. Various landlords could see the difficulties that faced their tenants in times of depression and reacted with compassion. Walter Joyce of Corgary House, for example, gave his tenants a reduction in rent in 1883. This led to a huge party, attended by Joyce and his family, with fireworks, bonfires, music, dancing, a balloon ascent and much drinking of stout.[36] Good relations between some landlords and their tenants extended to sport, although hunting had been stopped locally at the height of the Land War.[37] One of the finest cricket pitches in the country was laid out in front of Longford Castle in Tiernascragh, a few miles from Meelick. It was a honeypot for the local elite – but it was also peopled by the finest sportsmen drawn from the agrarian hinterland. At least three of the Meelick hurlers were reputed to be superb cricketers. Indeed, one of their best players, Pat Mannion, was regarded by the local cognoscenti as an immense prospect, a man capable of playing first-class cricket.[38]

In James Lynam's adopted home town of Eyrecourt, local Protestant landlords had provided money for the repair of the Catholic church in the town, renovated the old courthouse for use as a theatre, and provided funding to stage amateur productions.[39] Links between the local landlords and many townspeople exasperated Lynam, who believed that too many locals were willing to throw themselves beneath 'the wheels of the juggernaut of landlordism'.[40] He wrote to the press, with great rhetorical flourish and ignoring all evidence of a good relationship between some landlords and their tenants in the area, complaining that the people around Eyrecourt had been too afraid of their landlords to establish a branch of the National League. He wrote that the result was that their once-flourishing town was now in ruins.[41] In a series of speeches, Lynam condemned Irish landlords as 'simply the champions of rackrent, confiscation and robbery'. He condemned the police who protected them as a disgrace to themselves and to the mothers who reared them. Finally, he pronounced that his ambition was 'to meet the English government and the Irish landlords with something more important than speeches'.[42]

Lynam often made reference in speeches to his revolutionary intentions, and was reported by the police for involvement in apparent Fenian-related conspiracies.[43] Unlike many Fenians, however, he did more than simply write letters, make speeches and attend meetings. Even before the Plan of Campaign got under way, Lynam refused to pay rent on the two hundred acres he rented from Lord Clanricarde at Feaghmore, near Eyrecourt. More than fifty police turned up to evict him from his home in May 1886. Fr John Kirwan, the local parish priest, conducted negotiations between Lynam and Lord Clanricarde's agent, Frank Joyce, which resulted in Lynam being allowed to retain possession of his farm.[44]

By the end of November 1886, the Plan of Campaign was in operation in the hurling heartlands of Meelick and Eyrecourt. On behalf of the tenants on the Clanricarde Estate, James Lynam presented a demand that their rents be reduced by 40 per cent.[45] David Sheehy, MP and John Dillon, MP came to Eyrecourt and spoke in support of the move on a platform where they were joined by all the local priests and by James Lynam. As darkness fell, the streets of the town were illuminated by candles that had been lit in every window.[46] Lynam had once been considered an outsider in the town, but was now a central figure.[47] He suffered a serious leg injury in January 1887, which exacerbated the damage inflicted in the American Civil War. As he recovered from his injury, local people brought him baskets of turf and ploughed his farm for him.[48] It was symbolic of their gathering support for his land agitation.

Through the early months of 1887, more and more tenants around Meelick and Eyrecourt began to withhold their rents. The area filled with stories of intimidation and agrarian outrage.[49] In early 1887, Frank Joyce was replaced by Edward Shaw Tener as agent of the Marquess of Clanricarde. Joyce was reported to have tried without avail to get Clanricarde to reduce his rent and to negotiate settlements with his tenants.[50] His departure did not suggest a peaceful future, and evictions were considered to be imminent. As a high-profile agitator, James Lynam was sure to be a target when evictions commenced. Nonetheless, in tandem with Patrick Larkin, Lynam made the arrangements for the Meelick hurlers for their trip to Dublin to play the champions of Wexford.

VI

The spread of the GAA in the 1880s across the towns, villages and rural parishes of Ireland was a most uneven affair. It happened in different counties in different ways – and, in some, scarcely at all. And, of course, within counties, there was no single way in which the GAA took hold. Wexford is a perfect case in point.

Although there had been hurling played in Wexford apparently as recently as the 1870s, following the foundation of the GAA in 1884 the newly formed clubs of the county played only Gaelic football.[51] A Gaelic football match between teams from New Ross and Ryleen in March 1885, probably the first to be held in the county, ended in a scoreless draw. Football spread quickly and was played across Crossabeg, Oulart, Glynn Barntown and beyond.[52]

Wexford was ahead of most counties organizationally, establishing a County Committee in October 1885. In June 1886, delegates from across the county examined such matters as the payment of affiliation fees, the registration of clubs and the playing of tournaments. Interestingly, the matter of whether cricket matches could be conducted by GAA men was raised and the chairman of the committee, newspaper editor Edward Walsh, said that he saw no rule against it. It noted that it was not an Irish game, but with no hurling or football being played in the summer and most areas having no means of playing handball, he 'saw no reason why cricket should not be played'.[53]

The sense of the GAA as a narrow nationalist organization does not hold in Wexford. The town of Enniscorthy is a case in point. On 30 January 1886 the *Watchman* newspaper reported that a meeting had been held to form a new athletics club in Enniscorthy and eventually to affiliate it to the GAA. The first chairman was Denis P. Murphy, a young doctor; the first secretary Michael J. Whelan, a local businessman; and the first treasurer William Doyle, a local veterinary surgeon.[54] All of these men had previously held the same positions with the Vinegar Hill Harriers, an athletics club which was affiliated to the GAA's great rival, the IAAA.[55] The balance of the committee was drawn mostly from shopkeepers, merchants and tradesmen such as the cooper Thomas Keegan.[56] The meeting pronounced an ambition to 'embrace all the athletes in the town'.[57] By May 1886, more than fifty men had joined the new club – the Enniscorthy Gaelic Athletic Club – and it had acquired rooms on Irish Street and had them refurbished.[58] The rhetoric of nationalism was not apparent. Indeed, one of the first acts of the Enniscorthy Gaelic Athletic Club was to donate £1.1s to the fund for the Enniscorthy Steeplechases, an annual event in the town which was dominated by the local landed gentry.[59] From the beginning, the members of the Vinegar Hill Harriers and the Enniscorthy Gaelic Athletic Club enjoyed an excellent relationship. In August 1886, members of the two clubs came together and organized an athletics meeting on the New Fair Green in the town. A large crowd turned out to the venue, where two specially erected stands were 'well-patronised by the rank and fashion of the town and neighbourhood'.[60]

VII

At the November 1886 meeting of the Wexford Gaelic Athletic Club (popularly known as the 'Blues and Whites', based in Wexford town), two men – R. Goodison and John Coleman – stood up and enquired if there were any objection to a new GAA club being formed in the town for men from the Hill Street and John Street area of Wexford town. The men who wished to establish the club were all labourers and could not afford the existing subscription fee. When asked whether they would join the existing club if the fee was lowered, they replied that they thought that the members of the club, who were shopkeepers and clerks, might not like to play with labourers. They wondered further if it would be possible to establish a team of their own within the club, if it was not deemed appropriate to agree to the establishment of a new club.

Edward Walsh, president of the Blues and Whites, reacted vehemently against the idea. He said the club was composed of every class within the community; that whether someone was a labourer or a shopkeeper they were all still working men; that it was injudicious of any labourer to seek to create such distinctions between men; and that any labourer who wished to don the blue-and-white jersey of their club would be treated with perfect equality. He noted in conclusion that labourers in the town of Wexford had been part of the team which had played in Avondale the previous weekend.[61]

Walsh's objections notwithstanding, the labourers' petition made clear that the divisions of class in Wexford town were a factor in the GAA club, even if through no conscious effort. Walsh's remarks, even if well meant, could not alter the broader dynamics of life in Wexford. Ultimately, R. Goodison was one of the men who led the John Street Football Club into the GAA, where they were nicknamed 'The Coalporters'.[62]

VIII

In his columns in *Sport*, P. P. Sutton, himself a Wexford man, regularly exhorted his fellow countymen to take to hurling. It was to no avail.[63] There was an attempt to establish a club – the 'Ninety-Eight Hurling Club – in Enniscorthy in the summer of 1887, but it collapsed after a few practice sessions.[64] In July 1887 Sutton lamented the death of twenty-two-year-old Nick Murphy, star footballer and secretary of the Oulart Club, who died from rheumatic fever. Only a month previously, Murphy had met Sutton in Dublin to tell him that he had arranged for a hurling ball and hurleys to be made, and that he was intent on getting the Oulart men to play hurling.[65]

The failure to play a county hurling championship – the lack, indeed, of any hurling club in the county – should, in ordinary circumstances, have meant that Wexford would not compete in the All-Ireland championship. But nothing was ordinary about the GAA in 1887; everything, it seemed, was possible.

In early July 1887, Edward Walsh wrote to J. B. O'Reilly, secretary of the GAA, to enquire regarding the first round of All-Ireland championship matches. Wexford were due to play Galway in football and in hurling on Sunday 24 July, at Elm Park. O'Reilly replied on 11 July, saying that Galway 'would send up a Hurling Club but will not send a Football

Team, as they don't encourage football kicking. So now, what are we to do? I suppose Wexford will get a bye in football and Galway in hurling. I am extremely sorry that we cannot have the match. Could Wexford send a Hurling Team? If not all falls through.'[66]

The following evening, the members of the Castlebridge team, who had won the county football championship in controversial circumstances, called a meeting. After some discussion, the secretary of the club wrote to J. B. O'Reilly to say that his team of footballers would play the Galway men in hurling. O'Reilly wrote back: 'It's a plucky reply and well worthy of the approval of all Gaels.' The Castlebridge men then went and made hurleys for themselves. The match against Meelick was to be the first game of hurling they had ever played.[67]

IX

The fact that neither Meelick nor Castlebridge had won a county championship was politely overlooked in the run-up to the first-ever inter-county hurling championship match. The biggest crowd in the history of Gaelic games in the city was expected to attend a Sunday triple-header, arranged after the GAA wisely abandoned its original plan of playing most of the inter-county first-round matches on weekdays. Two football matches – Louth vs Waterford, and Limerick vs Meath – would be followed by the clash between the aristocrats of East Galway hurling, and a team of Wexford footballers who had never hurled competitively before.

The Galway hurlers arrived by train at Kingsbridge station on the Saturday night and stayed at the Midland Hotel.

On the morning of the match, the Wexford men arrived by train to Harcourt Street station, where they were met by a huge crowd of Wexford émigrés, who escorted the team to the grounds at Elm Park. In brilliant sunshine they arrived to find a crowd of thousands – up to ten thousand, according to P. P. Sutton – waiting to see the first-ever inter-county matches.[68]

On arrival in Elm Park, the Castlebridge players were brought to their own tent for dressing and for refreshment. From the tent, they had a good view of the two football matches that preceded their own game. Dundalk Young Ireland Society from Louth defeated Ballyduff Lower from Waterford, and then the Limerick Commercials defeated Dowdstown, the champions of Meath. For Castlebridge, it was an opportunity to study teams whom they might encounter later in the football championship.

Finally, the hurlers took the field. The Castlebridge men were wearing green jerseys, with a harp surrounded by a wreath of shamrocks on the breast. They also wore white buckskin breeches, black stockings and green-and-white caps. The Meelick men – almost all barefooted, and wearing unmatched working shirts – had only green caps to distinguish them as a team.

Remarkably, the match was not completely one-sided. The early play was described as 'brilliant, fast and fierce, intensely exciting, full of furious charges and stubborn repulses'. After Meelick drew first blood with a point, Castlebridge scored a goal. The experience and skill of the Meelick hurlers soon shone through, and Castlebridge would not score again. As the match progressed, it 'could now be seen that the Castlebridge men were little removed from novices in the tactics of the game, and that they were ignorant of the modes of defence and attack'. By the time the game was over, the Meelick men had scored a total of three goals and eight points, to just the single goal for Castlebridge.[69]

It was remarked that the Wexford men appeared somewhat ignorant of the rules. There was much comment on the interpretation that the Castlebridge players put on the rule which disallowed 'pushing or tripping from behind'. This they evidently read as allowing pushing and tripping from the side and the front. It was not an approach which sat well with their opponents, or with the supporters. Indeed, there were reports of 'a good deal of heated temper shown on both sides', culminating in one of the Meelick players, John (Jack) Lowery, having his front teeth knocked out. Such assaults (or accidents) were something of a commonplace in hurling and football matches. Jack Delahunty, the Faughs hurler, almost lost a leg when a simple scrape on the shin worsened into blood poisoning, apparently because his opponent's hurley had been bound with copper.[70] After a hurling tournament in Kilmallock, 'a great many hurlers came in for nice wounds and they were speedily attended to by Dr. Clery'.[71] Sometimes injuries had fatal results: following a face-to-face collision with a Dalkey man, the captain of the Wolfe Tones team, Sam Payne, burst a blood vessel and died the following day in St Michael's hospital in Kingstown. Payne, a Protestant who lived in Bluebell, was just twenty-one years old. In the wake of his death the Wolfe Tones club disbanded.[72]

Jack Lowery suffered no such fate. Indeed, in a way he profited from the loss of his teeth. Lord Ffrench, the owner of the lands at Elm Park, sent his agent to the Midland Hotel with £2 to give to Lowery to get his teeth fixed. Lowery said afterwards that he drank the money.[73] Lord Ffrench also gave £3 to the Meelick team to treat the players with refreshments. This surely aided their celebrations, which extended at least until the Monday. When the hurlers arrived off the train in Ballinasloe on Monday night, the whole area was reported to be ablaze with bonfires acclaiming their victory. Later, the *Western News* rather hilariously told its readers the Meelick team had beaten 'the champion team of Wexford which was hitherto considered invincible'. It also reported that this victory against the odds was largely the work of their captain James Lynam, 'a man who can surmount any obstacle, and by his pluck and energy he succeeded in placing the laurels on the brows of the men of Meelick'.[74] For their part, the Castlebridge men had no luck in the All-Ireland football championship either, losing in the next round to Dundalk Young Ireland Society.

Michael Cusack, father of modern hurling, was an avid cricketer and rugby player before turning against 'everything foreign and iniquitous' in Irish sport. He is pictured here – in the front row, with a big, bushy beard – with the Phoenix Rugby Club during the 1881–2 season.

Minutes of the second meeting of the Dublin Hurling Club, held on 3 January 1883.

Dublin Hurling Club

A general meeting of this club was held on Wednesday 3 Jan 188- at 35 York St a 6.30 Cl Dr Auchinlick in the chair. A draft of rules was submitted by Mr F.A. Patterton + after some discussion was with some slight alterations adopted temporarily. On the Motion of Mr F.A Patterton seconded by Mr Cusack Dr Auchlen Auchinlick was elected President of the club on the motion of Mr F.A. Patterton + seconded by W. Bell Mr M Cusack was elected vice President + on the motion of Mr Cook seconded C E Rowland Mr L H Christian was elected Hon Sec + Treasurer The following gentlemen were elected on the committee Messrs W Bell Bodkin, Burke, Cook, L Hamilton, C E Rowland, E P Rowland, F A Patterton R M Patterton + W Patterton, The subs was then fixed at 5/ per annum + it was decided to hold the first match in the Phoenix Park on Saturday 13 inst

Hugh Auchinleck M.D 83
Chairman

DUBLIN UNIVERSITY HURLEY CLUB 1879.

STANDING. G.Y. Dixon,   John Ross,   Geo. Thos. Fitzgerald,   Wm.H. Kelly,   Travers Smith.
(K.C.)   (Bart. Lord Chancellor   (F.T.C.D.)   (M.D.)
of Ireland)

SITTING: (Back row):   C.W. Welland,   T.S. Lindsay,   A.F. Blood,
(CER.)   (Archdeacon of Dublin).   (K.C.)

SITTING. (Front row): George Searight,   R.J. Polden,   F.W. Caulfield,   G.H. Garrett,   F.S. Searight.
(C.E.)   (M.D.)   (CER.)   (CER.)   (CER.)

EARLIEST KNOWN PHOTOGRAPH
OF A HURLING TEAM.

The closest thing to hurling in the capital in the early 1880s was a game called hurley. The Dublin University Hurley Club is pictured here in 1879. Hurley players were present at the first meetings of the Dublin Hurling Club, but the graft didn't take, in part because Cusack referred to them as 'civilised eunuchs'.

An illustration from a March 1884 issue of the London-based *Illustrated Sporting and Dramatic News*, depicting hurling skills and match situations. The artist was probably observing the Metropolitan Hurling Club, founded in Dublin in 1883; Tom Molohan and Michael Cusack are shown, as captain and president.

Ballinasloe Fair Green, where the hurlers of Killimor, in East Galway, played a match against the Metropolitan Hurling Club in April 1884 – arguably the first significant hurling match of the modern era.

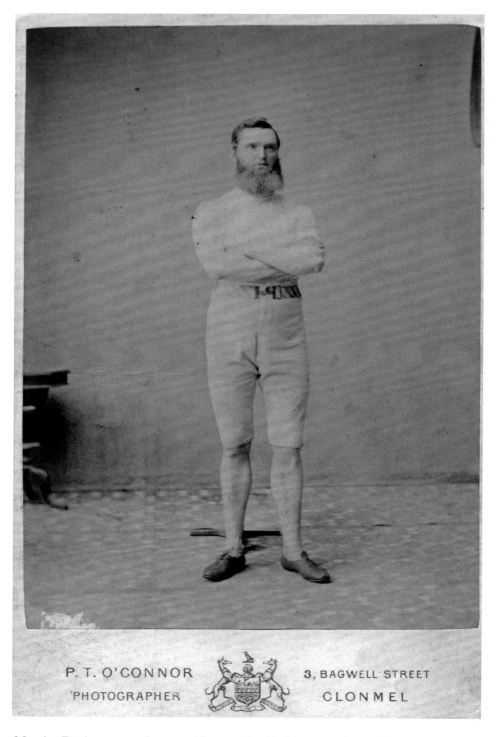

P. T. O'CONNOR   3, BAGWELL STREET

'PHOTOGRAPHER   CLONMEL

Maurice Davin – rower, boxer, cricketer and athletics star – pictured in 1878. Davin was
Michael Cusack's key partner in the founding of the GAA, and remained an admired
figure through the power struggles of the association's early years.

Michael Cusack – schoolmaster, journalist, and Irish-language and hurling revivalist – photographed with his trademark blackthorn stick and working boots. He was acutely conscious of his appearance and, somewhat to the GAA's detriment, quick to take offence.

Hayes' Hotel, where the GAA was founded on 1 November 1884.

A depiction of hurling at Inchicore, in Dublin, with insets featuring two key elements of the early GAA: its patron, Archbishop Thomas Croke, and 'What Dr Croke fears' – hurlers getting drunk after a match.

John Boyle O'Reilly, a Fenian who shared Cusack's obsession with the idea that the British had taken hurling away from the Irish in order to 'unman and degrade' them. Boyle O'Reilly ended up in Boston, where hurling was played under GAA rules as early as 1886; teams in that city competed for a trophy named after him.

J. K. Bracken – Fenian, stonemason and key figure in Tipperary hurling.

Three hurlers and a dog, from the 1885–9 minute book of Dublin club Faugh-a-Ballaghs.

P. N. Fitzgerald, the Fenian who chaired the GAA's annual convention in November 1887, at which the IRB seized firm control of the association.

The hurlers and other athletes who toured the United States in 1888, in what became known in the GAA as the 'American Invasion'. Intended as a money-spinner, the tour lost money, and twenty of the original fifty-one tourists remained in the States.

9. Match Abandoned

On the same day that Galway and Wexford played in Elm Park, the champions of Kilkenny and the champions of Cork were fixed to play in Dungarvan, Co. Waterford. Special trains drew thousands of supporters from both counties. Over the succeeding decades, the rivalry between Cork and Kilkenny would emerge as central to the development of hurling. Nothing that subsequently happened between them was quite as bizarre, however, as the first time they were drawn together in championship hurling.

I

As part of his crusade to promote hurling in as many parts of Ireland as possible, Michael Cusack had travelled to a match in Kilkenny city in April 1887. He was appalled by what he saw, condemning it as 'a positive disgrace'. The first problem was the men of Kilkenny. Walking through the city, he found 'pale, emaciated figures'. On the steps of the Bank of Ireland were a 'crowd of persons, who probably call themselves men, slothfully reclining with their faces towards the sun', while 'the huge pillars of the town hall supported the dead weight of a lot of fellows'. Cusack's mood darkened further when he eventually found the hurling field: 'The hurling of both teams was the worst and most spiritless ever witnessed on an Irish hillside.' During the play a half-dozen of the hurlers lay down in the centre of the field for a rest in 'a contemptible perversion of the grand old dashing game of hurling'. In fact, far from being interested in hurling, 'the local people sneak about the corners, with humps on them, to play flying visits to the shebeen'.[1]

Today we know Kilkenny as the county that has won more All-Ireland hurling titles than any other – and as the only county that does not participate in the football championship. But in the early days of the GAA, such a future would have seemed unimaginable. It was in Kilkenny that the first-ever football match under GAA rules took place, when Callan and Kilkenny played out a scoreless draw on the Fair Green at Callan.[2] Huge crowds regularly turned out for monster football tournaments.[3]

The state of hurling in the county, meanwhile, was not quite as bad as Michael Cusack's article might suggest. The match which Cusack wrote about was probably one organized by the hurlers of the Kilkenny Workingmen's Club, who had played their first practice match just two months earlier.[4] In other parts of the county – notably Mooncoin and Tullaroan – hurling was played with a passion which rivalled any other part of Ireland.

The Mooncoin club was based in a rural parish in the south of Kilkenny. The Mooncoin men were accomplished enough as hurlers to be invited to big tournaments outside their home county, playing against teams such as Moycarkey from Tipperary.[5] The club had been formally established in January 1886 by two local farmers, a teacher and a publican, and organized a regular series of matches, including those between married and single men.[6] In Tullaroan the tradition of hurling long pre-dated the establishment of the GAA. A field – known locally as Bowden's Bog – was famed in ballad and lore as a venue for hurling going back generations. In the years immediately before the founding of the GAA, however, hurling had disappeared from the local village green.[7]

The decline of hurling in Tullaroan can at least partially be explained by the growth of cricket in the parish. At the time of the founding of the GAA, cricket was the most popular game in Kilkenny. The men who emerged as the best hurlers in Tullaroan were much the same men who had previously starred on its local cricket teams. Henry Meagher (whose son Lory became one of the most famed names in the history of hurling) was acknowledged as Tullaroan's best batsman and was also a considerable bowler. Others from Tullaroan who played cricket before turning to hurling were Tom Martin, the Graces, the Walshes, the Gaffneys, the Hoynes and the Comerfords.

The formation of the hurling club, however, did not spell the end for cricket in Tullaroan. Players regularly crossed between the two games and there was a close relationship between cricket and several GAA clubs across Kilkenny. In 1887 – even as the first championships were in full swing – Kells GAA club played a cricket match against a team from Tullaroan.[8] Henry Meagher and other leading hurlers continued to play cricket for teams around Tullaroan well into the 1890s.[9]

II

On Monday 5 March 1887 the newly formed Kilkenny County Committee made the draw for the county championships. While nineteen clubs signed up for the football championship, just four teams entered the hurling draw. It was decided to play two semi-finals on the same day, with Mooncoin play-ing the Kilkenny Workingmen's Club and Tullaroan playing Castlecomer.[10] The matches were played at the Workingmen's Club grounds, rented from a farmer, Matt Murphy, on the Freshford Road in Kilkenny city.[11] Two football champion-ship matches were fixed for the same venue on the same day, and involved three of the clubs who were to compete in the hurling matches. The Kilkenny Workingmen's Club played football against Conahy in the first match of the afternoon (and were well beaten). This was hardly ideal preparation for their hurling match against Mooncoin, which proved to be the most one-sided match played in any county that organ-ized a championship: six goals and thirteen points to no score.[12]

Both Tullaroan and Castlecomer were accompanied by huge crowds of supporters for their semi-final. This match was more evenly fought, but the score-line was one-sided: four goals and four points for Tullaroan to no score for Castlecomer.[13]

The county hurling final was fixed once more for the Workingmen's Club grounds for the middle Sunday in April 1887. The crowd was reckoned to be the largest yet seen at GAA matches in Kilkenny. Many Mooncoin supporters had come from the south of the county on a special train run by the Waterford and Central Ireland Railway Company.

The hurling final was the fifth match on the fixture list, being preceded by four second-round ties in the Kilkenny football championship – one of which involved the Moon-coin club. At least three of the men who played on the Mooncoin football team that day later turned out for the hurlers.[14] Influenced no doubt by the fact that it had a large readership in the south of Kilkenny, the *County Tipperary*

Independent had predicted in its preview of the match that Mooncoin 'should win easily'.[15] What ensued instead was a close contest, 'one of the fastest hurling matches ever witnessed'. Almost from the start, spectators spilled out onto the pitch, forcing the hurlers to weave through them.

Mooncoin seemed to have seized the initiative when they took a three-point lead in the second half, but Tullaroan responded with three or four strong attacks, 'and just before the expansion of the allotted hour they scored a goal and at the same time became the champion team of Kilkenny'.[16]

III

Winning the Cork hurling championship was no straightforward matter. Twenty-two teams entered the draw that was made by the executive of the Cork County Committee in the first week of February 1887. In April 1886, P. P. Sutton had dismissed a hurling match he had seen in Cork as 'lazy, indifferent play' which was watched by 'a handful of ill-conditioned, ill-conducted, ignorant spectators'.[17] But by July 1886 Sutton was writing of immense crowds, vigorous hurling and great excitement there.[18]

As in other counties, the Cork hurling championship was slow to get up and running. On the last two Sundays in the month, three championship matches were played.[19] On Sunday 17 April, there were two more matches played at Cork Park in the eastern part of the city, drawing more than 5,000 spectators; it was reported that the sounds of the various gaming and roulette tables set up all along the sidelines filled the air throughout the afternoon.[20] It was only in the last week in April that the entire first round of the hurling championship was completed, and the draw for the second round was not made until the middle of May.[21]

By then, the Cork correspondent for the *Celtic Times* was writing: 'I have reason to believe that the Cork championship contests will not conclude before the middle of June.' Even this prognosis was to prove optimistic. The reasons for the delays were many. The first related to grounds: finding pitches for hurling championship matches proved difficult, and Cork Park ended up being used for every single match.[22] When games were played at Cork Park in the first two years of the GAA, it was maligned as 'an exaggerated pig-stye', which held merely 'one rickety set of goal posts'.[23] By the summer of 1887, it was considered much improved; but the problem remained that Cork Park was not always available to the GAA – and when it was available it was not always in suitable condition for hurling. The grounds were shared with other sporting associations, and were sometimes commandeered by the British army based in the city. In May 1887 the loyalist *Cork Constitution* thundered that the Sunday matches in Cork Park 'amount to a grave public scandal', which causes 'no little distress and annoyance to many of the residents in the vicinity'. The paper lamented the gambling and card-sharping that attended the matches and said that the matches had 'led to several disturbances and free fights of a very discreditable character'. It called for the GAA matches to be stopped. In reply, the Cork correspondent of the *Celtic Times* said he was going to respond only because of the principle that 'curs should sometimes be honoured with a kicking'. And respond he did: the *Cork Constitution* was a 'disreputable and discredited rag', 'a puny and ignorant disciple of the Brigade of Liars', whose 'public career has always been characterised by a brazen disregard for truth, and whose impudent lying has been invariably directed against everything Irish'.[24] Three days after this riposte was published, Cork Park was used for a celebration of the birthday of Queen Victoria. Michael Cusack then weighed in to complain that the pitch had been ruined. He wrote that the British army had 'wanted some place to manoeuvre and to waste powder in commemorating the advent of a squealing baby a trifle of 68 years ago. Consequently, Tommy turned his eyes to the Park and, with the instinct of the brave British soldier, when he wants some place or something not exactly his own, [he] laid violent on the goal posts of the Cork Gaels, and threw them in a mangled heap in a sheep bin outside the Park gate.'[25]

Politics was also a factor in some of the postponements that dogged the Cork championship. For example, the ties fixed for Sunday 3 April clashed with a major demonstration to mark the twentieth anniversary of the death of Peter O'Neill Crowley, a Fenian leader from East Cork who had died in a skirmish with crown forces during the 1867 Fenian Rising. All GAA matches in Cork were cancelled to allow for attendance at the ceremonies, which were to end with the unveiling of a monument in his honour at Ballymacoda in Cork.[26] In July, a huge crowd turned up to Cork Park to see the Glasheen hurlers play St Finbarrs. It was expected to be the finest game yet played in the championship – but the Glasheen hurlers failed to turn up.[27]

IV

For all the delays, the Cork championship attracted huge interest as it rumbled along. On the Sundays when matches were played, big crowds turned out to watch the men from

Tower Street, Ballinhassig, Little Island and beyond play out their matches.[28] Things finally came to a head on Sunday 17 July, when St Finbarrs and the Cork Nationals were drawn to meet in a semi-final at 1 p.m. The winner would progress to play Passage in the final later in the afternoon.[29] With the championship winners already fixed to represent Cork in the All-Ireland championship in Dungarvan the following Sunday, there was no room for error.

An extraordinary crowd came to Cork Park for the hurling finals; the biggest of the summer. The semi-final meeting of St Finbarrs and the Cork Nationals was expected to be the greatest hurling match yet seen in the city. The two teams had played for a silver cup in the summer of 1886 and the Nationals had emerged victorious. Since then, their rivalry had been acute.[30] St Finbarrs had prepared for the championship by renting a field for £5, setting up a clubhouse on the Bandon Road, getting a set of jerseys and buying timber for hurleys.[31] Despite this, the Cork Nationals were strong favourites to win — after all, they had players from an area where 'they have been playing hurling since the time of Fionn Mac Cuil'.[32] According to the Cork correspondent of the *Celtic Times*, St Finbarrs would make a good fight of the match, but the Cork Nationals had elevated the art of hurling to a higher plane.[33]

Before the match had even started, the St Finbarrs men lodged an objection against the eligibility of some players of the Cork Nationals. This was rejected and the ball was thrown in at 2 p.m. The Cork Nationals scored an early point. St Finbarrs, wearing dark blue jerseys, then attacked. The ball flew around the Cork Nationals' goal area. Amid great confusion, the referee ruled that the ball had crossed the line inside the point posts and accordingly awarded a point to St Finbarrs. Spectators rushed onto the field and the umpire standing at the goalposts was asked his opinion; he said he believed the ball had not crossed the line and that no point should be awarded. This view was corroborated by two clergymen standing nearby.

The upshot was that the Cork Nationals refused to accept the decision of the referee while St Finbarrs refused to accept any decision but the referee's. Attempts to resolve the impasse proved fruitless and the match was abandoned. Both of the disputing teams and their supporters remained on the field, claiming victory. Both also challenged the captain of the Passage team, seeking to compete in the final. The Passage men, rather than make an impossible choice of opponent, decided to await the decision of the referee and the County Committee.[34]

In Dublin, Michael Cusack saw the debacle as an opportunity to run the knife through the ruling executive of the GAA. The match referee was J. E. Kennedy, a vice-president of the GAA and one of the former friends with whom Cusack had fallen out. For Cusack, it was Kennedy – and Kennedy alone – who was to blame for what happened. He claimed that the match had been played in good spirits from the outset. Then a dispute arose because of the 'absurdity' of the referee; the two clubs were 'blameless'.[35] The problem which now presented itself was that, not only were the two most important hurling clubs in the county in dispute and the county championship left unfinished, but the prospect was now looming that Cork would be unable to field a team in the All-Ireland hurling championship.

V

The Cork County Committee met the following evening, and decided that the match should be resumed the following Friday afternoon. It was decided that twenty minutes had elapsed in the match, so forty more would be played. The score at the commencement of the forty minutes would be Cork Nationals one point, St Finbarrs no score. In other words, the Cork County Committee was overruling the referee and disallowing the point that had been awarded to St Finbarrs. Further, it was stated that should either team fail to attend, the match would be awarded to their opponents.[36] It was also decided that the winners of the semi-final would line out again the following day at 3 p.m. against Passage Hurling Club for the final of the Cork championship. The winners of that final would then head to Dungarvan to play Tullaroan in the All-Ireland championship.

Appalled by the decision, James Dennehy, captain of the St Finbarrs club, wrote to the newspapers on the Tuesday and Thursday of the following week, and set out his version of events. Dennehy said that what had happened the previous Sunday was that the ball had initially been struck against the post by his men and had rebounded out, before being driven once again towards the goal and crossing the goal-line about two feet inside the post. He said the point was then awarded by the referee, who explained that the position of the goal umpire was such that he could not have seen the score. Dennehy said that it was at this point that the Cork Nationals refused to play on. The referee gave them five minutes to puck out the ball. They refused, at which point the referee declared St Finbarrs the winners and left the field.

Dennehy also argued that the Cork Nationals had had the opportunity of playing out the match and then objecting within twenty-four hours of the final whistle to the awarding of the score. Instead, he said, they fell back on the fact that their club secretary, D. M. Lane, was also the secretary of the County Committee. A mere five members of the committee were present when the decision was made to disallow the St Finbarrs point and restart the match with Cork Nationals a point ahead. Dennehy added that many of the players in his team had to work until after 7.00 in the evening and could play only on a Sunday. Finally, Dennehy noted pithily that his team 'have in no way violated any rule of the GAA, but stuck to the referee's decision'. [37]

The upshot was clear: St Finbarrs would not be turning up on Friday afternoon. Despite this, on Friday at 3 p.m., a large crowd assembled in Cork Park. The Cork Nationals took the field at the appointed time, but there was no sign of St Finbarrs. The Nationals played a match among themselves for fifteen minutes and then left the field. They were due to line out again the following afternoon at 3.00 to play against Passage Hurling Club for the final of the Cork championship.[38] That match did not take place either. The Passage Hurling Club declined to play, in light of the disputes of the previous week.[39]

An emergency meeting of the Cork County Committee was held on the Saturday evening at the business premises of Alderman D. Horgan, who was also the chairman of the committee. A huge crowd gathered outside as the meeting took place. As well as three other members of the County Committee, T. O'Riordan, who was also national secretary of the GAA and a Cork man, was present to 'render assistance in arriving at an amicable settlement'. Representatives of

Passage, St Finbarrs and the Cork Nationals were brought before the meeting. After some discussion, Passage withdrew from the competition, as they would be unable to get together a team to go to Dungarvan at such short notice. There is no further evidence as to why Passage – who had earned their right to play in the Cork final and would have known of the fixture in Dungarvan for weeks – now made such a seemingly inexplicable decision.

Either way, St Finbarrs agreed to a proposal that lots be drawn between themselves and the Cork Nationals to decide who would go to Dungarvan the following day to represent Cork. The Cork Nationals rejected the idea. They told the meeting that they would agree to accept whatever decision the County Committee made, but they would not draw lots. And there the meeting reached an impasse, for the quorum to make a decision at a County Committee meeting was five, and there were but four members present.[40]

When news of the impasse filtered from the meeting to the crowd waiting outside, there was 'the greatest dissatisfaction that no agreement could be come to for the purpose of sending a team to Dungarvan to represent Cork'. A special train had already been organized by the Cork Butter Exchange Band and Reading Room Society to travel in support of the Cork champions, whoever they might be. The train was to leave at 8 a.m. The band and the members of the society were booked to travel, as were the players and supporters of the Lee Football Club, the county's football champions. It was widely speculated that both St Finbarrs and the Cork Nationals intended to travel also and assert their right to play the Kilkenny men.

VI

In some respects, Dungarvan was an ideal venue for the first-ever meeting of Cork and Kilkenny in the All-Ireland hurling championship. As early as July 1885, the Dungarvan GAA club announced that it had secured the use of the old cricket grounds in the town for the playing of Gaelic games.[41] The club had developed its grounds to the point at which, by the time the matches between Cork and Kilkenny were fixed for the venue, the field was fully roped off and a stand had been erected along one sideline. The Waterford County Committee was run by officials whose attention to detail and vision far exceeded the standard in other counties. W. G. Fisher, the county secretary, was also the proprietor of the *Munster Express* and the *Mail*, and his papers gave the GAA huge coverage in the area.

On the other hand, there was no hurling being played in Waterford at the time. The game did have a history in the county: in 1887, an old hurler wrote to the press describing matches he had seen played in Mothel in the 1820s and 1830s. He recalled seeing sixty men stripped to the waist, hurling in a field amongst themselves and also travelling to play matches against a team from North Tipperary.[42] But by the time of the foundation of the GAA, hurling had no presence in the area. In an attempt to foster the game, the hurlers of Mooncoin in Kilkenny had offered to send down a team to give an exhibition before the Waterford county football final of 1887. The invitation was accepted, but for whatever reason, the exhibition did not take place.[43] All of this heightened the sense of excitement at the prospect of a match between the hurling champions of Cork and Kilkenny.[44]

VII

A second critical reason for the choice of Dungarvan as the venue for the championship matches was rooted in its position on the railway lines. The majority of supporters travelling from both Cork and Kilkenny did so by rail, although five members of the Cork Gaelic Bicycle Club cycled more than sixty miles from Cork city to the match. The Tullaroan hurlers and their supporters gathered on Sunday morning at the Waterford and Central Ireland railway station in Kilkenny city. There was, reported the newspapers, 'something martial in their thread, and it was easy to perceive that they were men who had a task before them'. By the time the train passed Mullinavat, the smoke belching from its engine bore testimony to the scale of the crowd on board.

At Kilmacow, the champion footballers of Kilkenny were waiting. When the people on the train saw the players already dressed in their green-and-amber jerseys, they gave a great cheer. At Waterford city, the passengers left the train and walked across a small wooden toll-bridge that spanned the river Suir, 'at considerable profit to the lessee'. They continued across the city to another station and boarded the train to Dungarvan. Soon there was no room left in the carriages and those who wanted to travel to the match were forced to climb onto the roof of the train. After Kilmacthomas, the approach of a tunnel left some of the passengers atop the train somewhat nervous. As the train steamed through the darkness, a rumble of cheering passed from the carriages and, as it emerged once more into the light, the rumble grew into huge volleys of cheers.[45]

VIII

The train from Cork had reached Dungarvan at noon, carrying 500 passengers. They were greeted by the Dungarvan Brass Band which led a procession through the town to the Gaelic Field, with the Butter Exchange Band bringing up the rear. Included in the procession were the Lee Football Club, the hurlers of St Finbarrs, and several members of the Cork Nationals. The newspapers estimated that up to 20,000 people – probably a gross exaggeration – were present by the time the footballers representing the Lee Football Club and Kilmacow took the field.

The hurling match was due to take place next. It ended in a dreadful anticlimax. The St Finbarrs men had travelled, not to insist that they had the right to play as the champions of Cork or even to represent Cork, they said, but to play a challenge match against the men from Tullaroan. The Tullaroan team were having none of this. They took the field and claimed victory. They then rejected the offer of a challenge match and left the ground. The men of St Finbarrs gamely played an exhibition match among themselves for twenty minutes. While the Kilkenny newspapers were entirely understanding of the decision of their champion hurlers not to play a challenge match in the circumstances, the Cork press were scathing, and lamented the attitude of the Kilkenny men, which they believed amounted to raising the 'white feather'.[46]

The story of Cork's hurling year had not yet ended, however. One month after their bitter dispute over the conclusion of the Cork hurling championship, St Finbarrs and the Cork Nationals were invited to play an exhibition match as part of a great athletics meeting at the County Kerry Athletic Club

Grounds in Tralee, Co. Kerry. There was no doubting on the day which was the superior team: Cork Nationals prevailed by four goals and five points to the four points scored by St Finbarrs.[47] The ease of their triumph must have made the Cork Nationals regret their decision not to accept the referee's decision in the Cork semi-final.

10. Death and Resurrection

The champions of Dublin, Metropolitans, and those of Tipperary, Thurles, were to meet on Saturday 30 July at Mountrath in Co. Laois. Both clubs had serious designs on winning the All-Ireland championship, and the absence of a team from Cork only made the prospect seem nearer. Metropolitans, however, were in turmoil. It did not appear likely that they could field a team.

I

The reasons for the difficulties facing Metropolitans were seasonal: they struggled in the summer to find men to play hurling. In part, this was a reflection of the widespread belief that hurling was a winter game and not a summer one. In his column in *Sport*, the Metropolitans player P. P. Sutton lamented that the championship was being played during the warmest time of the year: 'Under a broiling sun is certainly not the time for such vigorous pastimes as hurling and football.'[1] Early July 1887 was extremely warm by Irish standards – it was reported, for example, that three soldiers of the 11th Hussars had died from sunstroke on the Curragh while on sentry duty; and the *Nenagh Guardian* reported that the bogs around Birr and Tullamore were on fire.[2] Sutton wrote that it was 'little less than impossible to hurl or kick football due to the heat' and declared that 'hurling and football are dead for this season'.[3] Others pointed out that there were matches and tournaments being played in the heat all across the countryside. As one letter writer noted in the *Celtic Times*: 'There is no earthly reason why hurling should not be practised during the summer months as well as in the winter.'[4]

In truth, the agitation by Sutton against summer play did not arise from a simple aversion to playing in the sun. It was related to the fact that many Metropolitans would be away for stretches of the summer on their holidays. At a meeting of the Metropolitan club on 7 May, a motion was passed calling on the Central Executive of the GAA to speed up the playing of the championship as they would not be in a position to field a team after the second Sunday in June.[5]

In early July, the Central Executive of the GAA asked J. J. Kenny whether Metropolitans would be fielding a team to play the Tipperary champions in Mountrath. Kenny informed them that they would be unable to play as the majority of players – including himself – would be away on holidays.[6] On the day that the match was due to be played, *Sport* published a resolution passed by Metropolitans asking that the match with Tipperary be deferred until September.[7] The request was rejected by the Central Executive, who removed Metropolitans from the championship and gave Thurles a bye into the next round. It was a decision that left a residue of acute bitterness.

There were now just five counties with teams left in the All-Ireland hurling championship: Galway (whose representatives Meelick were the only team to actually have played a match at All-Ireland level, against a football team from Wexford), Kilkenny, Limerick, Clare and Tipperary. At a meeting of the Central Executive of the GAA in the Castle

Hotel in Nenagh on 15 August 1887, the draw was made for the next round of the competition. Meelick received a bye. Tullaroan from Kilkenny were drawn against the champions of Limerick, who at that point remained undecided, with the match to be played on 28 August; and the Tipperary champions, Thurles, were picked to play against the champions of Clare, also as yet unknown, on 4 September 1887.[8] Metropolitans, noting this schedule, argued that their request to play in September could and should have been acceded to. They were too late.

II

Kilkenny champions Tullaroan were set for a battle with the champions of Limerick, where the tradition of hurling was deep and powerful. On 1 May 1840, for example, the *Limerick Reporter* had noted that hurling was very prevalent among country people who played on Sunday evenings. The newspaper remarked that the hurling often generated bad feeling and always desecrated the Sabbath. Specific reference was made to a recent match at Ballinguard that had been particularly rough and had obliged many players to come into the city for surgery the following day.[9] The tradition of hurling seems to have endured in some rural areas right up until the founding of the GAA. Around the village of Castleconnell, for example, the Mackey family were recorded as being involved in traditional matches in 'Coffey's Field' at Sallymount, before 1884.

All across the towns and villages of rural Limerick, the GAA quickly took hold through 1885 and 1886. Clubs were founded in Adare, Bruff, Murroe and beyond.[10] The Mackeys were involved in the founding of a GAA club in Castleconnell.[11] It became one of the most progressive and active GAA clubs in the county, running the prestigious Castleconnell Hurling Tournament for which two silver cups were awarded as prizes. One of the cups, valued at £10, was played for between 'top-class teams'; the second, valued at £5, was for teams 'who have never won anything'.[12] At this tournament – and at others played across Limerick on Sunday afternoons – there was music and marching and huge excitement. At the heart of all the excitement was hurling. It is right that Gaelic football also spread into the county, but it was hurling that drew the greatest number of players and spectators.[13]

This was true for the city as well as for the rural parts of the county. By October 1886, it was claimed that there were fourteen GAA clubs affiliated in the city of Limerick alone. These were considered to be particularly active. In 1886, for example, St Michael's Temperance Society Hurling Club played eleven matches.[14] It is a mark of the standing of the club in the city that it had as its patron the Most Rev. Dr O'Dwyer, the Lord Bishop of Limerick, while its president was James O'Mara, the High Sheriff and Mayor of Limerick.[15] This was no guarantee of good behaviour, and a match between the club and the Treaty Stone Hurling Club ended in such bad temper that an entire programme of events had to be suspended.[16] But for all the arguments on the field, there was nonetheless fellowship and a broader unity of purpose. The St Michael's club – together with other clubs such as O'Connells, Shamrocks and St John's Temperance Society – formed a committee to run the GAA in Limerick city. When a County Committee was established to oversee the 1887 championship in Limerick, the city committee disbanded and handed over the money it had collected to the new County Committee.[17]

Hurling in the city was played at the Markets Field. The fact that it was enclosed was of vital importance to any sports organization seeking to charge admission fees. The problem for the Limerick County Committee was that the lease on the field was held by the Limerick Artisan Dwellings' Committee, given to them with a view towards building houses there. The construction work had not begun because the Board of Works had refused to advance the money to allow the project to proceed. Instead, the company was leasing the field to sports organizations. The GAA took it on Sundays at an annual rent of £16.[18] In late February 1887, with the Limerick hurling and football championships about to commence, there were genuine fears that the Markets Field was about to be lost to housing. The GAA clubs of the city held a meeting of protest. It was said at the meeting that the 1,500 men of Limerick city who played hurling were themselves working men who needed the labour and needed the homes, but that the houses being planned should not be built on the Markets Field. After all, it was noted, there was only one suitable field in the city for sport, but there was abundant waste ground on which houses could be built. The protests were successful and the Markets Field was saved as a venue for sport.[19]

III

The Limerick hurling championship took a long time to get up and running, and in early July it was still at the semi-final stage. By then, the matches were being played in the newly leased field of the Grocers' Association, near the Limerick Workhouse. The ground was not able to cope with the number of spectators who attended, and this was to have a huge impact on the outcome of the championship when the semi-finals were played on 3 July 1887. In the first semi-final

Murroe defeated Plan of Campaign, a club based in New-town, in something of a surprise result. Murroe had taken an early lead in the match, scoring a goal and two points, and then retreated to protect their own goal, to the point where scoring a goal in reply became essentially an impossibility for Plan of Campaign.

In the second semi-final Castleconnell were drawn to meet a Limerick city team, South Liberties. The match was chaotic as the crowd continuously surged in among the play-ers: 'The field was at no time clear during the match, and hurling was only carried on at some periods in the midst of a crowd, the players themselves having to push back the people with one hand while with the other they raised the hurleys to strike the ball.' South Liberties won by one goal and five points to two points.[20]

In the week following the match, a letter to the *Munster News* from a man who claimed to be 'an outsider and a city man' alleged that the crowd had begun to swarm onto the field only when the Castleconnell men were getting the upper hand, and that they did so deliberately to prevent a fair match from being played. The writer – who operated under the pseudonym of 'Gaelic' – suggested that the Castle-connell men were entitled to seek redress from 'whoever the proper parties are'.[21] The letter might have seemed quixotic at the time; but in retrospect one suspects that the author knew something that other people did not.

IV

If the semi-finals were somewhat chaotic, the final – on 17 July – was a scene of pure mayhem. The match between

South Liberties and Murroe lasted almost three hours, primarily because the players were, in the words of the *Munster
News*, 'grossly offensive to one another'. After two minutes a
Murroe player had to leave the field with a bad head wound
and thereafter there were frequent scuffles. The South Liberties captain later complained that the Murroe men had been
shouting: 'Break their hurleys!' and 'Cut the legs of them!'
and that five of their players had been severely injured in the
game, with several still receiving medical treatment a week
later.[22] Fighting extended to the crowd, who were considered
most partisan in favour of the South Liberties team. The
reporter for the *Munster News* considered it likely that country
teams would refrain from coming into the city of Limerick if
such a hostile atmosphere were to become typical.

At the full-time whistle, both teams claimed victory, and
they chaired their respective captains off the field amid cele-
bratory cheers. The dispute centred on a goal claimed by
Murroe but disputed by South Liberties. Under the system
that had developed, the referee did not have to give his decision until later in the evening. On this occasion, the referee
was also the County Committee chairman, P. O'Brien. He
duly announced his decision: the score was allowed and
Murroe were proclaimed the first champions of Limerick.[23]

V

Unsurprisingly, that was not that. Indeed, the dispute in
Limerick was only just beginning. In a remarkable move, the
Central Executive of the GAA declared that the champions
of Limerick were not Murroe, nor South Liberties, but the
defeated semi-finalists Castleconnell. There is no clear evidence

of how or when the executive arrived at such a bizarre ruling, but the only plausible explanation is that Anthony Mackey – a member of both the Castleconnell club and of the Central Executive of the GAA – was behind it.

Baffling as it was, the decision was entirely in keeping with other decisions being made in the summer of 1887. By then, the IRB was in complete control of the Central Executive of the association. And the Central Executive had taken to making such decisions as it pleased. Both Moycarkey in Tipperary and Metropolitans in Dublin had exited the championship without losing a match. Neither of those clubs had IRB men prominent in their ranks, while the clubs who benefited from their exit did. But the crowning of Castleconnell was the clearest example of all of the influence of the Fenians on the running of the first All-Ireland hurling championship.

The upshot was that the All-Ireland quarter-final hurling match between Castleconnell (as champions of Limerick) and Tullaroan (as champions of Kilkenny) was now fixed for the grounds of the St Patrick's Club at Inchicore in Dublin on 28 August 1887. At the appointed time for the match, there was a dramatic turn of events: the hurlers of Murroe – declared Limerick champions by the match referee, then inexplicably denied by the Central Executive of the GAA – made a flamboyant entrance. They marched to the centre of the field in their playing gear and carrying hurls. Meanwhile, there was no sign of the Castleconnell team, the official county champions by ruling of the Central Executive. The Murroe men, 'with a look of the fiercest determination', said that they would hold the field, if necessary, for two days, until one of two demands was met: either they be allowed to play Tullaroan, or Tullaroan be given a bye. They desired the former, but would accept the latter 'sooner than allow a team to play that had no right whatever to the championship of Limerick'.[24]

For almost an hour and a half, the Murroe men remained in place on the field. The way they held their hurls in front of them and the utter seriousness of their demeanour suggested to those in charge of the day that they should make no attempt to move them by force. The hurlers explained their position and drew sympathy from the crowd, but many spectators asked them to leave, to allow the next fixture to go ahead: a football match between the champions of Louth and Wexford.

The Tullaroan team were present also, but declined to take the field. They had no need to – they were, after all, fixed by the Central Executive to play Castleconnell. Eventually, the Murroe men marched from the field. Their point had been made. They were not allowed to compete in the All-Ireland championship, but they had prevented Castleconnell from fulfilling their fixture. Tullaroan, meanwhile, had made it through to an All-Ireland semi-final without having played a match outside their county. Twice they had turned up to play matches (first against Cork and now against Limerick), and twice there had been no match. If there was a further silver lining, it was that at least they were not out of pocket for the train fares: the Kilkenny County Committee had passed a resolution calling on all clubs to subscribe 10s for the purposes of defraying the cost borne by the champions in travelling outside the county for All-Ireland matches.[25] The Tullaroan men would have to travel again for the All-Ireland semi-final; perhaps on the third time of asking they would actually get to hurl.

The dispute in Limerick rumbled on for several years in the form of a bitter split of the County Committee. Attempts by the Central Executive to resolve the dispute came to nothing. Indeed, in the following year – 1888 – both committees ran county championships.[26]

VI

The remaining quarter-final match was between the champions of Clare and the champions of Tipperary. It was fixed initially for Limerick on Sunday 4 September, but (for reasons that are not recorded) was not actually played until Sunday 25 September, in Nenagh. The hurling match was being played in tandem with a football match between the champions of the two counties. Advertisements in the local press proclaimed that the match would take place on Church Road in Nenagh, at a field owned by A. Nolan, a local solicitor, with admission charges of 6d for the field and 1s for the stand.[27]

The Thurles team, champions of Tipperary, arrived to the field attended by local bands and a huge crowd of followers. The Clare men had already arrived there at 11 a.m. in a series of horse-drawn cars. They were from the Smith O'Brien club, based at Garraunboy in the parish of Killaloe, on the banks of the river Shannon. Long before the founding of the GAA, the men from the area had used the level meadows along the banks of the river to play hurling: a survey from 1838 designated these meadows as 'Hurling Fields'.[28] The Smith O'Brien club was founded during the summer of 1886 and played its first match in July of that year on a field owned by a local landlord, William Spaight.[29] The club played challenge matches against teams from Clare, Tipperary and Limerick in the following months and also competed in the Castleconnell Tournament.

The Smith O'Brien club was also represented at the meeting on Monday 14 February 1887, in the Town Hall in Ennis, to establish a Clare County Committee. There were twenty-two entries for the hurling championship and just three for the football.[30] This delighted Michael Cusack, who looked with relish at everything that was happening in his home county of Clare. When he went to Barefield, he painted a vivid picture of a match which started late because of the difficulty in securing a good enough ball. When it did start, however, the play was outstanding and he was struck by the way the women waved their hankies in the air in support of the players.[31] Cusack was also quick to assert the good behaviour of Clare's hurlers, praising their moderation and kindly feeling. This was somewhat overstating matters – the *Munster News* reported that when two Clare parishes met in hurling, it was nearly sure to end up in a free fight with broken skulls and bloodletting.[32] Even sports days ended up in rows. *Sport* reported one such meeting held in October 1886, when 'a lot of rustics' had got their hands on sticks which they used as shillelaghs to smash everything in their path: 'Apple-stands, roulette boards, and everything of the kind were reduced to matchwood, and when these valiant Vandals had nothing more to smash they commenced on each other's heads.'[33]

In the first round of the championship, the Smith O'Brien club defeated Daniel O'Connells from Feakle, and in the second round they defeated the Wolfe Tones club from Bodyke. That game ended in dispute, with Wolfe Tones alleging that the winning goal had been scored after full-time and should therefore be disallowed. In a move that was at once bizarre and entirely typical of GAA administration that year, the Clare County Committee directed that *both* teams be allowed to proceed to the next round of the championship.[34]

VII

The Clare championship was then derailed by a land crisis at Bodyke. From early in the year, land and hurling had been tied together in Clare. At GAA matches, banners were flown which read 'The Land for the People', and 'Plan of Campaign'.[35] Mounting tension exploded on the estate of Colonel John O'Callaghan, a section of which stood at Bodyke. While relations on the estate between landlord and tenants had traditionally been good, the Land War of 1879–82 had changed that. Colonel O'Callaghan granted a rent reduction in 1879, but it was not enough to save himself from being boycotted. Things escalated through 1881 and in June of that year police arrived to serve writs on tenants for the non-payment of rents. A violent confrontation ensued and a tenant, John Moloney, was killed by the blow of a rifle butt.

While the situation settled somewhat for a number of years, it flared again in 1886 and 1887 with the instigation of the Plan of Campaign. Just as with other landlords in other counties, Colonel O'Callaghan was offered a reduced rent, but he declined to negotiate. He argued that rent reductions would bring about the financial ruin of his estate, and sought instead to evict non-paying tenants, beginning on 2 June 1887 when the sheriff arrived with police, soldiers and 'emergency men' (workers brought in to an area and usually associated with the landlord Property Defence Association). A huge crowd gathered to support those resisting eviction and to jeer the police. As the walls of the cottages were attacked with crowbars, tenants threw boiling water and cow dung from behind barricades. The evictions continued day after day until 15 June, by which time twenty-eight tenants had been evicted. More than twenty people – most of them women – were charged in connection with the violence on the estate. Some were convicted and given hard labour of up to three months; others were freed.[36]

Before the evictions, hurling had become a huge part of life in Bodyke following the founding of the Wolfe Tones club in 1886. Wearing scarlet-and-blue jerseys, they played tournament matches in their own village and beyond. There was huge local pride in their prowess. When they defeated a team from Mountshannon in Galway, much was made of a stroke from James Burke, 'the Bodyke Giant', who reportedly hit a ball in the air 'like a skyrocket' before it fell 320 feet from where he stood.[37] It was said that Burke stood 6 foot 8 in his stockinged feet and that his hurley was as tall as an ordinary man.[38] They had played a championship match on the weekend before the evictions began, but were then unable to continue to hurl thereafter, such was the turmoil in the area with protests continuing day after day. Among the people who had supported the tenants were the hurlers of Crusheen, who were unable to fulfil their planned championship match against Killanamona because they spent the day at Bodyke.[39]

The Clare championship had proceeded without Bodyke Wolfe Tones and the County Committee ruled that they could not be readmitted. In the circumstances, it is unsurprising that this was a most controversial decision. The objections brought no change of tack and the championship progressed to the point where the Clare county final was fixed for the Mill Field in Broadford on 17 July 1887, with the Smith O'Brien club playing Ogonnelloe.[40] Smith O'Briens wore green jerseys with gold hoops and Ogonnelloe wore blue and white. The teams were level at just one point apiece at half-time. In the second half, Smith O'Briens managed to score two more points without reply and were crowned champions.[41]

The Clare champions had been due to play against those of Wicklow in Athlone in July, but Wicklow had not run a hurling championship; so Smith O'Briens did not have their first outing in the All-Ireland championship until the semi-final against Thurles. The captain of the team was Matthew Crowe, who was twenty-three; he later emigrated and joined the Chicago police force. His brother Michael, a farmer, also played on the team. Other farmers or farmers' sons on the team included Jack Sheedy, Corney Hayes, Thomas Hayes, Tim Crowe, Paddy Smyth, John Hayes, Paddy Vaughan, Paddy Scanlan, James McKeogh, Michael McKeogh and Michael Ryan. Paddy O'Brien was a farm labourer who emigrated to America, as did Jack Molloy. William Scanlan went to Australia, where he died in 1901. Martin and Michael Dwyer's father had a shoe and boot business in Killaloe, and the brothers emigrated to America. James Nihill had a millinery and drapery shop on Killaloe's Main Street. Martin Crowe was remembered as having marked the Ogonnelloe player 'Hero' Madden in the county final; he later left for America where he rose to the rank of captain in the fire brigade of Houston, Texas.

Edmund Scanlan, then a clerical student in Maynooth, would be ordained as a priest in 1890.[42] He was the team's goalkeeper, and had been brilliant in the county final; but when it came to the match against Thurles, he was unavailable: he had now gone back to the seminary in Maynooth. His absence entirely undid the team's defence. According to the newspapers, the Smith O'Brien club 'did not play in anything like their old form', and Thurles coasted to a straightforward victory by one goal and seven points to three points. Michael Cusack reported: 'I could not honestly congratulate them, for I would rather see Clare winning; but since my native county could not win, I like Thurles next.'[43] And so Thurles joined Meelick and Tullaroan as the only teams left in the All-Ireland championship.

When the draw was duly made for the remaining teams, Thurles were pitted against Tullaroan in the only semi-final, and Meelick were given a bye through to the All-Ireland final.

VIII

Initially, the semi-final between Thurles and Tullaroan was scheduled for Clonmel, Co. Tipperary, on 23 October. The teams arrived by a special excursion train at the Drill Field there only to find it already occupied by the hurlers of Clonmel and Moycarkey, who were playing out a match that had been postponed from a local tournament. Frank Maloney, from Nenagh and North Tipperary, as well as being a vice-president of the GAA, was due to referee the All-Ireland semi-final, and he asked that the field be vacated. The hurlers insisted that they would play out their match first. Likewise the newly arrived teams persisted in asking that their match be allowed to proceed immediately. Unsurprisingly, given the way they had been treated earlier in the year, the men from Moycarkey again declined to move. The result was that the hurlers of Thurles and Tullaroan decided they would not wait to play – and so they left. Was this a deliberate ploy by the Moycarkey hurlers to frustrate a match that they must have felt they should have been playing in?

It was agreed that the semi-final would now be played the following Thursday afternoon, 27 October, in Urlingford, Co. Kilkenny.[44] The Tullaroan men had played no championship hurling since their match against Mooncoin in the Kilkenny final back in May, though they had played challenge and tournament matches. When the Kilkenny GAA held their annual sports day in late August 1887, they did so at 'Duke's Meadows' on Canal Walk, which belonged to the Marquess of Ormonde, James Butler. Tullaroan, as county champions, played a challenge match on the bank, while spectators were entertained by the local military band.[45]

For their part, the Thurles team was now much stronger than the one that had taken the field during the Tipperary championship. This was because Thurles had taken some of the best hurlers from their neighbouring clubs and put them in their own jerseys. Thurles had beaten Two-Mile Borris in the first round of the Tipperary championship. Reports in the newspapers noted that, although defeated, players such as Tommy Healy, Dan Ryan, Jack Maher, Tom Stapleton, Tim Dwyer, Ned Bowe, Jer Ryan and John Mockler had played superbly for Two-Mile Borris.[46] The Thurles club duly recruited these very men.

But the Tullaroan hurlers were wise to the machinations of Thurles. The last of the rain had cleared from the skies when the two sets of players lined up opposing one another, with a reported 6,000 people in attendance.[47] The Tullaroan captain objected immediately to the presence in the Thurles team of players from Two-Mile Borris. It was one thing to use players against a team from Clare who would not have known the men they were facing. It was entirely another to use them against Tullaroan, a club from just a few miles away in West Kilkenny. The Thurles contingent claimed that the hurlers to whom objections were being raised lived on the outskirts of Thurles parish and were members of the club. Nonetheless, they agreed to remove the disputed players and replace them with men from Thurles town.

The loss of the Two-Mile Borris players in no way impaired Thurles, who won by four goals and seven points to no score.[48] Visiting Thurles in the days after the final, Michael Cusack remarked how the victory over the champions of Kilkenny and the prospect of an All-Ireland final against Meelick was the general topic of conversation in the town, with 'rich and poor, young and old, laymen and clergymen, women, children and everyone . . . nearly wild with delight'.[49]

But not everyone was looking forward to a Thurles–Meelick final. J. J. Kenny, the captain of Metropolitans, champion hurlers of Dublin, called one more time for the All-Ireland draw to be reopened. He argued that because the championship had run so far behind schedule already, the sensible thing was to allow back in all those teams which had never been defeated. In this list he included St Finbarrs, Passage Hurling Club and the Cork Nationals, all from Cork; Moycarkey, who had never been beaten in Tipperary; Murroe, who were considered to be the true champions of Limerick; and, of course, his own Metropolitans. These teams, he wrote, had never been fairly and honestly beaten on the field of play.

It was a damningly long list, but whatever justice Kenny's argument carried, it was ignored by the Central Executive: the All-Ireland hurling final would be played out between Thurles and Meelick.[50]

11. Gunfire in Hayes' Hotel

With the semi-finals finally out of the way, the stage should have been set for the first All-Ireland hurling final. Yet more than six months actually passed before that match was eventually played. The delay was caused by a vicious civil war within the GAA that lasted all through the autumn and winter of 1887.

At the heart of this conflict lay the politics of revolution. The Irish Republican Brotherhood had maintained a consistent presence within the GAA from the time of the very first meeting in November 1884. At the beginning, Fenians mostly worked in the shadows of the GAA, but from February 1887 onward, as we have seen, they were increasingly open about their intention to dominate the association – pushing through rule changes, forcing out Maurice Davin as president, and favouring IRB-linked teams when disputes arose in the hurling and football championships.

In the late summer of 1887, the IRB moved to exercise complete control. They faced resistance from moderate nationalists, the clergy, and people who were involved in the GAA for a simple love of sport and did not wish to see their association used as the pawn of any political faction, Republican or otherwise. What ensued was a bitter battle that soon spilled into violence. Against this backdrop of revolutionary intrigue, the hurling final between Meelick and Thurles was left to one side.

I

In a secret report, titled 'Overview of Sedition in Ireland' and completed in October 1882, the Royal Irish Constabulary warned of the dangers posed by secret societies in a land 'honey-combed with Fenianism': 'There is reason to believe that Fenians, the Irish Republican Brotherhood, Ribbonmen, Moonlighters and kindred societies by whatever name called, are disposed to amalgamate in one general society having for its object the extirpation of landlordism, and the subversion and final overthrow of British rule in Ireland.'[1] As the GAA gathered momentum in the years after its establishment in 1884, panicked reports from sections of the police claimed that the association was evolving into that 'one general society' of revolution. The GAA, the police believed, was 'a most dangerous association', led by 'a gathering of the dangerous members of the IRB'.[2] They had good reason for their fears and beliefs. The names of some of the revolutionaries cited in that original 1882 report on sedition – P. N. Fitzgerald, P. J. White, James Lynam and others – were those of the very men who were increasingly prominent in the GAA locally and nationally by the middle of 1887.[3]

Inspector Henry Bourchier was the policeman charged with writing reports for the south-eastern division of the Royal Irish Constabulary. In July 1887 he reported that the GAA was prospering and that the interest being taken in it could not be wholly accounted for by the love of sport. Two months later he reported that, across the southeast, the leaders of the GAA, the IRB and the National League (the party structure which supported Charles Stewart

Parnell) were one and the same body of men.[4] Such claims need to be read with some caution. Bourchier, and inspectors in every police division in Ireland, received intelligence from a small army of informants. Some of these informants clearly sought to justify their retainers by supplying information that was an embellished version of reality. But it is clear that the authorities took seriously the GAA's role in revolutionary politics, and that they had good cause to do so.

As the leaders of the British administration in Ireland, based at Dublin Castle, sought to assess the political aspect of the GAA, they took an interest in the revenue that was generated by the playing of matches in front of thousands of spectators. Informers had little doubt where this money was going. Reports from Clare and from Kerry recorded the belief that the GAA was a money-making machine for the IRB. One informer, Maurice O'Halloran, wrote from Clare: 'As the cool, moderate people say, "'Tis only a swindle for Fenian organisers to make money out of."'[5]

As well as raising money, the GAA was seen as a fertile recruiting ground for the IRB. Over the years informants painted vivid (occasionally fanciful) pictures of how GAA players were sworn into the IRB. One informer described the process as follows. Firstly, hints are given to a player that the person they are talking to is involved in 'a higher club'. Later, the discussion is moved towards Irish patriots such as Robert Emmet, Lord Edward Fitzgerald or the Manchester Martyrs, and 'a close watch is kept on the patient to observe how the bait takes'. Then, if the player appears a suitable candidate, he is plied with drink, to see if he can hold his tongue or if he is given to blabbing. Finally, if all is well, the candidate is brought to some dark place and asked will he 'join the IRB and fight for the Republic'.[6]

A spy in the Kerry GAA, whose code-name was 'Emerald', told how he was playing Gaelic football in a field in Tralee when he was approached by Maurice Moynihan, the secretary of the GAA in Kerry, and was asked did he want to become 'a man'. When 'Emerald' said he did, Moynihan brought him behind the stand and swore him into the IRB.[7]

II

The reality of the GAA's politics was much more moderate than either the IRB wanted it to be or some policemen believed it to be. The great majority of men who joined the GAA did so to play football and hurling; the great majority of spectators who came to GAA matches were drawn by the spectacle of the games and for the pure enjoyment of a day out. Accordingly, it was one thing for IRB members to assume positions of power within the association; it was an entirely different matter to exercise that power in a way intended to benefit the IRB in its political aims. As Bourchier reported from the south-eastern division during 1887: 'Informants, who have attended numbers of GAA meetings at my direction, say that nothing practical of a Fenian character is carried on at them.'[8]

Some GAA players actually were policemen, notably in Dublin's Kilmainham Club and the Metropolitan Hurling Club.[9] By the beginning of 1887 there were over 400 clubs affiliated to the GAA, so it is scarcely a surprise that the politics of the association should reflect the range of political sentiment across the nationalist community.

In Wicklow, for example, the Bray Emmets GAA club was accused of flying Union Jacks above the fields during a sports day, and for carrying out the event in a 'thoroughly West British fashion'. The club was also derided for giving the use of its rooms for unionist meetings, and it was alleged that in its politics it was 'a Unionist club'. These allegations were made by a 'Bray Nationalist' who wrote to the *Drogheda Independent* in advance of a proposed match between Bray Emmets and the Drogheda Gaelic Club. Upon publication of this letter – and despite the fact that the allegations were unproven – the Drogheda Gaelic Club refused to play the Bray team. It says much for the shades of nationalist opinion within the GAA and the political priorities (or lack of such priorities) of its members, that another Drogheda club, Davitts, were more than willing to play Emmets. A huge crowd turned out to the match, played at Shamrock Lodge a mile outside Drogheda town.[10] The imagery of Emmets was also reported on another occasion to be anything but British. When the team paraded before playing a match in the 1887 Wicklow football championships, they walked behind four banners: one bearing a likeness of Robert Emmet, an American flag recently imported by ship from across the Atlantic, and two green banners with embroidered harps.[11]

The evident diversity of political allegiance within the GAA was everywhere to be found, even in the names chosen by the clubs. There were clubs named for Republican martyrs (Wolfe Tones, Robert Emmets, Henry Grattans) and for constitutional nationalists (Daniel O'Connells, Parnells). Many clubs were named for saints, or for places of work and professions. And many clubs simply took the name of the locality in which they were based. A few – such as Dauntless of Rathmines – seemed to have borrowed their names from the lexicon of British public school sport. In Westmeath, Kinnegad Slashers met on Sunday afternoons to play matches amongst themselves and divided their number into Tories versus Liberals. And, finally, there was the club named after a British prime minister: Gladstonians.

Gladstone may have been unsuccessful in his attempts to introduce Home Rule to Ireland, but he was viewed as a hero by many moderate nationalists. In the summer of 1887, a deputation from the Cork Executive of the GAA travelled to Swansea in Wales to present a miniature gold hurley to Gladstone, in conjunction with the Cork Protestant Home Rule Association. Gladstone immediately fixed the hurley to his watch-chain. They also presented him with a shield bearing the inscription: 'To the Right Hon. W E Gladstone, M.P., from the Cork County Executive of the Gaelic Athletic Association, 1887'. The shield carried the Cork coat-of-arms, surrounded by emblems of a wolfhound, a round tower and a harp, and the entire production rested on a spray of shamrocks. Finally, the GAA delegation – at least one of whom was an IRB man – presented Gladstone with a regular match ball and hurley, and a copy of the GAA rules.[12]

III

As the summer of 1887 developed, the GAA began to divide on clear political lines. Two of Dublin's leading athletics clubs – the Grocers' Assistants club and the Freeman's Journal club – refused to submit to the rule of the executive in the running of their annual sports. The executive responded by expelling Grocers' Assistants from the association, along with all members of the Dublin GAA County Committee who had supported them; and all the athletes who had competed at the events were suspended for three months.[13] From that moment on, the GAA was divided between those who supported the IRB-controlled executive and those who began to organize against it.

The next flashpoint came in August 1887, when the Moycarkey hurlers were invited to play Faugh-a-Ballaghs at the Dunleary Sports in Dublin.[14] They accepted the invitation and, on arrival at Kingsbridge station, were marched through the city behind the Dunleary Brass Band. They beat Faugh-a-Ballaghs with a brilliant display and were presented with silver medals to mark their success. After a banquet that evening in Brazil's Hotel in Kingstown, Major O'Kelly, the president of Moycarkey, made a speech saying that they had travelled to Dublin for the love of hurling and to protest against the behaviour of the GAA executive.[15] It was their last act as members of the GAA that summer. On the eve of the Dunleary Sports, the GAA executive had expelled the Dunleary club from the GAA. Moycarkey had travelled and played anyway, as an act of defiance. For this act, they too were expelled from the GAA. The Faugh-a-Ballagh club knew in advance that they would also be expelled if they played Moycarkey, but voted unanimously to proceed with a game nonetheless.[16] Later in the year, other clubs sought to ignore this expulsion and invited Moycarkey to play them in hurling matches. In response to those invitations, Moycarkey's star hurler, Tom O'Grady, wrote back that they were currently not in a position to play matches following their expulsion: 'I am not able this time to give you any assistance in promoting the hurling in Kilkenny and Waterford.'[17]

The IRB used its newspaper, the *Gael*, to promote everything that it was doing in the GAA. In response, many members of the GAA kept quiet or sought consensus, but Michael Cusack was having none of it. He may have been ousted from his position as secretary, but he still regarded the GAA very much as his organization. He had fought with many GAA people, of every political persuasion and none, but he reserved particular contempt for the way the Central Executive of the GAA had been captured by the IRB. He called them illiterate, idiotic, contemptible and falsely patriotic.[18] And, as we have seen, he called them shitfaces, in print.[19] During the summer and autumn of 1887, Cusack launched a series of vitriolic attacks against the IRB. It would have been dully repetitive, if it hadn't all been so brilliantly written and so utterly devoid of fear.

The IRB was never likely to turn a blind eye to Cusack's attacks. At a match in Dublin in September 1887, an IRB man promised to 'amputate the limbs' off Cusack. Cusack sneered back that he presumed his challenger was a medical student wanting to talk shop, and informed him that he was at his service and ready for the 'threatened process of amputation'.[20] On that occasion there was no fight, but on others there were. Cusack got into a scuffle with J. E. Kennedy, by then a vice-president of the GAA, on O'Connell Street in Dublin one afternoon. Cusack said later that he grabbed Kennedy by the throat and threw him to the ground, and passed off his claimed victory in this fight as a minor thing: 'Those who can swallow a camel need not strain at a gnat.'[21]

In the face of repeated IRB threats, Cusack never blinked. He kept the abuse flowing in the pages of his newspaper, describing the IRB-run executive as 'drunken corner boys', 'a junta of knaves and fools', and 'a miserable, mischievous, traitorous gang'.[22] Cusack did not blindly follow the opponents of the executive – he was capable of turning on any man at any time – but he offered a counterpoint to those elements of the GAA who remained very active within the association despite being entirely at odds with its leadership. From the middle of the summer, those elements had targeted the GAA's annual convention in November 1887 as the moment when they would act to regain control of the GAA. All through the autumn, the cry rang out: 'Wait till November!'[23] By the time November came around, the scene was set for a showdown.

IV

In the weeks before the convention, two different articles in the *Gael* contained what amounted to threats of personal violence against those GAA men who did not follow the lead of the IRB. No GAA member was at greater risk from such threats than Michael Cusack. On Tuesday 8 November, he took the train from Dublin to Thurles for the annual convention, just as he had done three years previously when founding the GAA. The pull of the association and Cusack's unique personality meant that he was always going to attend the meeting. Still, it was a brave decision to travel – and Cusack was happy to praise his own courage in his newspaper column. In his account, he noted how, in the aftermath of his fight with J. E. Kennedy on O'Connell Street, Kennedy had pledged that he would eventually have his blood. Pat Hoctor swore to Cusack that he would wipe him out at the first opportunity. Stephen Smithwick promised to put a bullet through Cusack's head. And another Dublin IRB man, J. B. O'Reilly, attacked Cusack around public-house closing time on a city street. But, as Cusack wrote: 'These idiotic proceedings of cowards and bastards did not keep me from Thurles.'

His version of what happened in Thurles is the only one that survives. On arrival in the town, he wrote, he headed straight to Hayes' Hotel, where just three years earlier he had been the driving force behind the establishment of the GAA. He saw a group of IRB men in consultation outside the bar area and was immediately confronted by one of their number, Anthony Mackey, from Castleconnell in Limerick, and asked why he was watching the group. Cusack denied having any interest in watching 'a corner glugger of clucking hens'. The confrontation worsened to the point where J. B. O'Reilly walked over, pulled a pistol from his pocket and let off a shot in the air. The women who ran the hotel immediately shut the bar. Cusack left the hotel and headed for the room that had been engaged for him in the town. On the way he discussed the situation with a number of people and it was resolved that the best course of action was for Cusack to return on that night's mail train to Dublin. He left Thurles, he later said, not because of the threats to his personal safety, but because of 'the unconscionable ruffianism of the cowardly scoundrel who could, in our age, without notice, fire a pistol in a private room and in the presence of ladies'.[24]

The altercation was a symptom of the tension that was building in Thurles. The IRB had prepared extensively for the annual convention. The GAA's constitution allowed that every affiliated club in the country could send two delegates to it. The IRB spent the second half of the year organizing and affiliating clubs all across the country in order to rig the convention in their favour, and by November there were reputed to be over six hundred clubs in Ireland, with fifty-five in Co. Louth alone. Many of these were mere vehicles for the IRB to preserve its position of power within the GAA and fulfilled no genuine sporting function.

On 1 November – eight days before the convention – IRB leaders had met in Limerick to review their progress and to 'arrange for the Thurles convention to support the Executive, and exclude all but IRB men'. They appeared well placed to achieve their ambitions. In the days before the convention, police around the country reported that men who were under their surveillance were departing for Tipperary. In all, more than seven hundred men travelled to Thurles and on the morning of the convention – Wednesday 9 November – the town was filled by IRB delegates marching through the streets in 'perfect military order'.[25]

V

Victory for the IRB was anything but assured. Over the previous month their opponents within the GAA had launched a counter-attack. A meeting of the GAA in South Tipperary passed a motion of 'no-confidence' in the executive and called for the return of Maurice Davin as president. This was supported by a meeting of Dublin clubs and by the clubs of Waterford. A meeting of Wexford clubs went further and derided the IRB men in charge of the executive as 'scoundrels'.[26] Political moderates within the GAA trusted Davin to safeguard its integrity as a progressive sporting body with nationalist allegiances. For that to happen, they had to defeat the IRB at convention.

The convention was held in the courthouse in Thurles. By 1 p.m. there were about seven hundred delegates present, filling it beyond capacity. As if to emphasize divisions within the association, the executive occupied the judicial bench at the head of the room with their supporters crammed into the body of the court. The gallery, meanwhile, was filled with their opponents. (For reasons that are unexplained, Davin – the figurehead of the anti-IRB elements – was not present.) At the clerks' desk were members of the press, who set about recording the extraordinary proceedings. The reporters had the best view in the house of the disorder that followed – and they relished every minute of it.[27]

Opponents of the IRB suffered an early defeat. When representatives of various expelled clubs approached the front door of the courthouse, they were refused admittance on the grounds that they were not affiliated clubs of the GAA. A letter of protest was composed and passed in to the meeting, but it was never read out. The representatives of the expelled clubs spent the afternoon in the yard outside the courthouse.

Inside, the IRB confirmed their grip on proceedings by appointing one of their number, P. N. Fitzgerald, as chair of the meeting. A number of priests who had seen the GAA slide away into IRB hands had mobilized for the meeting and moved immediately to reject Fitzgerald. Led by Fr John Scanlan, a curate in Nenagh, they attempted to have him replaced by Major John O'Kelly from Moycarkey. Fitzgerald refused even to allow the proposition of O'Kelly as chairman to be put to the meeting, on the grounds that he was a member of the suspended Moycarkey club. Fr Scanlan then climbed up on a bench in the courtroom to decry the decision and was met with shouts of opposition. As the noise in the courtroom grew, he said that he had been playing hurling since before many in the room had even been born and he would bow to no one. He alluded to the fact that Fitzgerald was a well-known Fenian who was followed by the police and said that he was not a suitable chairman for the meeting.

Fitzgerald replied:

'I think I have given our reverend friend sufficient latitude . . .
I am very sorry that a gentleman of his profession should be
the first to throw in the apple of discord. I know that I am
watched by the authorities (loud cheers). But I consider it no
crime to be watched by the authorities (loud and prolonged
cheers). And though I take part in your proceedings here
today, it's purely from a non-political point of view. I rule
the gentleman out of order, and the business of the meeting
is open (cheers and noise and interruptions).'[28]

Fr Scanlan attempted to further his case, gesticulating
wildly from the back of the court. As Fitzgerald replied, the
meeting descended into pantomime farce with each sentence
cheered and booed, alternately, by opposing factions within
the courthouse:

Fitzgerald: 'I would appeal to you, now, Father, to allow us
    to conduct our business.'
Fr. Scanlan: 'There is no chairman. I cannot hear you.'
Fitzgerald: 'I regret our opening proceedings should be
    interfered with by one whose mission is to preach good-
    will to all mankind. It is not the first time in the history
    of Ireland that individual clerics have been found . . .
    (loud cheers which drowned out the rest).'
A voice: 'Hear the Priest.'
Fr. Scanlan: 'There is no chairman.'
Fitzgerald: 'I again ask our reverend friend to sit down and
    we will take his protest.'
Fr. Scanlan: 'No. No.'

By this point, Fr Scanlan was standing on top of the benches in the middle of the courtroom, and was joined there by at least three more priests and by other supporters. They pushed their way along the tables towards the head of the room where the members of the Central Executive were seated. As they neared the top, a brawl developed. The priests were shoved about the place and sticks were wielded ominously. Reporters at the front of the room had to jump up on the benches to save themselves as 'things looked extremely threatening'.[29]

Pat Hoctor, an IRB man and vice-president of the GAA, jumped up on a bench and condemned the conduct of Fr Scanlan as nothing short of disgraceful. He described the meeting in Thurles as the 'First Home Government Convention that has met for many a day', and called for a vote to be taken to decide whether Fitzgerald should be chairman. It was clear by a show of hands from the body of the crowd that the great majority favoured the IRB.

Fitzgerald: 'Now, gentlemen, I hope our reverend Father is satisfied.'

Fr. Scanlan: 'I claim to be heard as well as he was.'

Fitzgerald: 'Now, we will have to make it rough if this goes on.'

A voice: 'Rough we will make it.'

Fitzgerald: 'Are you satisfied with a show of hands?'

Fr. Scanlan: 'I am not.'

Fitzgerald: 'This must end somewhere. I will hear no-one further.'

A voice (thought to be Anthony Mackey): 'We'll pulverise the priests.'

Meanwhile, altercations broke out in the body of the court. Things got more menacing. The crowd swayed. The priests were nearly driven off the table. Reporters were pushed into a position of defence, trying to write the detail of what was happening, even as delegates seemed certain 'each moment to fall off the table and on to the Fourth Estate'. Eventually, Fr Scanlan was shoved down onto a table, other men were seized by the collar, sticks were again brandished, and loud cries filled the room, as the priests were driven roughly about. It was a 'scene of excitement that threatened every minute to develop into a riot'.[30]

> Fr. Scanlan: 'If this is persevered in, you will break up the organisation.'
>
> A voice: 'There will be other things broken up too.'
>
> Fitzgerald: 'I regret to say to you, Fr Scanlan, that you are the cause of all the disturbance here today.'
>
> Fr. Scanlan (folding his arms): 'I will stop here as long as I like.'
>
> Fitzgerald (hotly): 'Then we will remove you, sir.'
>
> Fr. Scanlan (defiantly): 'Take care of yourself, sir.'
>
> Fitzgerald (loudly): 'There are limits to human endurance even if you are a priest. When a clergyman comes on this platform he is a layman, and if he meets with rough usage, let him take the consequences (renewed cheers).'
>
> Fr. Scanlan: 'One word is all I ask.'
>
> Fitzgerald: 'I will allow Fr. Scanlan to say one word and no more.'

As Fr Scanlan began his speech, the reporters' table he was standing on collapsed on the ground beneath him. He was then lifted up onto the bench beside Fitzgerald and made a speech saying that he was being denied his right to propose an alternative chairman to Fitzgerald. The meeting again dissolved into noise and confusion.

A voice: 'You want to smash the Gaelic Association.'
Fr. Scanlan: 'I have been refused a right to reply.'
Fitzgerald: 'Now, Fr. Scanlan, you have made your protest.'

At that point, almost two hours after the meeting had begun, Fr Scanlan left the top of the room and headed down through the courthouse and out to the yard. He was followed by the three priests who had been with him in the scuffle, and by up to two hundred supporters. As they left the courthouse they were heckled by many who remained. Fitzgerald resumed the meeting, saying that he regretted the unseemly scenes of violence but that he 'thanked God that we have got in Ireland today men who would not have clerical dictators'.[31]

The IRB then got down to the business of electing a new Central Executive for the GAA. Pat Hoctor proposed that Edmond Bennett from the Clare IRB be elected president. Bennett was a surprise nominee. He was regarded by police as a 'broken-down farmer of bad character . . . a '67 Fenian . . . a bad lot'. His choice as president seems to have been a decision made on the spur of the moment as the IRB had actually intended that Fitzgerald would be elected president. The police informers, who were present throughout the meeting, believed that Fitzgerald had deemed it necessary, in the wake of the fight with the priests, to step aside as an act of discretion,[32] and that Bennett was 'a mere tool in the hands of Hoctor and Fitzgerald'.[33]

VI

Not all the opponents of the IRB had left the hall with the priests.

A third body of men was present – men whose loyalty lay neither with the priests nor with the IRB. And they were now finally able to push for the election of their champion, Maurice Davin, as president. Tempers frayed once more and supporters of Davin and Bennett exchanged abuse. Amid some confusion, with one delegate claiming that unauthorized persons had come into the room through side doors and broken windows, an attempt was made to take the vote by a show of hands. It proved impossible and the meeting dragged on through argument and counter-argument.

It was now almost 6 p.m. (five hours after the meeting had begun), and the courthouse had slipped into darkness. The reporters' table had been broken in pieces and was scattered across the front of the courthouse. The huge crowd had created an oppressive heat and the air hung with the stale smoke of pipe tobacco. Finally, at a quarter to seven, came a resolution of sorts. A division was taken in the style of the House of Commons. Supporters of each candidate were sent through opposite doors that led away into separate yards. Tellers had been placed at each door to count the men as they passed. The result was a clear one, though not a rout: 210 votes for Davin, 316 for Bennett. If the priests and their supporters had not stormed out of the hall, Davin would most likely have won the vote.

Edmond Bennett, the newly elected president of the GAA, took the chair at the top of the room and proceeded with the rest of the elections. Every other position was now

unopposed. The non-IRB elements of the GAA appear to
have focused solely on the election of Maurice Davin, neglecting every other office. Their disorganization is striking. With
Davin defeated, the IRB took charge of the entire Central
Executive of the GAA. Only the proposal to appoint
Anthony Mackey as treasurer brought an objection, relating
to Mackey's role in causing the split in Limerick. A voice from
the floor cried out: 'We object to him. He put Limerick out
of the hurling championship.' Mackey was declared elected,
however, amid booing from a section of the assembly.

The convention ended with a remarkable display of effront-
ery. As if to completely ignore what had transpired over the
previous hours, P. N. Fitzgerald moved a motion which
ordained that the GAA was to be a purely sporting body and
that no club of the association was to engage in a public
political meeting or demonstration. The motion was unanimously passed. And, as if to throw an olive branch to the men
against whom they had fought for the afternoon, the executive offered to allow suspended clubs to re-enter the GAA
provided they sent a letter of apology for breaking the rules of
the association.

Leaving the meeting, various IRB men had no doubt
that their hold on the GAA was now complete. One of their
number remarked to an undercover detective that he was
proud that the priests had been thrown out and that the
GAA was now composed only of Fenians rather than of
'rotten nationalists'. Pat Hoctor, who had been re-elected as
vice-president of the GAA, was even more direct. He headed
to the post office and sent a telegram to John Torley, a Glas-
gow IRB leader. It simply read: 'Victory all along the line.'[34]

VII

The day was not done, however. When Fr John Scanlan had led his contingent from the meeting, he joined the members of the suspended GAA clubs who had remained in the yard at the front of the courthouse. Fr Scanlan called an impromptu meeting and said that he believed, without fear of contradiction, that the GAA was being made into a Fenian organization. He related the details of the meeting to those who had not made it inside, claiming that IRB men had threatened to 'pulverise the priests'. He called on all around him to set up a new organization without the Fenians, saying: 'If you form a new association, I promise you we will hurl these fellows anytime.'

The gathering then decamped to the market place in Thurles, where they were joined by hundreds of local people who had been drawn to the spectacle. Fr Scanlan announced that he was calling for a meeting to be held in Hayes' Hotel later that evening to formalize a new association. Speeches by him and other priests denounced the IRB men, before the group crossed the main square to the hotel. They were cheered as they walked by the large crowds of people gathered in the square.[35]

Inside, Fr Scanlan was appointed chairman, and he opened the meeting with another long and eloquent speech about the importance of opposing the IRB. One of the roughly 200 people present was a Wexford man who described the behaviour of the executive – with its determination to centralize power and to coerce men – as being the same as that of the British government.

There were some unexpected faces at the Hayes' Hotel

meeting, including two GAA vice-presidents. J. K. Bracken told the gathering that he strongly protested against the actions of the executive in the courthouse: 'These men should have listened to the priests of Tipperary.' J. E. Kennedy, for his part, claimed that he had come to the meeting to defend himself against the allegation that he had manhandled priests. He produced to the meeting a letter of resignation from the Central Executive of the GAA which, he said, would be published in due course. It wasn't. The contents of that letter and the reason for the resignation were never made clear.[36]

The presence of Bracken and Kennedy at the 'Priests' Convention' illustrates the notorious capacity of Irish Republicans to split. The political divides, personal intrigues, and outright animus that divided the IRB were real. Bracken and Kennedy must have understood, too, that what had happened in the courthouse earlier that afternoon was unlikely to bring popularity to either the GAA or its newly elected Central Executive.

As the meeting concluded, Fr Scanlan and his supporters stopped short of establishing a rival sporting organization. Instead, they contented themselves with making a series of pledges of opposition to the IRB-led GAA – with the implication that they would continue to resist from within. The 'rotten nationalists' were not finished yet.[37]

VIII

The full implications of the events of that day in Thurles soon became clear. On the following day, Archbishop Croke wrote a letter to the *Freeman's Journal* in which he recounted his 'pain and humiliation' at what he had heard had transpired at the convention. He concluded: 'Nothing, then, remains for me but to dissociate myself, as I now publicly do, from the branch of the Gaelic Athletic Association which exercised such a sinister influence over yesterday's proceedings.'[38] Croke later said that what had happened at the convention had put '50,000 young and enthusiastic Irishmen under the irresponsible control . . . of not less than a dozen men of whom . . . the very best and most charitable thing that can be said is that they are either wholly unknown or not favourably known to the country'.[39]

Croke's words signalled an almighty backlash against the IRB-run executive. National and local newspapers had carried lurid accounts of the sensational happenings in the Thurles courthouse across several pages. The behaviour of Fitzgerald and his cohort, the actions of the priests, and the meeting in Hayes' Hotel provoked intense interest in what was happening to the GAA, even among those who had no interest in its games. Almost immediately it became apparent that the IRB – in their words and in their deeds – had made a significant tactical error. It was one thing to manipulate the GAA from positions of power that had been acquired with relative ease; it was entirely another matter to maintain those positions amid scenes of violent conflict with priests, and in opposition to men as popular as Maurice Davin and Archbishop Croke.

The assault on the priests provided the opponents of the Central Executive with the perfect weapon with which to retaliate. Michael Cusack saw this immediately. In a venomous editorial in the *Celtic Times*, he wrote that 'the irreligious, socialistic set of Hoctor and O'Reilly will be shown that they cannot, with impunity, publicly insult, jeer and mock the devoted priests of our land'. He continued by saying that it was clear from the reaction of clubs all over the country that the executive had gone too far and that the enthusiasm against them was 'spreading like wildfire'.

Cusack's prediction that the GAA would be reclaimed by a group uniting under the banner of 'Priests and People' was lent credence by the torrent of resolutions passed by clubs from counties all over Ireland, calling for the return of Maurice Davin as president of the GAA and the removal of the Central Executive.[40] By the end of November 1887, over 250 clubs had sent resolutions calling for Davin's restoration; a mere two clubs had published resolutions supporting the executive.[41] Assailed from every quarter, the executive met for the first time since the annual convention when they gathered at Limerick Junction on Wednesday evening, 23 November. Following the meeting, Edmond Bennett, the newly elected president, issued a statement to the press in which he denied that priests had been treated with insult and violence and railed against the way the enemies of the GAA had sown discord in its ranks. The executive passed a motion which said that there had been a deplorable misinterpretation of their motives and that their opponents were shamefully using the name of Archbishop Croke as a stick 'to force this association into an attitude of abject servility, unworthy of any body of independent Irishmen'.[42]

The members of the executive were, of course, correct in their opinion that the enemies of the GAA hoped to contribute to its dissolution. There had been at least one police infiltrator stirring up trouble at the November convention, while a police inspector wrote to officials in Dublin Castle, as relations within the GAA continued to worsen, advising that 'we may hope for good results from the animosities and jealousies which the split will occasion'. Michael Davitt later claimed in the *Freeman's Journal* that police across the country had been instructed by a coded message to worsen the divide between the GAA's competing political factions and, in Cork, at least, a clear instruction was given to policemen to facilitate the GAA down the path of self-destruction.[43]

Nonetheless, it was clear that the executive had itself created almost all of the problems it now faced, and its internal opponents sensed vulnerability. Michael Cusack wrote that its members were 'living in a fool's paradise, encouraging one another with a little noise, as cowards and children do in the dark'.[44] More importantly, Croke and Davin were moving back to centre stage. With the executive on the defensive, Croke organized a meeting in Cashel with Davin and his fellow GAA patron, Michael Davitt. Davitt appears to have been acting as a sort of intermediary between the disputing factions.[45] In the wake of that meeting, Davin drafted the outline of a new constitution for the GAA and pursued a public campaign to reconstruct the association.

Croke wrote approvingly to the press of Davin's initiatives, but was careful to offer room for future compromise by acquitting the executive of 'any and every deliberate intent to annoy or insult me'. It was an important gesture, intended to leave open the possibility, as Croke put it, of securing the support of all nationalists for the GAA: 'I dread and deprecate disunion amongst Irishmen . . . Strictly speaking, I am no party man. As long as one loves and labours for Ireland, according to his lights and within the limits of prudence and righteousness, he may count me as a friend and fellow-labourer. Ireland, anyhow, needs all our energy today. Let us not foolishly expend it in squabbling with and thus weakening each other.'[46]

IX

For all that the Central Executive had attempted to see off opponents, the public intervention of Archbishop Croke and the moves towards conciliation now gathered momentum. Five IRB men travelled to Thurles and, over two days in the last week in November 1887, held a series of meetings with Croke and Davin.[47] The upshot of those meetings was the establishment of a four-man Provisional Committee drawn from supporters of the executive and of Davin. At its first meeting, this committee agreed that a Reconstruction Convention would be held in Thurles on Wednesday 4 January at 1.30 p.m. In the interim, every county was to organize to hold a meeting on Tuesday 27 December to pick its delegates for the convention. It was now agreed that this convention would stage fresh elections for every office and that a new constitution would be put in place.[48]

Inspector Henry Bourchier wrote to Dublin Castle saying that his informants were telling him that, in the battle for the GAA, the IRB was losing.[49] This was true in that it was now apparent that the IRB would no longer have complete control of the association. But the Reconstruction Convention made it clear that they were in the GAA for the long haul.

In contrast to the vast crowd at the November convention, there were just eighty delegates present when the convention opened in the hall of the Young Men's Society in Thurles. Things started harmoniously, with Maurice Davin unanimously elected to chair the meeting. There was general agreement to the new constitution as outlined by Davin, which streamlined the rules governing the administration of the GAA and devolved much power from its Central Executive to the County Committees. This decentralization was clearly an attempt to stop the IRB (or any faction) running the GAA by claiming control of its executive.

Only when the elections were held did trouble arise. Davin was elected president, without opposition. Soon enough it became apparent that only about a quarter of the delegates were affiliated with the IRB, and that the Fenians would lose much of their representation on the executive.[50] P. N. Fitzgerald protested that 'the convention was rigged' and claimed, unconvincingly, that 'if we were in a majority we would not trample on the rights of a minority'. He made an ominous prediction that, though they were clearly beaten on that day, they would rise again, maybe in twelve months or two years, to reclaim the GAA.[51]

Otherwise, the Reconstruction Convention passed off in relative calm. Davin's men held most of the key positions, but several IRB men were voted onto the newly formed Central Executive of the GAA. And, in a motion proposed by Frank Dineen, a Fenian, and seconded by Rev. Fr J. Clancy, a clergyman based in Clare, it was unanimously agreed to formally ratify the rule, passed in February, that no member of the police could join the GAA or play in its games. The various factions within the organization were able to unite against what had now become (even if only briefly for some sections of the GAA) a 'common enemy' at a time of evictions, shadowing by the special branch and the imprisonment of nationalist MPs.

It seems remarkable in the light of everything else that was going on, but a group of men within the GAA had spent the previous two months revising the playing rules. The changes in hurling were straightforward. The 'forfeit point' – awarded when the defending team knocked the ball over their own end-line – was now replaced by a forty-yards free puck. The rule on tackling was changed in an attempt to make the game less physical. Most importantly, the referee was to be issued with a whistle and given greater individual responsibility to enforce the playing rules. This was a significant response to the on-field controversies that had blighted the staging of the first All-Ireland championships.[52]

As a final act, the meeting decided that the new playing rules would come into immediate effect. There was, however, to be one exception to this rule: the final of the All-Ireland hurling championship, between Meelick and Thurles, would be played out under the old rules. Finally, the men of the GAA were back talking about hurling. In his GAA column in *Sport*, P. P. Sutton sounded a sanguine note: 'Out of evil often cometh good.'

12. The First All-Ireland Hurling Final

It took several months for the newly reconstructed GAA to sort out arrangements for the first All-Ireland hurling final. But, eventually, the match was set for Birr on Easter Sunday, 1 April 1888.

Birr, the largest town in the south of King's County, was gloriously divided in everything it did – even in its name, for the Birr of nationalist Ireland was equally the Parsonstown of unionism, the seat of the Earls of Rosse. The political, economic and religious fault lines of Irish society were readily apparent in the culture of Birr, and the backdrop to the first All-Ireland hurling final was the clash of cultures in small-town Ireland.

I

Birr was the oldest town in King's County and, by the 1880s, home to just under 5,000 inhabitants. In its architecture and its planning, it was genuinely unique. The main streets and squares of the town had been laid out by successive generations of the Parsons family, who had been granted several thousand acres of land there by the Crown in the 1620s. The idea was to introduce a sense of 'English civility' to an area with a long tradition of rebellion. Introducing civility meant bringing in 'undertakers' to farm the land and, over the following decades, Birr and its surrounds became home to waves of settlers. By the 1800s it had both Protestant and Catholic churches, two Methodist chapels, a Presbyterian meeting-house and a Quaker hall.

At the heart of the town was Birr Castle, the home of the Earls of Rosse and a place of real innovation. In the 1840s the largest telescope in the world had been constructed in the castle grounds by William Parsons, the 3rd Earl. The telescope retained its record status for seventy-five years and, by the 1880s, the observatory at the castle was of international importance, attracting renowned scientists and visitors curious to study the far reaches of the universe. In the week before the hurling final, one of the social events taking place in the town was a lecture in the Parochial Schoolroom by astronomer Dr Otto Boeddicker, of the Birr Castle Observatory, entitled 'Are there any worlds inhabited except our own?' The lecture opened with the Rev. French leading the large attendance in singing the hymn 'The Heavens Declare Thy Glory', and then Dr Boeddicker used his magic lantern to present numerous illustrations of the 'heavenly' bodies. The lecture was just part of an evening's entertainment for the elite of Birr. Later, some budding dramatists in the town staged a series of sketches in the Printing House Buildings, which began with a farce entitled 'The Mischievous Nigger', and concluded with another, 'The Haunted House'. And later still, there were dancing classes organized in Dooly's Hotel by Monsieur Delplanque, 'a Gallic gentleman', where the presence of the Countess of Rosse was perceived as a guarantee of their success.[1]

For the general populace of the area, there were other, more basic concerns. Emigration agents advertised cheap fares for passage by ship to America on a weekly basis and then recorded the names of those who departed. It became a

ritual in the town to send emigrants off in a certain style.
When fourteen people emigrated from Birr in April 1887,
they were played off by the band of the Roman Catholic
Young Men's Society. Although the area was not as disturbed
as other parts of Ireland, the farms outside Birr were a site
of conflict. There was agitation there during the Land
War and more, again, during the Plan of Campaign. For
example, when a tenant farmer called William O'Brien was
evicted from lands near the town, local people erected a
roadside hut for him and his family. The eviction had brought
big demonstrations with 'any amount of bands and banners
present'.[2]

The presence of two newspapers in the town underlined
the manner in which Birr was divided. The *Midland Tribune*
carried on its masthead the legend 'Ireland for the Irish and
the Land for the People'. It appealed for support from the
tenant farmers of the Midlands, stressed that it was the only
Catholic newspaper in the region, and proclaimed that it
would never shrink from conflict with 'haughty landlordism'. It noted, for example, an attempt to develop a gun club
in nearby Tullamore, and suggested caustically that the young
landlord who was leading the enterprise was sure to enjoy
success 'if he devotes to it but half the zeal that he has displayed in evicting some of his tenantry'.[3] Naturally, the
Midland Tribune gave substantial uncritical coverage of hurling, and repeatedly commended the various clubs of the
region for their patriotic endeavours.

The *King's County Chronicle*, on the other hand, was avow-
edly unionist, devoted to coverage of the local elite. The
natives of town and country were regularly portrayed as
feckless, drunken, insubordinate and treacherous Catholics.
The *Chronicle*'s treatment of hurling is a lovely mix of

condescension, outrage and obvious interest. On the evening after the King's County championship second-round matches in 1888 (there had been no championship organized in 1887), the paper would detail the presence of 4,000 people and note the results. Having satisfied its interest in the game, the paper then returned to type, lambasting the desecration of the Sabbath and condemning events that happened in the hours after the game. It claimed that 'some of the hurlers stepped into St. Brendan's Church at night while Mr. Sykes was giving an organ recital. So little respect had they for the House of God that they entered hat on head, and behaved in a manner so irreverent that Dr. Myles removed them personally, along with their formidable looking iron-bound "hurleys". Such are the class to whom the Gladstonians would consign the destinies of the loyalists of Ireland.'[4]

II

Nothing was beyond division in Birr. In the spring of 1888, the members of the Parsonstown Cycling Club held their first jaunt of the season when they toured down to Banagher and enjoyed a fine dinner. Not to be outdone, the newly formed Birr Cycling Club announced that it, too, would be taking its inaugural voyage the following Sunday, also to Banagher, where dinner would once more be served. Its supporters remarked: 'Now Birr has its own iron greyhound club as well as "Parsonstown".'[5]

Sport was everywhere in the lives of the townspeople. It was reported that 'the favourite amusement of the inmates of Birr Workhouse is pitch-and-toss'.[6] The local press also carried complaints that the chaplain based in the workhouse spent his days playing tennis, to the extent that he generally wandered about dressed in his tennis gear.[7]

Indeed, tennis was a big game in Birr, and the championships and tournaments run by the King's County and Ormond tennis club were major social events. Huge marquees were erected and regimental bands attended. There were flavoured ices and cocktails for sale, and the local gentry descended on the town, some arriving in four-horse carriages, with 'spanking horses and full-liveried coachmen and frontmen'.[8] The less prestigious Wilmer Tennis Club, which had taken the pavilion from the old cricket club in the town and brought it to its grounds, noted – by contradistinction – that its membership was open to all, 'respectability being the one desideratum'.[9]

The largest military barracks in the Midlands – Crinkle Barracks – was based on the outskirts of Birr. It had been built during the Napoleonic wars and could house up to 2,000 soldiers. As well as being a huge boost to the economy of the town, it also shaped the sporting landscape. On the week of the hurling final, Galway Grammar School played a rugby match against a Birr team that was a combined selection of locals and soldiers stationed in Crinkle Barracks. Then, on the day of the All-Ireland final, two teams drawn from the Scots Fusiliers played their first cricket match of the season on a pitch attached to the barracks.[10]

By 1888, the *King's County Chronicle* was reporting that Assheton Biddulph, the Master of the King's County and Ormond Hunt, was moving to stop the hunt's activities because its members were nervous of attack and of bad publicity.[11] The dispute around hunting was obviously related to land agitation, and attacking the hunt had become something of a pastime around Birr. In January 1888 a large crowd had gathered at a crossroads near the town to prevent the King's County and Ormond Hunt from carrying out their regular meeting. There were numerous police present, and the protest ended with the demonstrators spending the afternoon playing hurling.[12]

III

For the nationalists of Birr, there was no doubt that theirs was a hurling town, the capital of a hurling area. By March 1888 there were fifteen clubs affiliated to the King's County GAA, most of them hurling clubs based within ten miles of Birr,[13] and in 1887 and 1888 a series of highly successful hurling tournaments was played in and around the town.[14] There were two hurling clubs based in the town itself: St Brendan's, and Allen, Larkin and O'Briens, both of whom entered the King's County hurling championship. In 1888, the two clubs worked together to prepare Birr to stage the hurling final.

On 8 March an advertisement appeared in the *Midland Tribune*: 'Wanted: A field suitable for hurling, within a mile of Birr. For a suitable field £10 will be given for the season, ending December 1888. Apply to the secretary, St. Brendan's Club, GAA, Birr.'[15] Within a fortnight, the club was holding matches in a field given by local man Johnny Farrell, on Railway Road on the outskirts of the town. The field was 'level and not too grassy', and measured 100 yards wide by 200 yards long. It was first used for hurling on 24 March 1888 – the week before the All-Ireland final – when three of the second-round matches in the King's County championship were played there. On that occasion, the members of Birr's two clubs stewarded the 3,500 spectators without any problems. In the week before the All-Ireland final, further improvements were made by officials and players from the clubs. Preparations were not assisted by the weather. During March there had been ten days of snow in Birr, and three days of hail. But the worst of the weather had passed by the week of the final, and on the morning of the match, Johnny Farrell's field was good and dry.[16] For the players about to take to it in their bare feet, this was a welcome prospect.

IV

The town of Birr was ready, but were the hurlers of Meelick?

In the months before the All-Ireland final, land agitation in East Galway had worsened once more. The battle with Lord Clanricarde over the payment of rents had intensified. Police reports had noted that 'intimidation prevails to a large extent and no rent is being paid'.[17] James Lynam continued to lead the agitation. He told a meeting in December 1887 in the nearby town of Portumna that he had received threat after threat of eviction and that his blood froze at the thought of what his family had been subjected to for refusing to become slaves and sycophants.[18]

Despite the agitation, the hurlers had continued to play. There had been hurling tournaments and practice matches in Meelick during 1887 and this continued into 1888. Newspapers carried hurling reports in columns parallel to others that told of ongoing evictions and life-threatening confrontations in the fields all around East Galway. One Sunday afternoon's playing consisted of four hours of matches refereed by James Lynam. The only criticism was that there was no clean water for drinking, which was an inconvenience to those who were not drinking porter.[19]

The man chosen to captain the Meelick hurlers in the All-Ireland final was Pat Madden, a tenant farmer who lived in Meelick. He, too, was on the verge of being evicted from his farm. Other players worked as farmers and farm labourers, or as blacksmiths and carpenters. The team's goalkeeper was the publican's son, Pat Larkin, who had played in goal for Killimor against Michael Cusack's Metropolitans on Easter Monday 1883, some eighteen months before the GAA had been founded. Paddy Cullen, who later emigrated to America, was just eighteen when the final was played. He and his brothers were carpenters and the hurleys used in the final by the Meelick men were made in Cullen's house in the week of the game.[20]

In local lore, the Meelick players are also reputed to have made the ball used in the match. A story handed down tells of how three hurlers, John Lowery, John Callanan and John Mannion, were drinking in Patrick Fitzpatrick's public house in Killimor. Talk turned to hurling, notably to the problem of the heaviness of all existing hurling balls. Different balls had been tried but none had been of any use, particularly in wet conditions. John Callanan was sipping his whiskey when he looked at the bottle and the cork and had an epiphany: he could wrap a cork in twine and cover it with leather, thus producing a lighter ball.

Pat Hardiman of Killeen, it is remembered, had a certain fame in the area as a man skilled in cutting and sewing leather. The three players and Hardiman adjourned to the back room of the pub armed with corks, leather, twine and – naturally – with whiskey and porter. Even the music and laughter in the front of the pub did nothing to deflect them from their endeavour. Once the cork was bound, Pat Hardiman cut out the leather and, using awl and waxen hemp, sewed the ball tightly. On completion it was hopped across the floor of the pub. Later, it was brought to Birr by James Haverty and used in the final.[21] This story is not contradicted – though neither is it even remotely confirmed – by the Thurles captain, Jim Stapleton, who recalled in the 1940s that the ball used on the day of the final was of red leather with a worsted thread centre over a cork core, bigger than the modern *sliotar*, and neither hard nor heavy.[22]

The Meelick club arranged for their players to be brought to Birr by McIntyre's Brake, a horse-drawn coach that operated from McIntyre's Harp Hotel in Banagher, which was separated from Meelick by the river Shannon. The arrangements were straightforward. The brake, with the capacity to carry twenty-five passengers, would cross the Shannon and collect the players at various points along the roads between Killimor and Finney's Cross at the Banagher–Eyrecourt Road.[23]

It all went wrong. Two of the Killimor men, John Lowery and John Mannion, were late in arriving at their collection point, Mannion's Cross in Maheranearla. The two had mistakenly gone to Moorfield Cross and had only headed to Mannion's Cross when they realized their error. They were too late: the brake had travelled on without them. The hurlers rushed to Finney's Cross, only to find that, again, the brake had left half an hour previously. Not to be deterred, the pair headed off to Birr on foot, walking and running by turns. In Banagher – the halfway point of their journey – they stopped in Galbraith's pub, drank a pint each, bought a penny loaf and ate it as they resumed walking.[24]

Lowery and Mannion were not the only ones running late.

According to local tradition, the curate in Meelick, Fr Mullins, was late coming to the church to say 9.30 a.m. mass. As the minutes rolled on, the players attending realized that they were going to be late for the pick-up. Just as the priest came into the church, he saw the hurlers leaving by the back door. He made no attempt to stop them, beyond, possibly, the invocation of special powers: 'They won't win today,' Fr Mullins prophesied, 'and they'll be lucky if they ever win.'[25]

The hurlers knew nothing of this supposed curse as they headed off in McIntyre's Brake. On arrival in Birr around noon, the Meelick players were, according to the *Midland Tribune*, 'very cordially received' by local people. Too cordially, perhaps, for they headed immediately for a drink. While in a public house, it appears that they were led to believe that the Thurles men were most likely not coming to Birr, due to a row in the club. It was not, of course, unusual for matches to be postponed at the last minute and in all manner of circumstances.[26] The Meelick men took the news in their stride. They continued to drink bottles of porter in the belief that a game was now unlikely.

V

Rumours of a row in the Thurles camp were rooted in fact.[27] On the Friday night before the final, the team had been selected. It included fifteen players from Thurles and six from Two-Mile Borris – this even though Thurles had had to drop a pair of Two-Mile Borris players from the side that faced Tullaroan. Long Dinny Maher was to captain the team, as he had done throughout the championship. As the meeting concluded, Maher asked that players be reimbursed for the considerable cost of travel to previous matches in the championship. The club management would not agree. Faced with blank refusal, certain players reacted furiously. Long Dinny Maher, his brother Black Jack Maher, and five other hurlers from the Killinan end of Thurles parish (Red Dinny Maher, Ned Maher, Little Matty Maher, Pat Ryan and Con Callanan) said that they would not play in the final.

The officials in the Thurles club were ruthless in their response. The men in charge of the team, Hugh Ryan and Andrew Callanan, travelled by horse and trap to recruit the best hurlers from the clubs based in the villages and parishes around Thurles. By Sunday morning they had secured the services of seven celebrated hurlers from the surrounding areas. This was against the laws of the GAA, but the chances of it being challenged were extremely low, as the Meelick men would be unfamiliar with the identity of their opponents.

The upheaval in the Thurles camp had continued even on the morning of the match. Led by Long Dinny Maher, the seven Killinan hurlers had a late change of heart and arrived at Thurles station shortly before the special excursion train was due to leave for Birr, declaring that they were willing to take their places in the team. The offer was refused: the other hurlers were already on the train, they were told, and there could be no change. The train pulled away from the station leaving the Killinan men standing on the platform. As Long Dinny Maher later wistfully recalled: 'There were men from Gortnahoe, Drombane and Moyne called in and their expenses paid, while seven of the old hurlers . . . were left standing on the platform. These were the backbone of the club.'[28]

VI

When the special excursion train arrived from Thurles to Birr station at around 1 p.m., the hurlers were met by a large crowd of enthusiasts and officials, including Patrick White, the match referee, and Patrick Ryan, the vice-president of the County Committee of King's County GAA.[29]

The Thurles hurlers were led in procession down Railway Road, past the match field and into the centre of Birr where they entered Cunningham's Hotel. Word was sent to the Meelick men that the Thurles team had arrived in Birr and that, after all, the match would now be played. A huge shout filled the air and they headed for the appointed meeting place of Cunningham's. When they walked through the front door of the hotel, they were loudly cheered by the Thurles men. The hurlers shook hands and then retired to a room where, in the words of one newspaper report, they 'dressed themselves in Gaelic costume'.[30] Folk memory in Meelick makes no mention of jerseys; rather it recalls that the players in the final were 'the strong silent type who played in shirt and trousers and were identified only by green tam-o-shanters – knitted caps with tassels'.[31] However, another observer on the day commented on the 'beautiful and appropriate costumes' of both teams, the Meelick hurlers with their green jerseys and white stripes, and the Thurles hurlers also wearing green jerseys, but with 'a little galaxy of stars artistically worked around the centre'.[32]

Having changed into their playing gear, the teams gathered in front of the hotel. James Lynam, a veteran of the American Civil War, then took charge of affairs, organizing the two teams to fall into parallel lines in front of the hotel. He called:

'Right, about,' and the two teams turned and marched shoulder to shoulder in military formation away from Cunningham's. They were led through the streets of Birr by Lynam, and by the leading officials of the Thurles club, Lynam's fellow Fenians Hugh Ryan and Andrew Callanan.[33]

Ordinarily, the teams would have been conducted to the field by the Frankford Brass Band, but on the day of the hurling final that band was otherwise occupied. On the previous Wednesday, there had been evictions of tenants who had supported the Plan of Campaign at nearby Broughall, on lands owned by Christopher J. Bannon. One of the tenants, Rody Dooly, was reported to owe two years' rent, some £158. The sheriff, Richard Bull, and his bailiffs, accompanied by one hundred and fifty policemen, had moved to clear the Dooly family from their house and farm of fifty-four acres. By the time the police had arrived, the family, assisted by 'a crowd of country persons', had emptied the house of its furniture, but could not resist the eviction. On the day of the hurling final two thousand people marched together to a rally at Broughal Castle in support of the Doolys and other tenants who had been evicted. Instead of leading the hurlers through Birr to play in the All-Ireland final, the band led the procession to the eviction rally, and stayed on for a football match which the campaigners played in the shadow of the castle.[34]

VII

By the time the parade of players had passed across the Camcor river and down to Johnny Farrell's field, it was estimated that there were about three thousand people gathered around the pitch.[35] The new Thurles captain, Jim Stapleton, later remembered that the crowd gathered on the sidelines was enormous and, as there were no railings to keep the field of play clear, 'a friendly regiment of the Scottish Highlanders stationed in Birr at the time, volunteered to keep order and control the sidelines'.[36] Intriguingly, a newspaper report of the All-Ireland final remarks that 'the crowd, enormous though it was, kept as scrupulously outside the players' territory as if they had been guarded by a line of bayonets, and not as it was by a mere chalk line'.[37]

Newspaper reports from the time record members of the Highlanders regularly attending hurling matches in Birr. At the King's County championship matches the week before the All-Ireland final, the *King's County Chronicle* sneeringly noted that among the crowd were many Scottish soldiers who were attracted by the resemblance of hurling to their national game of shinty, and who were 'much amused at the "bhoys" playing with bare feet'.[38] It is possible that the Highlanders engaged in the stewarding at the All-Ireland final, but this is unconfirmed by newspaper accounts at the time, and stewarding at GAA matches was usually undertaken by local club members. In reports of the final, both Birr clubs – as well as the members of the executive of the County Committee of King's County GAA – were commended for the manner in which they organized the final.[39]

Waiting for the players at the field was Patrick J. White, a native of Toomevara in Co. Tipperary who was living and working in Birr. White initially declined the job of refereeing on account of his links with Tipperary, but was prevailed upon by both teams to carry on with the job, with the Meelick men assuring him of their absolute confidence in his impartiality. White, who was also secretary of the County

PAUL ROUSE

Committee of King's County GAA, was an experienced referee. Throughout March he had officiated at matches in the local championship, and the day after the Meelick–Thurles match he refereed the King's County senior hurling final at the same venue.[40]

It is unclear what part White played in a controversy that eventually shaped the course of the game. Indeed, it must be said that much of what is supposed to have happened across the hour's hurling of the final is contested. This is true not least because no journalist from a national newspaper travelled to Birr for the All-Ireland final. In the week before the match, E. D. Gray, the nationalist MP and owner of the *Freeman's Journal* and *Sport*, had died in Dublin. Even without the death of Gray, it is not clear that P. P. Sutton would have travelled to Birr to report on the final for *Sport*. Even though the principal national outlet for the coverage of hurling was his column in *Sport*, he remained deeply disillusioned at the manner in which his Metropolitans team had exited the championship. In the week after the final, Sutton included in his hurling notes an account of the match that was almost identical to the report of a local journalist which had appeared in the *Freeman's Journal* of the previous Tuesday.

Michael Cusack was not in Birr to write a report on the final. His newspaper, the *Celtic Times*, had added much to the excitement of the first hurling championship, but by the time that the final was played, it had disappeared. It is thought that the circulation of the *Celtic Times* may have reached 20,000 in early summer of 1887, but by the end of that year – and after just a year in existence – it was in free-fall. The reasons for this failure were many. Without financial backers, the paper was constantly fighting to keep its head above water. The relentless attacks on the IRB-controlled

224

Central Executive of the GAA and other targets took up so much space that other matters were squeezed to the side, and this may have alienated readers. This was a problem which Cusack recognized, but at too late a stage to avert its impact.[41] He was reputed to have pawned his watch in an attempt to get printers to publish the 21 January 1888 edition. They refused and the paper folded.

The GAA's own journal, the *Gael*, which had been the organ of the IRB men who ran the Central Executive during much of 1887, had also been dispensed with when Maurice Davin returned as president.

The two journalists who wrote brief accounts of the game for the *Midland Tribune* and for *Sport* agreed on the final score, but their descriptions of the play did not extend beyond one paragraph each. To these paragraphs can be added fragments of records and local traditions. The story of the game is, therefore, incomplete and disputed in parts – a fitting end to the way the championship unfolded.

VIII

Patrick J. White threw in the red leather ball at three o'clock. For eleven minutes the game was played in a frenzy, the ball 'whizzing in all directions, now here, now there, threatening one goal, now another'. The Meelick hurlers 'put forth much vigour', according to one observer, but when 'the Thurles men went to work with determination', they broke away and one of their whips struck a point. Thurles then pressed, but were repeatedly driven back by Meelick and for fifteen minutes before half-time, 'the play was simply fierce'.[42]

The teams changed ends for the second half. The contest

became even fiercer with 'some wonderful feats in manly prowess exhibited on both sides'.[43] Early in the half, Thurles pinned Meelick back near their own goal. There was a long skirmish in front of the Meelick posts and several times a goal seemed imminent. Meelick survived, but only at the expense of a forfeit point, which was awarded when one of their defenders hit the ball out over the end-line. Under the new rules introduced at the Reconstruction Convention four months previously, this act would only have resulted in Thurles being awarded a forty-yard free puck, but the All-Ireland final was played under the old rules and Meelick now trailed by two points.[44]

They suffered another blow soon afterwards. It seems that one of Meelick's best players, John Lowery, struck a Thurles man with his hurley, causing him to leave the field injured. Lowery was either sent off by the referee or – according to the *Midland Tribune* – removed from the fray by his own manager, James Lynam, for ten minutes.[45]

John Lowery later recalled that in the early stages of the match, when there was little to choose between the teams, a Thurles player began to cut lumps out of the Meelick men. He was, remembered Lowery, 'the wildest hurler he ever saw'. Eventually Lowery decided to take on the Thurles wild-man. The result was that the Thurles player was forced off the field, and Lowery too was made to leave by the referee. Lowery added that his capacity for displays of temper and impulse had not been diminished by the fact that he had been forced to walk much of the way to Birr.[46]

Whether Lowery was removed from the field by the referee or by his own manager, it seems that he continued to join in the play by rushing onto the field whenever the ball came near him – which was quite often, as he was following the play up and down the line. Patrick White remonstrated with Lowery on several occasions but to no avail. Lowery stopped interfering only when the referee warned that he would give a walkover to the Thurles team if the intrusions persisted.[47]

When Lowery was finally off the field, Thurles struck for the vital score. Jim Stapleton later recalled how he helped bring the ball down the field in a central rush of crowded men, before – seeing the chance of a score – he passed it out to Tommy Healy, who caught it and drove it hard and low through the goal.[48] But that may be a case of history being written by those who live the longest. The reporter for the *Midland Tribune* wrote that the crucial goal was actually scored by Jim Leahy, who struck the ball off his left side from the middle of the field, under the tape which served as a cross-bar, for the winning goal.[49]

This latter version is partly endorsed by the Meelick goal-keeper, John Mannion. Mannion's feet were paining him through the match – partly from the long walk to Birr, partly from the tightness of the new boots he was wearing. He was also constrained by the fact that this was the first time he had ever worn togs of any description, having previously played in his working breeches. Unfortunately, the togs were too tight around the waist, leaving him in discomfort and restricting his movement. Until the day he died, Mannion lamented the concession of a goal he would normally have stopped: 'The ball came down to me out of the sun and a 17 stone Tipperary man arrived at the same time. The ball went in between us, but they won it fair.'[50]

Losers, too, have their own way of recording the past. In Meelick the story was handed down that the actual final score was just one goal to no score.[51] The records of the GAA show, however, that when Patrick White blew the full-time whistle, Thurles had beaten Meelick by one goal and two points (including a forfeit point) to no score, and were duly crowned the first All-Ireland hurling champions.[52]

IX

After the winning captain, James Stapleton, had been carried through the field, and the two teams had cheered each other off, the forty-two hurlers were again lined up in military fashion by James Lynam and marched back to Cunningham's Hotel, where they were served with dinner.[53]

Back in January, the *King's County Chronicle* had been lured into untypical optimism when it commented favourably on the GAA's public expressions of determination to remove drink from the vicinity of its matches and tournaments. In an editorial, the *Chronicle* concluded: 'Truly we in Ireland are improving.'[54] Birr Petty Sessions on 13 April 1888 provided plenty of evidence to the contrary, as case after case of drunken and disorderly behaviour following the All-Ireland and King's County hurling championships came before the courts. The litany of crimes and misdemeanours was gleefully set out in the *Chronicle*. The paper recorded, for example, that Thomas Meara, from Roscrea, had been fined 10s for beating a man with a stick, and that Thomas Molloy had been 'one of the rioters in Parsonstown on the day of the hurling', but had given a false name and was now fined 26s, or, in default, one month in prison. In all, more than twenty men from all across South King's County and North Tipperary were fined between 5s and 30s by magistrates for their actions after championship hurling matches, and another was sent to jail for fourteen days. One publican lost his licence, and others were fined, for allowing drink to be sold on their premises during prohibited hours. Another publican was fined for selling drink to a man who was so drunk when he left the public house that he fell out of a cart. And then there was Thomas Coy, who was fined 7s.6d for being drunk in charge of a donkey and car.[55]

The police told magistrates that they 'were greatly harassed in the discharge of their duty' on the evening of the All-Ireland hurling final, and left the impression that the town of Birr was a very quiet one and didn't benefit from strangers coming into it and kicking up a row. The presiding magistrate, J. T. McSherry, RM, agreed that 'it was monstrous that people could not come into town for a day's amusement without carrying on such conduct'.[56] And the *King's County Chronicle*'s editor lamented once again the manner in which hurling desecrated the Sabbath and brought illegal trading in liquor to the extent that 'Easter has come and gone in a wild whirl of excitement and hurleys'.[57]

13. The Future

The first All-Ireland hurling championship was both a failure and a triumph. Its failure lay in the interminable disputes, the cancellations, the gross chicanery and the sheer disorganization that dogged so much of the competition. These failures limited the hurling championship to a grand total of four matches between clubs from different counties.

Nonetheless, its very completion was its enduring achievement. There was now an All-Ireland championship, and this had been contested despite the fact that the GAA was in its infancy; that basic requirements such as hurleys, balls and playing gear were in short supply; that the acquisition of grounds was anything but straightforward; and that the association was meanwhile being torn asunder by a dispute between extreme nationalists and their more moderate fellow members. The first All-Ireland championship was, ultimately, a triumph because it had happened at all.

I

In the week after the final in Birr, P. P. Sutton cast a jaundiced eye over proceedings in his newspaper column. He wrote: 'The hurling championship for 1887 has at last been decided and Thurles have won it. The history of this championship is a most disgraceful one, but the least said now about it the better.' For all his enduring regret, even bitterness, at the way his own Metropolitans team had been treated, he managed a tribute of sorts to the championship winners:

> In the early part of the championship Thurles were not dreamt of as likely winners, but in the final of the Tipperary championship they showed splendid pluck, stamina and science, defeating the hitherto invincible North 'Tipps'. In the inter-county championships they improved if anything ... For many reasons few will begrudge Thurles the championship. It was here the GAA was established, and since then the boys of the archiepiscopal city have given the greatest support to the movement for reviving our National games.

Sutton finished his review of the hurling championship by offering a piece of advice to the footballers: 'Now that the hurling championship has been finished, the Limerick Commercials and the Dundalk Young Irelanders should look alive and put the football championship out of its misery.'[1] That championship, too, had been riven by disputes, the finest of which involved J. K. Bracken, founding member of the GAA, active IRB man and leading figure in the Templemore club. In October 1887, Templemore were playing in the All-Ireland semi-final against Limerick Commercials. With the game nearly over and Commercials pushing for a winning goal, a Commercials player found himself alone with the ball in front of the Templemore goals. He was about to shoot the winning score when he was grabbed by Bracken and thrown to the ground. The tackle had already proved difficult to define in Gaelic football, but this was obviously a foul – one made considerably worse by the fact that Bracken was on the field as a match umpire, not as a player.[2] Although Templemore went on to win the match, the Central Executive of the GAA ordered that it be replayed on account of

Bracken's behaviour, and Commercials duly won out. The All-Ireland football final was played in Donnybrook, Co. Dublin, on 29 April 1888 and saw Limerick Commercials defeat Dundalk Young Irelands by one goal and four points to three points.

There was, unsurprisingly, an objection lodged by the Dundalk club. Maurice Davin was in the chair at a special meeting of the GAA's Central Executive at 15 Upper Gloucester Street, Dublin, at 1.30 p.m. on Monday 29 April 1888, when the executive considered the claim that Limerick Commercials had fielded an illegal player, W. Spain, in the football final. Ultimately, the appeal was dismissed on grounds of insufficient evidence. Similar appeals relating to other matches from around the country were deemed a matter for the County Committees. The meeting passed a lengthy motion which decreed that County Committees should act decisively to remove from their championships any club which used players from other parishes.[3]

II

The matter of providing medals for the 1887 All-Ireland championship winners was also on the agenda for the GAA Central Executive. J. F. O'Crowley from Cork, who had been charged with procuring the medals for all winners of the 1887 GAA Athletics Championships, reported on his failure to do so: 'It was the wish of the late Central Executive that the medals should be produced from dies and made in Ireland, and as the area in the art of die-sinking is somewhat limited, the preparatory work was delayed.'[4] The members of the executive were so satisfied by the explanation that they sanctioned O'Crowley to continue with his procurement of athletics medals from 1887, 'as well as similar medals for hurling and football of the same year, the first prizes in each case being gold and the second silver'.

The prizes won by hurlers for their endeavours were important. In certain eccentric cases unusual prizes were given. A tournament in Bray, Co. Wicklow, saw the winners receive fancy belts with silver buckles, and at a tournament organized in Ruan in Co. Clare the prize was a pony.[5] More usually, in tournaments all across the country, hurlers were rewarded with silver cups, and gold and silver medals for their successes.[6] It was counter-intuitive that championship medals should be inferior to tournament ones, yet this is what happened. There was an outcry against the quality of medals presented for the winners of the first Dublin championships, with Michael Cusack describing them as 'a disgrace and almost an insult'.[7]

III

The Central Executive's business continued through the day but remained unfinished by evening. When the members reassembled, this time in the Mansion House, the following day to complete business, they made the draw for the inter-county stage of the 1888 All-Ireland championships. The only significant decision was that the championship would from now on be organized on a provincial basis. It made draws which included five Munster counties – Tipperary, Cork, Limerick, Clare and Waterford – for both football and hurling; eight Leinster counties for football but only two – Dublin and Kildare – for hurling; three Connacht counties – Galway,

Sligo and Mayo – for football and hurling; and two Ulster counties – Cavan and Monaghan – for football, with none for hurling. It was agreed that the various provincial representatives on the Central Executive would take charge of all draws and match arrangements in their provinces. The draw for the interprovincial stage was also made and pitted Leinster against Connacht and Ulster against Munster.

As the second day was drawing to a close, Maurice Davin advanced an idea that was to have a profound impact on the immediate future of the All-Ireland hurling championship. Davin, according to a report in *Sport*, told the meeting that 'for some time past he had been considering a project of sending a body of representative Gaels to America to represent the association there and to afford our brethren at the other side of the Atlantic an opportunity of witnessing our old Irish pastimes'. His idea was that two teams of hurlers, to be selected from different parts of the country (by a means which could afterwards be arranged), as well as a number of the best all-round athletes that the country could produce, should be sent to America 'to give exhibitions in Gaelic pastimes, and also compete with the athletes in America'. The idea met with the approval in principle of all the members of the council.[8] Almost immediately, the venture became known as the 'American Invasion'.

Later that night, after the meeting was ended, Davin received enthusiastic support for his idea in an informal setting when the County Dublin Executive entertained the members of the Central Executive for 'supper at Corless's well-known restaurant'. After extensive toasting of Ireland, the GAA, its members, the press, the proposed American Invasion and 'the winners of the All-Ireland championships', the evening concluded with music and song, including Tim

O'Riordan singing 'The Boys of the Old Brigade', Fr Concannon singing 'An Irish Maiden's Lament', W. Burke singing 'Conger's Soup', and J. P. Cox singing 'A Gaelic Song'.[9] The mood in the association was buoyant and the omens for the 1888 championship were positive.

IV

By the time of that Central Executive meeting in late April 1888, most counties had already begun their new championships and the competition generally proceeded much more speedily than in the previous year. Nonetheless, it did not prove possible to complete the championship before many hurlers left Ireland as part of Maurice Davin's American Invasion in mid-September 1888 – and so the championship was suspended.

Davin's aim was to establish the GAA in America and to found an annual athletics and hurling contest between the US and Ireland. The undertaking was also seen as a money-maker: it was estimated that the American Invasion would net the association a projected £5,000 of profit from gate receipts. On 16 September 1888, fifty-one hurlers, athletes and officials set sail on the SS *Wisconsin* from Queenstown, Co. Cork. Maurice Davin was the head of the party, and his brother Pat travelled as well, to compete as an athlete and hurler. Pat Davin recalled the first night on the boat as idyllic – dancing on the deck till late in the evening with Germans and Russians and Swedes. And then came the storm. The hurlers – coming, as most of them did, from inland areas – were extremely badly affected, many of them vomiting continuously. At 1.00 in the morning the ship was almost lost when it was hit by a massive wave. Passengers were thrown about the place and, Pat Davin later recalled, most of the hurlers 'remained up saying their prayers and expecting every minute to be their last'.[10] Their state of mind was not improved by the sight of a small boat being tossed around the sea with only the stump of its mast remaining.

Things did not improve immediately upon arrival when, at their first practice in Manhattan, one of the Irish athletes lost control of a hammer throw and did serious damage to a spectator. (Maurice Davin gave hammer-throwing exhibitions throughout the tour, though it is unclear whether or not it was he who hit the spectator.) The hurling exhibition matches drew praise in the local press and seemed to be anything but exhibitions. For example, in the match in the Manhattan grounds, there were at least a dozen hurleys broken. Not long into the tour, the hurlers were running out of hurleys and had to get some made for them by the veteran Fenian Bob Kelly. Unfortunately, the only wood available was hickory. The clash of the hickory did not have quite the same ring to it and in the first melee all the hurleys splintered to matchwood.

But the hurling matches were not just about sport. In his diary of the tour, Pat Davin remembered three respectable old ladies with a hurley they had been given by one of the players. The sight of it was so evocative of home, he wrote, that 'each of them took it in turn and kissed it with reverence, while all three wept copiously'.[11] On their arrival in every city the Irish Invaders were met by piped and brass bands and were paraded to their hotels. In Boston they were dragged through the streets in carriages pulled by Irish immigrants.

And yet the tour was a financial disaster. Two rival bodies were then in dispute over who controlled American athletics.

The GAA attempted to stay neutral, but was hit by a boycott of sorts which limited the scope of the tour to just fifteen exhibition hurling matches, while the athletes only competed on nine occasions. As a result of heavy snow, the planned two-week foray into Canada was cancelled. All of these things hurt attendances, and by the middle of the tour the Invaders had run out of money. Maurice Davin was forced to wire Michael Davitt, a patron of the GAA, seeking a bail-out to the tune of more than £450. Clubs across Ireland were also asked to vote money to help defray the costs.[12]

It had been hoped to repay Davitt with money earned in an end-of-tour exhibition. On the night before sailing for home, there was an indoor sports festival staged by way of a 'send-off' for the Irish athletes. A huge crowd, numbering several thousand, filled Madison Square Garden. And yet, at the end of the meeting, the local American organizers presented the Irish Invaders with a bill for $75, which they claimed was the sum they had lost on the night. It was, wrote Pat Davin, 'a cruel and shameless trick'.[13] Worse than the loss of money, though, was the loss of men. More than twenty of the original touring party of fifty-one remained permanently in America, and several more returned to Ireland only to tidy up their affairs before going back to the States to live and work.[14]

V

The 1888 hurling championship, having been left in abeyance while the Invasion was in progress, was never finished. This was partly because of renewed IRB attempts to regain control of the GAA. The peace brokered at the Reconstruction

Convention of January 1888 allowed the GAA the space to make progress for much of the year, but this peace eventually unravelled and the Fenians moved again to seize control in late 1888 and early 1889.

Throughout most of his presidency, Maurice Davin had fought against ceding control of the GAA to the IRB. It was no straightforward task, but he presided over meetings, stuck rigidly to the rulebook, and defended his position with integrity and without fear. Before one early GAA meeting which threatened to be volatile, he had assured Michael Cusack that he would not be daunted by anyone who sought to deflect the GAA from its purpose, saying: 'Michael, I am not afraid of anything.'[15] Eventually, though, he wearied of fighting. At the annual convention of the GAA in January 1889, Davin resigned when it became clear that he would not be supported in his efforts to sort out the association's finances and to impose discipline on its clubs. He had been seriously weakened by the debacle of the American Invasion. Having resigned, he walked silently from the room, displaying no sign of emotion.[16]

VI

The loss to the GAA was immense. Without Maurice Davin to manage its affairs, the association began to fall apart and the battle between the Fenians and the clergy resumed. Equally damaging to the GAA was the sense that it was unable to organize itself without dissension and malpractice, and that it was run according to the desires of a cabal of men who wanted only their own to prosper.[17] On top of that, emigration continued to rise and the rural economy was in a

depressed state.[18] This was a far cry from the sense of enthusiasm, and the promise of equality, which had attended the
birth of the association. Despite the turmoil, the All-Ireland
hurling championship was held in 1889, 1890 and 1891. But
in the last of these years, only five counties participated.

In the summer and autumn of 1891, the country was convulsed by the sensational news of Charles Stewart Parnell's
affair with a married woman, Katherine O'Shea. Nationalist
Ireland was split over the scandal. The GAA at central level
sided with Parnell, a stance that induced outright hostility
from clergy and a further loss of support from political moderates. The most evocative image of the GAA's support for
Parnell came in death: when he died in 1891, two thousand
GAA men marched alongside the cortège with hurleys
draped in black.[19]

By that point the GAA, too, appeared on the brink of
death. P. J. Linnane, the president of the GAA in Co. Clare,
said as much at a County Committee meeting in Ennis.[20]
The twelve hundred clubs of 1888 fell to a mere two hundred
and twenty by 1892. A year later, in 1893, just fourteen delegates representing three counties were present at the GAA's
annual convention. As few as three teams entered the hurling championship played in that same year. Politics had all
but destroyed the GAA.[21]

VII

As it turned out, Maurice Davin was not entirely finished
with the GAA after his resignation as president. He laid out
a hurling pitch and an athletics ground on one of the fields
on his farm, where he and his brothers had done most of

their training. Over the years he erected a pavilion for athletes, enclosed the grounds with a wooden paling and erected a timber stand for the comfort of spectators. Davin often refereed the matches at Deerpark, and the venue was developed to such an extent that it was used to stage the 1901 and 1904 All-Ireland hurling finals.

Davin also remained extremely fit. When an American journalist, William Fletcher, called to Deerpark to interview him for the *New York Daily News* in 1907, Davin brought Fletcher out onto the sports field and demonstrated how to throw the hammer. His third attempt would have been good enough to win the Irish championships as late as the 1890s, which was impressive work for a man of sixty-five. After dinner, Davin took out his violin and played a series of Irish tunes.

In his later years, when women got the opportunity to play hurling through the formation of a national Camogie Association, Davin financially supported the development of a club in Carrick; and in July 1915, in his mid-seventies, he hired a motor car to take him to Clonmel to see Carrick play a camogie match. Indeed, he regularly hired cars to take him to hurling and football matches around Munster during his autumn years. He remained actively engaged in the river-haulage business, which struggled on despite the gathering competition from rail and road and steamboats, and there are entries in his books for boats hauling coal up the river Suir as late as 1922. When he died on 27 January 1927, he had been ill for barely a fortnight.

VIII

Michael Cusack's later life was much more complicated – and more tragic – than that of his great collaborator, Davin. The time and energy that Cusack expended on GAA-related matters and on his newspaper the *Celtic Times* deflected his attention from his school, which inevitably suffered. He moved from Gardiner Place to a house on nearby North Great George's Street in 1888 and advertised in the paper that the school – 'famous for 10 years' and 'now thoroughly reorganised' – was open for day and evening classes.[22] The school, however, was unable to recover the status which had seen it considered the finest grinds school in Dublin for getting its pupils through the entrance exams for the British civil service, and eventually it, too, closed its doors.

Infinitely worse was to follow. Michael Cusack's wife, Margaret, died from TB on 16 September 1890. By then the couple had six children (several others having died in infancy) who ranged in age from six to thirteen years. A month after the death of his wife, Cusack also suffered the loss of his eight-year-old daughter, Mary, also from TB.[23] Two of his sons – John and Frank – were placed in St Vincent's Orphanage in Glasnevin. A third son – Michael – most likely remained living with Cusack. His two surviving daughters – Bride and Clare – were sent to live with relatives in England.[24]

Living at various addresses across Dublin over the next sixteen years, Cusack earned a precarious living from journalism and teaching. In 1901, for example, he was one of three boarders living in a house on Mountjoy Street in Dublin's north inner city, with a retired policeman as his landlord. By then, three of his children were back living together at nearby St Teresa's Road. Clare (twenty-three), John (twenty) and Frank (seventeen) were all living together, and on the night the census was taken they were being visited by their sister Bride.

He remained a striking figure around the city, but his days of pomp had passed. His later journalism often harked back to the founding and early years of the GAA. Sometimes, these articles are bathed in an almost unbearable melancholy of loneliness: 'I thought I could write a little, in a short article, about the friends of my early manhood. I can't. They are swarming and trooping round me – mostly from the universe viewless to our eyes. I sympathise with the Persian king of old – Xerxes, I think, was his name – who wept at the thoughts of death.'[25]

IX

In 1899 and again in 1902, Michael Cusack wrote articles in the Dublin press in which he recounted how and why the GAA was founded, and set about smoothing the jagged edges of his own history into a neat story, simply and alluringly told. He recalled that in the 1860s cricket had made 'regrettable' inroads on the domain of hurling. Then, in the 1870s, rugby football came as a 'further denationalising plague, to carry on through the winter the work of ruin that cricket was doing during the summer'. And then, on top of that, there was the elitist form of athletics that was developing in the country all the better 'to complete the work of national and physical ruin more thoroughly'.[26]

Cusack freely admitted that he had been 'in and through all these camps' during these years, but he then moved to square his involvement with 'denationalising' games and the imperialists who ran them. He explained: 'Their mission was to absorb into their systems all that was manful in Ireland and have them chalked down as British. My purpose was to learn as much as I could from friends and foes, and to bide the hour at which Ireland could hear me.'[27] And, of course, it was the degraded state of Ireland which ultimately moved Cusack to act when he did to found the GAA: 'I essayed to rouse the people from the appalling torpor that was creeping over them and, vampire-like, thinning out the heart's blood of the Irish nation . . . I took it into my head to strike one smashing blow on behalf of Ireland.' It was then that he 'declared war against the foreign faction' and established the GAA.[28]

Michael Cusack was adopted by a new generation of cultural nationalists who became prominent in the GAA after 1900. In fact, he was nominated to return as secretary of the association in 1901, but fell short by just two votes. He attended the annual convention as a Dublin delegate in every year bar one between 1901 and 1906, while he also appeared at hurling matches in the Phoenix Park, encouraging the young hurlers: *'Ar an dtalaimh!'* ('On the ground!') and *'Tarraing a Mhic'* ('Pull on the ball, son').[29]

But tragedy was never far from Cusack's life. His beloved son Michael died, aged twenty-seven, in January 1906. Later that year, Cusack attended the GAA's annual convention in Thurles, and subsequently wrote a letter of thanks:

> The convention condoled with me over the death of my eldest son. To most people this may appear formal – to me it was the quiet prayer of a hundred thousand Gaelic men. A very substantial money grant was passed to me in recognition of hitherto unremunerated services of nearly a generation ago.

The Gaels are just to themselves and to me. I desire to acknowledge their kindly generous recognition of my efforts to make Ireland a place worth living in. I can never know any Ireland but the kindly Ireland – Irish heart so real, so warm, so true that I knew when I was young and that I find in my wracked off days in the Gaelic Athletic Association.[30]

Shortly afterwards, Michael Cusack himself was gone, dying suddenly on 28 November 1906, a few months short of his sixtieth birthday. He was buried beside his wife in Glasnevin cemetery. Around one hundred Dublin hurlers were present at the funeral, while Tipperary and Kilkenny hurling teams, who were due to play a match in Dublin, also formed part of the cortège.[31] Among the mourners was also Cusack's youngest son, Frank, who had been just six when his mother died and was now twenty-two. Having worked in the post office in Dublin for a time, Frank subsequently lost contact with the rest of the members of the family and was believed to have emigrated to America after 1911.[32]

The rest of his children lived until the 1950s. His eldest child, Clare, never married and eventually died in Dublin on 10 December 1955. A second daughter, Bride, entered the Sisters of Mercy in 1903, having been educated in England. Known as Mother Gabriel, she taught for many years in Doncaster and then lived at a convent in Yorkshire. Her death on 16 June 1956 was reported in the *Irish Independent* three days later as being the death of the last surviving child of Michael Cusack. The girls had been predeceased by their brother John, who had lived for many years in Dublin's Rathgar with his wife Kathleen. They had no children. John died on 30 October 1950 and was buried in Glasnevin cemetery. A file kept by John

Cusack shows that he and his two sisters kept in contact by letter and postcard. In it are original photographs of the Cusack family, of Margaret, of Michael as part of the Phoenix rugby team, and of Michael with his big, grey beard. The file also contains the 1883 minute books of the Dublin Hurling Club, which pre-dated the establishment of the GAA, and various notes which Michael Cusack made regarding the story of his family and their lineage. He ends his notes with the statement: 'The story of Ireland may tell the rest if it likes.'[33]

X

Even before Michael Cusack's death, the journalist and hurler P. P. Sutton had also passed away. He was just thirty-six years of age when he died from pneumonia in June 1901. His remains were brought to the Pro-Cathedral on Marlborough Street and then home by train to Gorey in Wexford, before being carried by hearse to Oulart. Before he died he had written, 'To Wexford I am bound by ties as strong as steel.' GAA men – some of whom had played with Sutton for the Metropolitan hurlers in the 1887 All-Ireland hurling championship – travelled every step of the way with his funeral and a reporter from the *Free Press* wrote: 'There is not a Gaelic Athletic club in Ireland where his name is not known and honoured.' While Cusack's writing in the *Celtic Times* had captured the spirit of the hurling revival, Sutton's role as GAA correspondent for *Sport* and for the *Freeman's Journal* was also vital. Sutton's columns through the 1880s tell the story of the birth of the GAA and within his words lies the story of a modern game in the making. He embraced almost everything about the way modern sport was organized. He was appalled at skulduggery and sharp practice and a failure to abide by rules. He was also brave enough to publish his views, even if this cannot always have earned him friend-ships. He had, for example, a tense relationship with Cusack, with whom he continued to have disputes in the 1890s.[34]

Sutton's modernity rested in more than just words, though; it was rooted in the practical aspect of his engagement with hurling. He bought his hurling balls from shops on Dublin streets, and took immense pride in his beautifully grained hurleys with their corded handles.[35] His experience was not the same as that of many of the men he played against, whose hurleys were made by local carpenters or simply cut from ditches. In December 1887, for example, a match in Carrick-on-Suir saw hurlers use everything from 'the polished and painted camáns to the less pretentious fir-bush crooks'.[36] 'Sceilg' (John J. O'Kelly, a nationalist politician and Irish language activist) recalled that on Valentia island, the hurls would be cut from furze stumps or whatever wood was avail-able in the nearest ditch, and also recalled that they used to make their hurling balls from cattle hair rolled hard into a ball and steeped in gutta-percha. He claimed even to have heard of a whale's eye used as a *sliotar* (hurling ball).[37]

In many of his newspaper columns Sutton campaigned for order off the field as well as on. He deplored the tendency of supporters to crowd onto the field while games were in progress, and reported with disgust the story that a hurler had been struck by a spectator at a match in Tipperary where Lorrha and Dorrha were playing against Ballingarry and Eglish.[38] And yet he understood why people became so involved in the game: 'It requires hurling to generate that keen and intense excitement among the spectators which makes them oblivious of everything save the game . . . The clash of *camán* against *camán*, the apparently dangerous aspects of the situations, and the terrible earnestness of the players visibly affect the spectators, so that their feelings are worked up to a far higher pitch of excitement than by any phase of a football match.'[39]

Sutton vehemently opposed the IRB men who assumed control of the GAA, not because he did not support the idea of an independent Ireland, but because he abhorred the way in which they had subverted the fair operation of the association. Nonetheless, he argued that 'all Gaels should sink petty personalities and sentimental grievances, and grasping the hand of friendship and brotherhood, stand shoulder to shoulder in their one common cause – the preservation and cultivation of our national pastimes'.[40] Hurling for Sutton was, in itself, an act of patriotism: 'Anyone who thoroughly understands hurling and the qualities necessary to make a brilliant player, must fully agree with what has been so often said about it – that it is a game for men, an inferior or sluggish race would never have thought of it.'[41]

XI

If P. P. Sutton was a man of his times, so was Pat Madden. Madden was the formidable hurler who had captained the Meelick team against Thurles in the All-Ireland final. Then, in the months afterwards, he was evicted from his small farm by Lord Clanricarde's agents, and for the following years, lived in a hut by the side of the road in Meelick. In August 1889, Madden was joined there, in another hut, by James Lynam, the man who had been the chief organizer of local hurling, and now also evicted by Lord Clanricarde.

For the following five years at least, Lynam fought to get his land back. In the summer of 1890, there were reports that the Loughrea IRB member John McCarthy had met with him to plan the murder of both Lord Clanricarde's agent, Mr Tener, and the man who had taken the lease on the land which Lynam had once farmed, John Horseman.[42] Attempts by Horseman to sell sheep in Banagher were impeded by Lynam and his supporters that same summer. The passage of time did little to ease the bitterness. In January 1894 two foxhounds belonging to John Horseman were poisoned in Eyrecourt and the local hunt club asked Horseman not to hunt with them.[43]

James Lynam stood for election as a radical Parnellite candidate for the East Galway constituency in 1892. He was defeated, as was the goalkeeper from the Meelick 1887 team, Pat Larkin, also a Fenian. (Another player from that day in Birr, James Cosgrove, a moderate nationalist, was more successful: he stood for the Irish Parliamentary Party and was elected as MP for East Galway.[44]) After he moved to Dublin in the mid-1890s, Lynam continued to attend public meetings and to campaign on behalf of people who had lost their farms.[45] He listed his own occupation always as 'farmer', even when living in the centre of Dublin.

Having contested an All-Ireland final in 1888, the Meelick club folded in 1889, although it did return in various incarnations in the twentieth century.[46] The players who contested that final never received the silver medals that were their due. Indeed, it is not even certain who exactly all of those players were. No match report has listed their names for posterity nor is there a surviving photo of the team. The most striking commemoration of their claim to history is a plaque that was erected on the gable end of the house from which

Pat Madden was evicted. It reads: 'This was the home of Pat Madden, captain of the Meelick team that represented Galway against Thurles of Tipperary in the First All-Ireland Hurling Final.'

XII

The only photograph that exists of the Thurles hurlers of the 1880s is one which was taken around 1908.[47] In it, the hurlers have pushed into middle age, as the receding hairlines and the press of their stomachs against the jerseys they have donned for the photograph makes all too apparent. The picture is a somewhat controversial one. It includes some of the men who played in the final and others who did not travel because of the dispute over expenses. Occasionally – then and later – that controversy was reignited. In 1913, for example, when winners' medals had still not been presented to the All-Ireland champions of 1887, the embers of dispute were stirred.[48] The *Tipperary Star* newspaper published a report from a meeting of the Tipperary County Committee from 5 January 1913 at which the matter of the distribution of the 1887 medals was discussed. The GAA had decided that the twenty-one players in that final – or their next of kin – should be presented with medals. There was a difficulty with this, as the famed Thurles hurler and administrator Tom Semple told the meeting: several other players who had played in the run-up to the final were also seeking medals. The Tipperary County Committee was refusing this as they did not have the means to pay for additional medals.

In the aftermath of the publication in the *Tipperary Star* of the report of the meeting, Long Dinny Maher wrote to the paper to explain why he and the men from the Killinan area of Thurles had not played in Birr. He set out the dispute over expenses and how men from other clubs had been brought in, concluding: 'I may also add that I do not expect or seek a medal, but I feel satisfied in explaining, as far as memory helps me, the cause of our absence from the 1887 final.'[49]

XIII

Long Dinny Maher now lies buried in a beautiful old grave-yard at the back of Killinan Hill, a little more than a mile outside Thurles. On the stone wall at the front of the ceme-tery, a small plaque commemorates the fact that five Tipperary hurling captains are buried there. The view falls back across town and countryside and into Semple Stadium, which has a terrace at one end named the Killinan End. In the middle of the graveyard, Long Dinny Maher is buried just eight feet away from Moycarkey's Tom O'Grady. Both married women called Joanna and they died within a few years of each other in the 1920s. If things had fallen just a little bit differently, either man might easily have held the honour of being the first-ever captain of an All-Ireland win-ning team.

The hurler who did win that honour – Jim Stapleton – wrote a letter in 1948 to P. D. Mehigan, a GAA journalist who wrote under the pseudonym 'Carbery'. In the letter, written shortly before his death, Jim Stapleton set out the full list of names of the men who did actually play in the first All-Ireland hurling final. He said that the team comprised eight players from Thurles, six from Two-Mile Borris, three from Drombane, and others from surrounding areas:

More than once I have seen the wrong names in print. We hurled for the honour of our county and wanted nothing more. I am anxious now that the full names of the men and their clubs, who played in that final, should be published. All I am concerned about now is to give honour where honour is due and clear all doubts. I had the honour of captaining them and I am the only survivor now of as fine a team of men as ever represented their county.[50]

XIV

The presence of forty-two hurlers in a field in the Irish Midlands playing a game unique to Ireland was the happy coincidence of the forces of history and of the extraordinary personality of one man, Michael Cusack. The hurling match which took place in Birr on Easter Sunday 1888 was a modern game, played between clubs which were affiliated to a governing body that organized the competition and set the rules by which it should be played.

The idea that a hurling contest could be organized in such a fashion would have been scarcely imaginable just a few years previously. Hurling was a marginal, diminishing presence in Irish life. At the start of the 1880s, the dominant sports in Ireland were manifestations not just of the power and prestige of the British Empire, but also of the increasing dominance of English culture across that Empire. The Gaelic Athletic Association was both an imitation of the British way of playing sport and a reaction against those sports. It was carried high on the rising tide of Irish nationalism and itself played a significant role in shaping that nationalism.

While Gaelic football soon proved the GAA's most popular activity, it was hurling which allowed the association to present itself as a thoroughly Irish organization – dedicated to promoting Irish nationalism, as well as providing games for ordinary people. For the GAA, hurling was more than just a game. It was depicted as something whose history extended back into mythology, a game that had survived the effects of conquest and colonization, and that in its modern form symbolized the resilience of native Irish culture. More than that, hurling was seen as emblematic of the rebirth of an Irish nation. It had been salvaged from the past to prosper against the overwhelming power of the games of the British Empire. Just before the playing of the first All-Ireland final, the Land League leader, Michael Davitt, wrote of what he believed was now happening: 'Old men have forgotten the miseries of the Famine and had their youth renewed by the sights and sounds that were evoked by the thrilling music of the camán.'

In 1882, when he embarked upon the revival of hurling, Michael Cusack wrote that if his mission proved to be successful, he had no doubt that 'the coming generations will bless us for the service we have rendered them'.[51] That service – the remaking of hurling, the founding of an association to foster the game and the organization of a national championship – was undertaken by pioneers whose legacy is the generations of hurlers who have followed in their wake. They set off something that has yet to end.

Abbreviations

AAA	Amateur Athletic Association
CBS	Crime Branch Special
DICS	Detective Inspector Crime Special
FA	Football Association
GAA	Gaelic Athletic Association
IAAA	Irish Amateur Athletic Association
IRB	Irish Republican Brotherhood
IRFU	Irish Rugby Football Union
NAI	National Archives of Ireland
NLI	National Library of Ireland
NUIG	National University of Ireland, Galway

Notes

Prologue: Forty-two Hurlers

1 The sources on which the prologue is based are fully detailed in Chapter 12 of this book.

1. 'Splendid and by no means dangerous'

1 Marcus de Búrca, *Michael Cusack and the GAA* (1989), pp. 36–43.
2 *Shamrock*, 24 June to 9 October 1882.
3 *Irish Times*, 22 December 1882.
4 *Irish Sportsman*, 1 January 1879.
5 *Irish Sportsman*, 1 January 1879.
6 *Irish Times*, 21 and 23 December 1882.
7 *Irish Times*, 22 December 1882.
8 *Irish Times*, 21 December 1882.
9 *Irish Times*, 15 May 1896.
10 *Irish Times*, 1 January 1883.
11 *Irish Times*, 23 and 27 December 1882.
12 *Irish Times*, 1 January 1883.
13 NUIG Archives, Michael Cusack Papers, Dublin Hurling Club minute book.
14 *Sport*, 3 February 1883.
15 NUIG Archives, Michael Cusack Papers, Dublin Hurling Club minute book; *Irish Times*, 10 January 1883.
16 *Irish Times*, 21 December 1882.

254

17 NUIG Archives, Michael Cusack Papers, Dublin Hurling Club minute book.

18 *Irish Times*, 27 January 1883.

19 NUIG Archives, Michael Cusack Papers, Dublin Hurling Club minute book.

20 *Irish Sportsman*, 24 February 1883.

21 *Sport*, 3 and 17 February 1883; *Irish Times*, 9 March and 5 April 1883.

22 NUIG Archives, Michael Cusack Papers, Dublin Hurling Club minute book.

23 *Sport*, 3 February 1883. Later, after the founding of the GAA, the game of hurley collapsed and just two clubs remained, King's Hospital and High School. By the early 1890s a Hockey Association had been founded in England and a code of rules developed. In the autumn of 1892 both King's Hospital and High School abandoned hurley and turned to hockey. Then, in February 1893, the two clubs drove the formation of the Irish Hockey Union, with the Rev. Gibson elected president.

24 *Irish Sportsman*, 27 January 1883; T. S. C. Dagg, *Hockey in Ireland* (1944), p. 39.

25 *Sport*, 3 February 1883.

26 *Celtic Times*, 14 May 1887.

27 See, for example, *Irish Sportsman*, 6 March 1880, for a match against Ordnance Survey in the Phoenix Park.

28 *Sport*, 8 October 1881.

29 R. M. Peter (ed.), *The Irish Football Annual* (1880), p. 79.

30 *Irish Sportsman*, 8 January 1881.

31 Liam Ó Caithnia, *Mícheál Cíosóg* (1982), p. 110.

32 *Irish Sportsman*, 18 February 1882.

33 Marcus de Búrca, *Michael Cusack and the GAA* (1989), pp. 30–1.

34 *Shamrock*, 8 July 1882.

35 *Shamrock*, 9 October 1882.

36 *Shamrock*, 8 July 1882.

37 *Shamrock*, 2 September and 9 October 1882.

38 F. S. L. Lyons, *Culture and Anarchy, 1890–1939* (1979), p. 8.

39 Anon., *Gaelic Union for the Preservation and Cultivation of the Irish Language* (1882); Paul Rouse, 'Michael Cusack: Sportsman and Journalist', in Mike Cronin, William Murphy and Paul Rouse (eds), *The Gaelic Athletic Association, 1884–2009* (2009), pp. 47–61.

40 NLI, Ms. 5605, Council of the Gaelic Union for the Preservation and Cultivation of the Irish Language minutes, 1882–6.

41 *Kildare Observer*, 12 May 1888.

42 *Shamrock*, 17 February 1883.

43 *Shamrock*, 10 March 1884.

2. A New Beginning

1 *Irish Weekly Independent and Nation*, 13 December 1902.

2 *Celtic Times*, 2 April 1887.

3 *Sport*, 8 December 1883.

4 *Irish Weekly Independent and Nation*, 13 December 1902.

5 Padraic Ó Laoi, *Annals of the GAA in Galway, Vol. 1, 1884–1901* (1983), p. 8.

6 *Western News*, 19 April 1884.

7 *Irish Times*, 15 April 1884.

8 *Irish Times*, 15 April 1884.

9 *Western News*, 12, 19 and 26 April 1884.

10 *Sport*, 6 August 1881.

11 See, for example, National Folklore Collection, Iml. 921, pp. 56–7.

12 *Irish Sportsman*, 26 October 1878.

13 *Irish Sportsman*, 3 May 1884.

14 See, for example, for the countryside, *Irish Sportsman*, 17 November 1877, and for the city, *Sport*, 30 July 1881.

15 John Lawrence, *Handbook of Cricket in Ireland* (1877–8), p. 150.

16 Peter Lovesey, *The Official Centenary History of the Amateur Athletic Association* (1981), pp. 40–4.

17 *Sport*, 11 June 1881.

18 *Irish Sportsman*, 28 February 1885.

19 *Irish Sportsman*, 17 and 24 May and 12 July 1884.

20 *Shamrock*, 24 February 1883.

21 *Irish Sportsman*, 9 April, 2 July and 1 October 1881.

22 *Irish Times*, 30 April 1884.

23 *Irish Times*, 14 April 1884.

24 See, for example, Cusack's article on his coat in *Celtic Times*, 16 April 1887.

25 *United Irishman*, 4 March 1899.

26 Séamus Ó Riain, *Maurice Davin (1842–1927): First President of the GAA* (1993).

27 *Sport*, 26 November 1887; Pat Davin, *Recollections of a Veteran Irish Athlete* (1938), p. 39. See also Séamus Ó Riain, *Maurice Davin (1842–1927): First President of the GAA* (1993).

28 Maurice Davin Notebook, GAA Museum and Archives, Croke Park; Séamus Ó Riain, *Maurice Davin (1842–1927): First President of the GAA* (1993), p. 19.

29 Pat Davin, *Recollections of a Veteran Irish Athlete* (1938), pp. 42–3.

30 *Irish Weekly Independent and Nation*, 13 December 1902; Pat Davin, *Recollections of a Veteran Irish Athlete* (1938); Séamus Ó Riain, *Maurice Davin (1842–1927): First President of the GAA* (1993).

31 *Irish Sportsman*, 3 November 1877.

32 Tony O'Donoghue, *Irish Championship Athletics 1873–1914* (2005), p. 14.

33 *United Ireland*, 11 October 1884.

34 *United Ireland*, 18 October 1884.

35 Séamus Ó Riain, *Maurice Davin (1842–1927): First President of the GAA* (1993), p. 55.

36 There is considerable dispute over how many people actually attended the meeting. It was, in any case, a small crowd and represented an inauspicious beginning for the association. See J. M. Tobin, 'Who was Present at the Founding Meeting of the GAA at Thurles in 1884?', *History Ireland*, Vol. 23, No. 5 (Sept/Oct 2015), pp. 32–4.

37 *United Ireland*, 8 November 1884; *Irish Sportsman*, 8 November 1884; *Shamrock*, 15 November 1884; *Freeman's Journal*, 3 November 1884; *Cork Examiner*, 3 November 1884.

38 See, for example, *Irish Sportsman*, 22 December 1877 and 9 April 1881, and *Sport*, 6 August 1881 and 22 July 1882.

39 *Freeman's Journal*, 13 February 1885.

40 Séamus Ó Riain, *Maurice Davin 1842–1927: First President of the GAA* (1993), pp. 40–51.

41 Michael Cusack, 'The Rise of the Gaelic Athletic Association', *Shan Van Vocht*, Vol. 2 (1897), pp. 147–8.

3. The Making of a Modern Game

1 *United Ireland*, 3 January 1885.

2 *Freeman's Journal*, 20 December 1884.

3 *United Ireland*, 7 February 1885.

4 *United Ireland*, 24 January 1885; *Freeman's Journal*, 13 February 1885.

5 *United Ireland*, 24 January 1885.

6 *United Ireland*, 21 February 1885. A plaque in the village of Ballyneale, Co. Waterford, claims that a match was played there in November 1884. This match may have been used by Davin to trial his proposed rules.

7 *United Ireland*, 28 March 1885.

8 *Nenagh Guardian*, 25 March 1885.

9 W. F. Mandle, *The Gaelic Athletic Association and Irish Nationalist Politics, 1884–1924* (1987), pp. 21–3.

10 *United Ireland*, 19 December 1885.

11 W. F. Mandle, *The Gaelic Athletic Association and Irish Nationalist Politics, 1884–1924* (1987), p. 24.

12 *Celtic Times*, 25 June 1887.

13 *United Ireland*, 25 July 1885.

14 *Celtic Times*, 19 November 1887.

15 Faugh-a-Ballaghs GAA Club Minute Book, 1885–9. I would like to thank Liam and Ann-Marie Fleury for allowing me access to this minute book. *Irish Times*, 3 April 1954.

16 *United Ireland*, 2 May 1885.

17 *United Ireland*, 14 February and 4 July 1885.

18 See, for example, *United Ireland*, 9 January 1886.

19 *United Ireland*, 11 July 1885.

20 *United Ireland*, 23 January 1886.

21 *Celtic Times*, 2 April 1887.

22 *Celtic Times*, 26 February 1887.

23 *Celtic Times*, 2 April 1887.

24 It has been repeatedly stated that these rules date from 1869, but the only evidence I can find of them in written form dates from 1885. Padraic Ó Laoi, *Annals of the GAA in Galway, Vol. 1, 1884–1901* (1983), pp. 10–12.

25 Padraic Ó Laoi, *Annals of the GAA in Galway, Vol. 1, 1884–1901* (1983), pp. 10–12.

26 *Freeman's Journal*, 21 April 1885.

27 *Western News*, 17 October 1885.

28 *Western News*, 30 May 1885.

29 Art Ó Maolfabhail, Roddy Hegarty and Dónal McAnallen, 'From Cú Chulainn to Cusack: Ball-playing, camán, shinny

and hurling in Ulster before the GAA', in Dónal McAnallen, David Hassan and Roddy Hegarty (eds), *The Evolution of the GAA: Ulaidh, Éire and Eile* (2009), pp. 62–78; Conor Curran, *The Development of Sport in Donegal, 1880–1935* (2015), p. 39.

30 *Freeman's Journal*, 21 April 1885; *Western News*, 30 May 1885.
31 *United Ireland*, 5 September 1885.
32 *Western News*, 3 October 1885.
33 *Western News*, 23 January 1886.
34 *United Ireland*, 24 October 1885.
35 *United Ireland*, 19 December 1885.
36 Liam Ó Caithnia, *Mícheál Cíosóg* (1982), pp. 45–6.
37 *Sport*, 20 February 1886; *United Ireland*, 20 February 1886.
38 *Sport*, 20 February 1886; *United Ireland*, 20 February 1886; *Celtic Times*, 29 October 1887.
39 Seamus King, 'Hurling in South-East Galway' (unpublished manuscript, n.d.). I would like to thank Seamus King for providing me with a copy of this paper, which he has delivered publicly on a number of occasions.
40 Daniel Grace, *Portrait of a Parish: Monsea and Killodiernan, Co. Tipperary* (1996), p. 212.
41 *Sport*, 20 February 1886; *United Ireland*, 20 February 1886; *Celtic Times*, 29 October 1887.
42 *Sport*, 20 February 1886; *United Ireland*, 20 February 1886; *Celtic Times*, 29 October 1887; Padraic Ó Laoi, *Annals of the GAA in Galway, Vol. 1, 1884–1901* (1983), p. 26.

4. The Triumph of Hurling

1 *United Ireland*, 27 February and 24 April 1886.
2 *United Ireland*, 3 April 1886.
3 *Western News*, 17 April 1886.

4 *United Ireland*, 13 March 1886.

5 Donal O'Gorman, 'The Game of Hurling', in William Nolan and William Corbett (eds), *Thurles: The Cathedral Town: Essays in Honour of Archbishop Thomas Morris* (1989), pp. 141–64, p. 146.

6 *United Ireland*, 1 May 1886.

7 See, for example, *Irish Sportsman*, 25 December 1886.

8 *Celtic Times*, 26 March 1887.

9 *Sport*, 18 December 1886, 15 October and 24 June 1887.

10 *Sport*, 19 February 1887.

11 *Sport*, 25 June 1887.

12 Faugh-a-Ballaghs GAA Club Minute Book, 1885–9.

13 Patrick Bracken, 'The Emergence of Hurling in Australia, 1877–1917', *Sport in Society*, Vol. 19, No. 1 (2016), pp. 62–73. I would like to thank Pat for his help with the book.

14 *Age*, 17 April 1878.

15 *Advocate*, 28 March 1885.

16 Patrick Bracken, 'The Emergence of Hurling in Australia, 1877–1917', *Sport in Society*, Vol. 19, No. 1 (2016), pp. 62–73.

17 *Boston Globe*, 6 August 1882.

18 John Boyle O'Reilly, *Athletics and Manly Sport* (1890), pp. 195–8.

19 *Boston Globe*, 8 September 1882.

20 *Boston Globe*, 20 November 1885.

21 Patrick Bracken, 'The Emergence of Hurling in Australia, 1877–1917', *Sport in Society*, Vol. 19, No. 1 (2016), pp. 62–73.

22 *Celtic Times*, 30 April 1887.

23 *Sport*, 25 June 1887.

24 *United Ireland*, January and February 1885, 8 and 20 August 1885; *Sport*, 21 August 1886 and 19 September 1885; *Munster News*, 10 August 1887.

25 *Celtic Times*, 30 July 1887.

26 See, for example, *Sport*, 5 February 1887.

27 *Sport*, 16 October 1886.

28 NAI CBS DICS, South-Eastern Division, monthly report, September 1888.

29 *Celtic Times*, 2 April 1887.

30 *Celtic Times*, 16 April 1887.

31 *Celtic Times*, 3 December 1887.

32 *Celtic Times*, 12 March 1887.

33 *Celtic Times*, 8 October 1887.

34 *Sport*, 21 May 1881.

35 *Nenagh Guardian*, 28 May 1887.

36 *Sport*, 1 September 1888.

37 *Celtic Times*, 26 March 1887.

38 *Celtic Times*, 12 March and 5 November 1887.

39 *Celtic Times*, 23 April 1887.

40 *Celtic Times*, 4 June 1887.

41 *Midland Tribune*, 29 March and 2 August 1888.

42 Neal Garnham, 'Accounting for the Early Success of the Gaelic Athletic Association', *Irish Historical Studies*, Vol. 34 (2004), pp. 65–78, p. 73.

43 See also Elizabeth Malcolm, *'Ireland Sober, Ireland Free': Drink and Temperance in Nineteenth-century Ireland* (1986), esp. chapters 5 and 6.

44 NAI CBS 2452/5, Copy of by-law passed by Longford GAA, 20 January 1891. See also T. F. O'Sullivan, *Story of the GAA* (1916), pp. 84–5.

45 *United Ireland*, 19 June 1886.

46 *Sport*, 5 February 1887.

47 *Sport*, 17 December 1887.

48 *Sport*, 10 December 1887.

49 *Sport*, 9 August 1884.

50 *Midland Tribune*, 9 August 1888.

5. The Fall of Michael Cusack

1 The idea that Cusack was a stooge of the IRB can be found, for example, in an article written by Thomas Markham – himself an IRB man – in the *Irish Press Jubilee Supplement*, 14 April 1934. The influence of that article and the claim that Cusack was removed by the IRB can be seen in W. F. Mandle, *The Gaelic Athletic Association and Irish Nationalist Politics, 1884–1924* (1987), chapter 2.

2 NAI CBS, Box 8 9057/S, Report on Michael Deering, 3 October 1894.

3 NAI CBS Box 9 9228/S, Report on P. J. Kelly, 18 November 1894.

4 *United Ireland*, 13 April 1885.

5 *United Ireland*, 31 October 1885.

6 *Sport*, 20 November 1886.

7 *Sport*, 13 March 1886.

8 *Sport*, 6 March 1886.

9 *United Ireland*, 13 March 1886.

10 *Sport*, 9 February 1885.

11 *Sport*, 27 March 1886.

12 *Sport*, 27 March 1886.

13 *Cork Herald*, 7 April 1886.

14 *United Ireland*, 3 July 1886.

15 *Celtic Times*, 2 July 1887.

16 *Sport*, 10 July 1886.

17 *Sport*, 10 July 1886.

18 *United Ireland*, 10 July 1886.

19 *United Ireland*, 31 July 1887.

20 *Sport*, 2 October 1886.

21 *Celtic Times*, 27 August 1887.

22 W. F. Mandle, 'The IRB and the Beginnings of the Gaelic Athletic Association', *Irish Historical Studies*, Vol. 20, No. 80 (1977), pp. 418–38, p. 420.

23 W. F. Mandle, *The Gaelic Athletic Association and Irish Nationalist Politics, 1884–1924* (1987), p. 31.

24 *Cork Examiner*, 30 August 1886.

25 *Sport*, 20 November 1886.

26 NLI, Ms. 15385, T. F. O'Sullivan Papers, 'How the GAA was Started in Kerry', n.d.

6. A New Era in Dublin

1 Evidence of this tendency is provided in a brilliant piece of research conducted by Jimmy Wren, which is published in William Nolan (ed.), *The Gaelic Athletic Association in Dublin, 1884–2000*, Vols 1–3 (2005), pp. 1202–78.

2 *Sport*, 30 April 1887.

3 William Nolan (ed.), *The Gaelic Athletic Association in Dublin, 1884–2000*, Vols 1–3 (2005), p. 7.

4 *Sport*, 19 February 1887.

5 *Sport*, 15 January 1887.

6 William Nolan (ed.), *The Gaelic Athletic Association in Dublin, 1884–2000*, Vols 1–3 (2005), p. 1226.

7 See Faugh-a-Ballaghs GAA Club Minute Book, 1885–9.

8 *United Ireland*, 22 May 1886.

9 Faugh-a-Ballaghs GAA Club Minute Book, 1885–9.

10 *Sport*, 25 September and 2 October 1886.

11 Faugh-a-Ballaghs GAA Club Minute Book, 1885–9.

12 William Nolan (ed.), *The Gaelic Athletic Association in Dublin, 1884–2000*, Vols 1–3 (2005), p. 1246.

13 *Irish Sportsman*, 18 December 1886.

14 *United Ireland*, 22 May 1886.

15 *Sport*, 22 January 1887.

16 *Sport*, 5 March 1887.

17 *Sport*, 1 November 1884.

18 *Sport*, 15 January 1887.

19 *Celtic Times*, 21 May 1887.

20 *Sport*, 15 January 1887.

21 *Sport*, 5 March 1887.

22 *Sport*, 23 April 1887.

23 *Munster News*, 14 September 1887.

24 *Celtic Times*, 27 November 1887.

25 *Celtic Times*, 16 July 1887.

26 *Celtic Times*, 2 and 30 April 1887.

27 *Celtic Times*, 19 March 1887.

28 Owen McGee, *The IRB* (2005), pp. 164–5.

29 W. F. Mandle, 'The IRB and the Beginnings of the Gaelic Athletic Association', *Irish Historical Studies*, Vol. 20, No. 80 (1977), pp. 418–38, p. 429.

30 *Celtic Times*, 22 October 1887.

31 *Celtic Times*, 13 August 1887.

32 *Celtic Times*, 23 July 1887.

33 *Sport*, 6 June 1887.

34 *Irish Sportsman*, 1 January 1886.

35 *Sport*, 25 September 1886.

36 *Irish Sportsman*, 18 December 1886 and 28 August 1887.

37 *Irish Sportsman*, 28 August 1887.

38 Faugh-a-Ballaghs GAA Club Minute Book, 1885–9.

39 *Sport*, 2 April 1887.

40 *Celtic Times*, 2 April 1887.

41 *Sport*, 2 April 1887.

42 Faugh-a-Ballaghs GAA Club Minute Book, 1885–9.

43 *Celtic Times*, 4 June 1887.

44 *Sport*, 23 April 1887.

45 *Celtic Times*, 23 and 30 April 1887.

7. The Home of Hurling?

1 See, for example, P. P. Sutton writing in *Sport* on 27 October 1886.

2 *Celtic Times*, 19 February 1887.

3 *Celtic Times*, 2 April 1887.

4 *Celtic Times*, 21 May 1887.

5 *Celtic Times*, 23 April 1887.

6 See, for example, Patrick Bracken, *The Growth and Development of Sport in Co. Tipperary, 1840–1880* (De Montfort University PhD Thesis, 2014). See also articles such as Liam Ó Donnchú, 'Hurling in Mid-Tipperary Pre-1884', *Tipperary Historical Journal* (2001), pp. 43–51, and A. T. Lucas, 'Hair Hurling Balls from Limerick and Tipperary', *Journal of the Cork Archaeological and Historical Society* (1971), No. 76, p. 70. Various histories of local GAA clubs in Tipperary also document the story of hurling in Tipperary before the foundation of the GAA. Among these are Daniel Grace, *Portrait of a Parish: Monsea and Killodiernan, Co. Tipperary* (1996). For the wider context, see, for example, Seamus King, *A History of Hurling* (1996); Liam Ó Caithnia, *Scéal na hIomána: Ó Thosach Ama go dtí 1884* (1980); and Art Ó Maolfabhail, *Camán: 2,000 Years of Hurling in Ireland* (1973).

7 See, for example, *Celtic Times*, 23 July 1887. See also Patrick Bracken, *The Growth and Development of Sport in Co. Tipperary, 1840–1880* (De Montfort University Leicester: PhD Thesis, 2014), chapter 6.

8 See, for example, NLI Ms. 9515 for the minutes of the Kilruane Rugby football club from the 1870s. See also Patrick Bracken, *'Foreign and Fantastic Field Sports': Cricket in County Tipperary* (2004).

9 *Tipperary Advocate*, January 1885. Quoted in Nancy Murphy, 'Frank R. Maloney – Nenagh's GAA pioneer', *Tipperary Historical Journal* (1997), pp. 74–82, p. 75.

10 *Sport*, 19 March 1887.

11 *Celtic Times*, 18 June 1887.

12 *Tipperary Advocate*, 15 October 1887.

13 Denis G. Marnane, 'Land and Violence in Nineteenth-Century Tipperary', *Tipperary Historical Journal* (1988), pp. 53–89.

14 *Nenagh Guardian*, 19 February 1887.

15 Gerard Moran, 'The Fenians and Tipperary Politics', *Tipperary Historical Journal* (1994), pp. 73–90.

16 See Nancy Murphy, 'Joseph K. Bracken: GAA Founder, Fenian and Politician', in William Nolan (ed.), *Tipperary: History and Society* (1985), pp. 379–93, p. 380.

17 R. V. Comerford, *Charles J. Kickham: A Study in Irish Nationalism and Literature* (1979).

18 Charles Kickham, *Knocknagow* (1873), pp. 450–3.

19 Donal O'Gorman, 'The Game of Hurling', in William Nolan and William Corbett (eds), *Thurles: The Cathedral Town: Essays in Honour of Archbishop Thomas Morris* (1989), pp. 141–64, p. 146.

20 *Celtic Times*, 12 March 1887.

21 *Sport*, 18 December 1886.

22 Séamus Ó Riain, *Moneygall* (n.d.), p. 5.

23 For an in-depth look at Maloney's career, see Nancy Murphy, 'Frank R. Maloney – Nenagh's GAA pioneer', *Tipperary Historical Journal* (1997), pp. 74–82.

24 See Patrick Bracken, *'Foreign and Fantastic Field Sports': Cricket in County Tipperary* (2004).

25 Nancy Murphy, 'Frank R. Maloney – Nenagh's GAA pioneer', *Tipperary Historical Journal* (1997), pp. 74–82, p. 76.

26 *Celtic Times*, 7 May 1887.

27 *Sport*, 9 July 1887.

28 *Sport*, 9 July 1887.

29 Philip Fogarty, *Tipperary's GAA Story* (1960), p. 23.

30 *Celtic Times*, 21 May 1887.

31 *Tipperary Advocate*, 1 January 1887.

32 *Nenagh Guardian*, 4 June 1887.

33 P. D. Mehigan, *Hurling: Ireland's National Game* (1946), p. 59.

34 See, for example, *Celtic Times*, 26 February and 9 April 1887.

35 *Sport*, 12 February 1887.

36 *Sport*, 24 December 1887.

37 *Celtic Times*, 12 November 1887.

38 *Sport*, 1 January 1887.

39 *Celtic Times*, 14 April 1887.

40 *Sport*, 21 January and 4 February 1888.

41 *Sport*, 12 February 1887.

42 T. F. O'Sullivan, *Story of the GAA* (1916), pp. 18–19.

43 *Celtic Times*, 1 October 1887.

44 *Sport*, 14 January 1888.

45 *Celtic Times*, 2 April 1887.

46 *Tipperary People*, 14 January 1887.

47 *Sport*, 12 February 1887.

48 See Nancy Murphy, 'Joseph K. Bracken: GAA Founder, Fenian and Politician', in William Nolan (ed.), *Tipperary: History and Society* (1985), pp. 379–93, p. 380.

49 NAI CBS 12844/S, Note on J. K. Bracken, 18-12-1896.

50 *Sport*, 20 November 1886.

51 *Tipperary Advocate*, 19 March 1887.

52 *Sport*, 1 January 1887.

53 *Tipperary Advocate*, 5 March 1887.

54 *Celtic Times*, 6 August 1887.

55 *Sport*, 12 February 1887.

56 *Celtic Times*, 16 April and 30 July 1887; *Sport*, 22 October 1887; *Nenagh Guardian*, 21 May 1887.

57 NAI CBS 1360/S, September 1890 and NAI CBS 13114/S, February 1897.

58 Interview with Mícheál Maher, Thurles.

59 See also Philip Fogarty, *Tipperary's GAA Story* (1960), p. 30.

60 *Tipperary Advocate*, 19 March 1887.

61 *Sport*, 5 March 1887.

62 *Sport*, 1 May 1886.

63 Philip Fogarty, *Tipperary's GAA Story* (1960), p. 22.

64 Philip Fogarty, *Tipperary's GAA Story* (1960), p. 21.

65 *Irish Sportsman*, 3 July 1886.

66 *Sport*, 21 May and 27 August 1887.

67 *Sport*, 27 August 1887.

68 *Celtic Times*, 2 April 1887.

69 *Sport*, 2 April 1887.

70 *Celtic Times*, 2 April 1887.

71 *Celtic Times*, 2 April 1887.

72 *Celtic Times*, 2 April 1887.

73 *Sport*, 16 April 1887.

74 *Sport*, 30 April 1887.

75 *Celtic Times*, 21 May 1887; *Sport*, 21 May 1887.

76 *Celtic Times*, 2 July 1887.

77 *Celtic Times*, 16 July 1887.

78 *Sport*, 16 April 1887.

79 *Sport*, 28 February and 5 November 1887.

80 *Sport*, 5 November 1887.

81 W. F. Mandle, 'The IRB and the Beginnings of the Gaelic Athletic Association', in *Irish Historical Studies*, Vol. 20, No. 80 (1977), pp. 413–38, p. 428.

82 *Sport*, 4 June 1887.

83 *Sport*, 13 August 1887.

84 *Celtic Times*, 23 July 1887.

85 *Celtic Times*, 25 June 1887.

86 *Sport*, 30 July 1887.

87 Philip Fogarty, *Tipperary's GAA Story* (1960), p. 28.

88 *Tipperary Advocate*, 30 July 1887; Philip Fogarty, *Tipperary's GAA Story* (1960), pp. 30–1; Seamus King, *A History of the GAA in the North Tipperary Division* (2000), pp. 13–16.

89 *Celtic Times*, 30 July 1887.

90 *Sport*, 13 August 1887.

91 *Sport*, 27 August 1887.

8. Aristocrats and Beginners

1 *Celtic Times*, 12 March 1887.

2 *Sport*, 4 June 1887.

3 *Sport*, 23 July 1887.

4 *Celtic Times*, 29 October 1887.

5 *Tuam News*, 25 November 1887.

6 *Midlands County Advertiser*, 31 March 1887.

7 *Celtic Times*, 19 February 1887.

8 *Sport*, 12 March 1887.

9 See, for example, an article in the *Evening Herald*, 8 March 1965.

10 *Celtic Times*, 23 July 1887. This interpretation is supported in Padraic Ó Laoi, *Annals of the GAA in Galway, Vol. 1, 1884–1901* (1983), pp. 44–6.

11 Sean Spellissy, *The History of Galway* (1999), p. 392.

12 *Western News*, 24 April 1886.

13 *Western News*, 16 April 1887.

14 *Sport*, 5 March 1887.

15 NAI CBS 3/716, box one, B. 122.

16 Hansard, House of Commons, 25 June 1896, Vol. 42, cc. 57–8.

17 Quoted in Laurence M. Geary, *The Plan of Campaign, 1886–1891* (1986), p. 139. See Thomas Brett, *Life of the Most Reverend Dr Patrick Duggan, Bishop of Clonfert* (1921).

18 NAI CBS DICS, Western Division monthly report, September 1889.

19 R. B. McDowell, 'Burgh, Ulick John de, First Marquess of Clanricarde (1802–1874)', *Oxford Dictionary of National Biography* (2004).

20 See L. Perry Curtis, *The Depiction of Eviction in Ireland, 1845–1910* (2011).

21 *Western News*, 28 January 1882.

22 S. L. Gwynn, 'Canning, Hubert George de Burgh, Second Marquess of Clanricarde (1832–1916)', *Oxford Dictionary of National Biography* (2004).

23 *Western News*, 1 and 8 July and 5 August 1882.

24 Laurence M. Geary, *The Plan of Campaign, 1886–1891* (1986), p. 18.

25 *Western News*, 28 October 1887.

26 Seán Ó Riain, *Killimor Hurling Club, 1884–1984* (1984).

27 *Western News*, 14 January 1882 and 8 March 1884.

28 NAI CBS DICS, Western Division monthly report, December 1887.

29 NAI CBS DICS, Western Division monthly report, February 1888.

30 *Western News*, 9 July 1887.

31 NAI CBS DICS, Western Division monthly report, October 1888.

32 NAI CBS DCCI, Report of the Western Division, April 1888.

33 *Western News*, 26 September 1885.

34 *Western News*, 26 February 1887.

35 *Western News*, 19 March 1886.

36 *Western News*, 20 January 1883.

37 *Western News*, 18 February 1882.

38 Meelick GAA Club, *Centenary 1888–1988: First All-Ireland Hurling Final* (1988), p. 5.

39 *Western News*, 5 April 1884.

40 *Western News,* 19 March 1887.

41 *Western News,* 5 April 1884.

42 *Tuam News,* 26 August 1887.

43 See, for example, NAI CBS Western Division monthly report, July 1890.

44 *Western News,* 29 May 1886.

45 *Western News,* 20 November 1886.

46 *Western News,* 4 December 1886.

47 *Western News,* 5 April 1884.

48 *Western News,* 15 January, 5 and 19 February 1887.

49 NAI CBS DICS, Western Division monthly report, November 1887; *Tuam News,* 30 March 1888.

50 *Western News,* 4 June 1887.

51 *Sport,* 14 January 1888.

52 Larry Larkin, 'The Early Days', in Anon. (ed.), *Comóradh an Chéid: Centenary Tribute to the GAA in Wexford* (1984), pp. 11–15, p. 11.

53 *People,* 19 June 1886.

54 *Watchman,* 30 January 1886; see also Sean Whelan, *The Ghosts of Bygone Days: An Enniscorthy GAA History* (1998), pp. 50–1.

55 *Watchman,* 10 October 1885.

56 Sean Whelan, *The Ghosts of Bygone Days: An Enniscorthy GAA History* (1998), pp. 50–1.

57 *Watchman,* 30 January 1886; see also Sean Whelan, *The Ghosts of Bygone Days: An Enniscorthy GAA History* (1998), pp. 50–1.

58 *Watchman,* 6 May 1886.

59 *Watchman,* 8 May 1886.

60 *Enniscorthy News,* 21 August 1886.

61 *People,* 6 November 1886.

62 Larry Larkin, 'The Early Days', in Anon. (ed.), *Comóradh an Chéid: Centenary Tribute to the GAA in Wexford* (1984), pp. 11–15, p. 13.

63 See, for example, *Sport,* 24 December 1886.

64 *People,* 2 July 1887; *Sport,* 14 January 1888.

65 *Sport*, 2 July 1887.

66 *People*, 16 July 1887.

67 *Wexford Independent*, 27 July 1887.

68 *Sport*, 30 July 1887.

69 *People*, 27 July 1887; *Sport*, 30 July 1887; *Celtic Times*, 30 July 1887; *Western News*, 30 July 1887.

70 *Sport*, 19 December 1887.

71 *Tipperary People*, 2 March 1888.

72 *Sport*, 25 February 1888.

73 *Western News*, 30 July 1887; Seán Ó Riain, *Killimor Hurling Club, 1884–1984* (1984).

74 *Western News*, 30 July and 20 August 1887.

9. Match Abandoned

1 *Celtic Times*, 16 April 1887.

2 Tom Ryall, *Kilkenny: The GAA Story 1884–1984* (1984), p. 11. It is also remembered that another football match was also played under GAA rules in Kilkenny that day and that it, too, ended in a scoreless draw.

3 See, for example, *Sport*, 4 December 1886.

4 *Sport*, 5 February 1887.

5 Tom Ryall, *Kilkenny: The GAA Story 1884–1984* (1984), p. 12.

6 Denis Kinsella, *The Mooncoin Story* (1990), pp. 2–3.

7 Antóin Ó Dúill, *Famous Tullaroan* (n.d.), p. 22.

8 Michael O'Dwyer, *The History of Cricket in County Kilkenny: The Forgotten Game* (2006), p. 46.

9 Michael O'Dwyer, *The History of Cricket in County Kilkenny: The Forgotten Game* (2006), p. 52.

10 *Sport*, 12 February 1887.

11 *Kilkenny Moderator*, 2 April 1887.

12 *Kilkenny Journal*, 6 April 1887.

13 *Sport*, 12 March and 9 April 1887.

14 *Kilkenny Journal*, 20 April 1887.

15 *County Tipperary Independent*, 16 April 1887.

16 *Kilkenny Journal*, 20 April 1887.

17 *Sport*, 24 April 1886.

18 *Sport*, 3 July 1886; and see, for example, *Celtic Times*, 2 April 1887.

19 *Celtic Times*, 26 March and 2 April 1887.

20 *Celtic Times*, 23 April 1887.

21 *Celtic Times*, 30 April 1887.

22 *Celtic Times*, 7 May 1887.

23 *Sport*, 24 April 1886.

24 *Cork Constitution*, 14 May 1887; *Celtic Times*, 21 May 1887.

25 *Celtic Times*, 4 June 1887.

26 *Celtic Times*, 2 April 1887. A hurling and football club that existed in the Clonard area of Belfast from 1902 to 1910 was known as Peter O'Neill Crowley Gaelic Athletic Club.

27 *Celtic Times*, 9 July 1887.

28 *Celtic Times*, 4 June 1887.

29 *Cork Herald*, 16 July 1887.

30 John P. Power, *A Story of Champions* (1941), p. 21.

31 Donal O'Sullivan, *Sport in Cork: A History* (2010), p. 15.

32 Newspaper report quoted in Donal O'Sullivan, *Sport in Cork: A History* (2010), p. 7.

33 *Celtic Times*, 16 July 1887.

34 *Cork Herald*, 18 July 1887.

35 *Celtic Times*, 23 July 1887.

36 *Cork Herald*, 21 and 22 July 1887.

37 *Cork Herald*, 21 and 22 July 1887.

38 *Cork Herald*, 23 July 1887.

39 *Cork Herald*, 25 July 1887.

40 *Cork Herald*, 25 July 1887.

41 *United Ireland*, 4 July 1885.

42 *Celtic Times*, 25 June 1887.

43 *Irish Press Golden Jubilee Supplement*, 1934, p. 68. It appears that such an exhibition may have taken place in Waterford city later in 1887, however.

44 Eventually, it was reported that the first Waterford hurling team to take the field was Carrickbeg, who played a challenge match against the Mooncoin reserves in a tournament at Piltown in early November 1887.

45 *Cork Herald*, 25 July 1887; *Kilkenny Journal*, 27 July 1887; *Munster Express*, 30 July 1887.

46 *Cork Herald*, 25 July 1887; *Kilkenny Journal*, 27 July 1887; *Munster Express*, 30 July 1887.

47 *Celtic Times*, 6 August 1887.

10. Death and Resurrection

1 *Sport*, 21 May 1887.

2 *Nenagh Guardian*, 6 and 16 July 1887.

3 *Sport*, 2 July 1887.

4 *Celtic Times*, 23 April 1887.

5 *Sport*, 14 May 1887.

6 *Sport*, 16 July 1887.

7 *Sport*, 30 July 1887.

8 *Celtic Times*, 20 August 1887.

9 Mark Tierney, *Murroe and Boher* (1966), p. 114.

10 Séamus Ó Ceallaigh, *History of the Limerick GAA* (1937), pp. 44–5.

11 Séamus Ó Ceallaigh, *The Mackey Story* (1982), p. 9.

12 *Munster News*, 22 January 1887.

13 *Munster News*, 2 February 1887.

14 *Sport*, 30 October 1886 and 22 January 1887.

15 *Munster News*, 19 January 1887.

16 *Sport*, 30 October 1886.

17 *Munster News*, 16 February 1887.

18 *Sport*, 8 January 1887.

19 *Munster News*, 2 March 1887.

20 *Munster News*, 6 July 1887.

21 *Munster News*, 9 July 1887.

22 *Munster News*, 27 July 1887.

23 *Limerick Chronicle*, 19 July 1887; *Munster News*, 20 July 1887.

24 *Sport*, 3 September 1887; *Celtic Times*, 3 September 1887.

25 *Sport*, 12 February 1887.

26 *Sport*, 5 May 1888. Such was the strength of following for each committee in 1888 that the GAA's Central Executive refused to choose between them and, instead, ordered that the winners of each of the rival championships should play off, with the winners going on to represent Limerick in the All-Ireland championships.

27 *Nenagh Guardian*, 17 September 1887.

28 Seán Kierse, *History of Smith O'Brien GAA Club, Killaloe, 1886–1987* (1991), pp. 39–40.

29 Seán Kierse, *History of Smith O'Brien GAA Club, Killaloe, 1886–1987* (1991), pp. 44–5.

30 *Sport*, 2 April 1887.

31 *Celtic Times*, 9 April 1887.

32 *Munster News*, 14 May 1887.

33 *Sport*, 30 October 1886.

34 Seán Kierse, *History of Smith O'Brien GAA Club, Killaloe, 1886–1987* (1991), pp. 45–61.

35 *Munster News*, 14 May 1887.

36 After something of a settlement was agreed for a time, the disputes later resurfaced in the 1890s when there were more

evictions, while cattle belonging to Colonel O'Callaghan were poisoned. Eventually, in 1909 the Land Commission acquired the land compulsorily and tenants were able to purchase their farms. The entire event was reported vividly in the national and international press.

37 *Clare Champion*, 26 March 1887.

38 *Clare Examiner*, 29 May 1887.

39 *Clare Journal*, 20 June 1887.

40 Seán Kierse, *History of Smith O'Brien GAA Club, Killaloe, 1886–1987* (1991), pp. 45–61.

41 *Sport*, 23 July 1887.

42 Seán Kierse, *History of Smith O'Brien GAA Club, Killaloe, 1886–1987* (1991), pp. 65–71. Kierse's study of the players of this club is a superb piece of work.

43 *Celtic Times*, 1 October 1887.

44 *Nenagh Guardian*, 26 October 1887; *Munster Express*, 29 October 1887.

45 *Kilkenny Moderator*, 3 September 1887.

46 Philip Fogarty, *Tipperary's GAA Story* (1960), p. 30.

47 *Sport*, 29 October 1887.

48 *Nenagh Guardian*, 29 October 1887. I would like to thank Tom and Nancy Murphy for sending me this newspaper cutting.

49 *Celtic Times*, 5 November 1887.

50 *Celtic Times*, 29 October 1887.

11. Gunfire in Hayes' Hotel

1 NAI CBS 3/716/Box 1, Report of Secret Societies, 4 October 1882.

2 W. F. Mandle, *The Gaelic Athletic Association and Irish Nationalist Politics, 1884–1925* (1987), p. 43.

3 NAI CBS 3/716/Box 1, Report of Secret Societies, 4 October 1882.

4 NAI CBS South-Eastern Division, monthly reports, July–September 1887.

5 NAI CBS 126/S, Maurice O'Halloran letter, 9 November 1887.

6 NAI CBS 296/S, Report 14 April 1890; see also NAI CBS 126/S, Secret Report, 12 April 1890 and NAI CBS Midlands, monthly reports, October 1889.

7 NAI CBS 126/S, Secret Report, 12 April 1890.

8 NAI CBS South-Eastern Division, monthly reports, July–September 1887.

9 *Celtic Times*, 5 and 26 March 1887.

10 *Celtic Times*, 8 October 1887.

11 *Celtic Times*, 14 April 1887.

12 *Celtic Times*, 11 June 1887; *Sport*, 11 June 1887.

13 W. F. Mandle, 'The IRB and the Beginnings of the Gaelic Athletic Association', *Irish Historical Studies*, Vol. 20, No. 80 (1977), pp. 418–38, p. 429.

14 See Éarnan P. de Blaghad, 'Cold War in Dublin GAA, 1887', in *Dublin Historical Record*, Vol. 22, No. 3 (Oct 1968), pp. 252–62.

15 *Sport*, 27 August 1887.

16 Faugh-a-Ballaghs GAA Club Minute Book, 1885–9.

17 *County Tipperary Independent*, 15 October 1887.

18 *Celtic Times*, 22 October 1887.

19 *Celtic Times*, 23 July 1887.

20 *Celtic Times*, 24 September 1887.

21 *Celtic Times*, 4 June 1887.

22 *Celtic Times*, 15 October and 5 November 1887.

23 W. F. Mandle, 'The IRB and the Beginnings of the Gaelic Athletic Association', *Irish Historical Studies*, Vol. 20, No. 80 (1977), pp. 418–38, p. 432.

24 *Celtic Times*, 12 November 1887.

25 W. F. Mandle, 'The IRB and the Beginnings of the Gaelic Athletic Association', *Irish Historical Studies*, Vol. 20, No. 80 (1977), pp. 418–38, p. 432.

26 W. F. Mandle, *The Gaelic Athletic Association and Irish Nationalist Politics, 1884–1924* (1987), pp. 43–4.

27 *Celtic Times*, 12 November 1887.

28 *Celtic Times*, 12 November 1887; *Sport*, 12 November 1887.

29 *Sport*, 12 November 1887.

30 *Celtic Times*, 12 November 1887.

31 *Sport*, 12 November 1887.

32 NAI CBS, 126/S, South-Eastern Division Reports, November and December 1887. See also W. F. Mandle, *The Gaelic Athletic Association and Irish Nationalist Politics, 1884–1924* (1987), pp. 50–1.

33 NAI CBS, 126/S, Secret Report, 11 November 1887.

34 W. F. Mandle, *The Gaelic Athletic Association and Irish Nationalist Politics, 1884–1924* (1987), p. 53. This account of the events of the annual convention is taken from a range of local and national newspapers, primarily drawing on *Sport*, 12 November 1887, and *Celtic Times*, 12 November 1887.

35 *Sport*, 12 November 1887.

36 *Celtic Times*, 12 November 1887.

37 *Sport*, 12 November 1887.

38 *Freeman's Journal*, 14 November 1887.

39 W. F. Mandle, *The Gaelic Athletic Association and Irish Nationalist Politics, 1884–1924* (1987), p. 62.

40 *Celtic Times*, 19 November 1887.

41 W. F. Mandle, *The Gaelic Athletic Association and Irish Nationalist Politics, 1884–1924* (1987), p. 59.

42 *Sport*, 26 November 1887.

43 W. F. Mandle, *The Gaelic Athletic Association and Irish Nationalist Politics, 1884–1924* (1987), p. 63.

44 *Celtic Times*, 3 December 1887.

45 W. F. Mandle, *The Gaelic Athletic Association and Irish Nationalist Politics, 1884–1924* (1987), pp. 60–1.

46 *Sport*, 3 December 1887.

47 W. F. Mandle, *The Gaelic Athletic Association and Irish Nationalist Politics, 1884–1924* (1987), pp. 60–1.

48 *Sport*, 10 December 1887.

49 NAI CBS DICS, South-Eastern Division monthly report, December 1887.

50 W. F. Mandle, *The Gaelic Athletic Association and Irish Nationalist Politics, 1884–1924* (1987), p. 4.

51 *Sport*, 7 January 1888; *Gael*, 7 January 1888.

52 *Sport*, 7 January 1888.

12. The First All-Ireland Hurling Final

1 *King's County Chronicle*, 29 March 1888.

2 *Nenagh Guardian*, 4 June 1887.

3 *Midland Tribune*, 5 April 1888.

4 *King's County Chronicle*, 29 March 1888.

5 *Midland Tribune*, 9 February 1888.

6 *Midland Tribune*, 16 February 1888.

7 *Nenagh Guardian*, 10 September 1887.

8 *King's County Chronicle*, 30 August 1888.

9 *King's County Chronicle*, 12 July 1888.

10 *King's County Chronicle*, 5 April 1888; *Midland Tribune*, 5 April 1888.

11 *King's County Chronicle*, 10 May 1888.

12 *Midland Tribune*, 19 January 1888.

13 *Midland Tribune*, 8 March 1888.

14 See, for example, reports on tournaments carried by the national and local press in July and September 1887, and in February and March 1888.

15 *Midland Tribune*, 8 March 1888.

16 P. D. Mehigan, 'Carbery', *Carbery's Annual 1948–9* (1948), p. 21; P. D. Mehigan, ed. Sean Kilfeather, *Vintage Carbery* (1984), pp. 59–62.

17 NAI CBS DICS, Western Division monthly reports, March 1888.

18 *Tuam News*, 16 December 1887.

19 See, for example, *Western News*, 5 March and 20 August 1887.

20 *Evening Herald*, 8 March 1965.

21 Seán Ó Riain, *Killimor Hurling Club, 1884–1984* (1984).

22 P. D. Mehigan, 'Carbery', *Carbery's Annual 1948–9* (1948), p. 21; P. D. Mehigan, ed. Sean Kilfeather, *Vintage Carbery* (1984), pp. 59–62.

23 Meelick GAA Club, *Centenary 1888–1988: First All-Ireland Hurling Final* (1988), pp. 16–17. McIntyre's brake, which was used to bring the Meelick players to the match, remained in use around the Banagher area for several decades after the final. Even after McIntyre's Hotel was converted into a private house for Michael Healy and his family, the brake was kept in storage in a back shed.

24 Paul O'Donnell, *The GAA in Mullagh 1884–1887* (n.d.), p. 4.

25 Meelick GAA Club, *Centenary 1888–1988: First All-Ireland Hurling Final* (1988), pp. 16–17.

26 *Midland Tribune*, 5 April 1888.

27 I owe a huge debt of gratitude to the late Micheál Maher, the nephew of Denis 'Long Dinny' Maher, for his help and information on this section.

28 *Tipperary Star*, 25 January 1913.

29 *Sport*, 7 April 1888.

30 *Sport*, 7 April 1888.

31 *Evening Herald*, 8 March 1965.

32 *Midland Tribune*, 5 April 1888.

33 *Sport*, 7 April 1888.

34 *Midland Tribune*, 5 April 1888.

35 *Sport*, 7 April 1888.

36 P. D. Mehigan, 'Carbery', *Carbery's Annual 1948–9* (1948), p. 21; P. D. Mehigan, ed. Sean Kilfeather, *Vintage Carbery* (1984), pp. 59–62.

37 *Sport*, 7 April 1888.

38 *King's County Chronicle*, 29 March 1888.

39 *Midland Tribune*, 5 April 1888.

40 Donal Shanahan, *Toomevara GAA* (n.d.), p. 163.

41 *Celtic Times*, 26 November 1887.

42 *Sport*, 7 April 1888; *Midland Tribune*, 5 April 1888.

43 *Midland Tribune*, 5 April 1888.

44 *Sport*, 7 April 1888.

45 *Evening Herald*, 8 March 1965; *Midland Tribune*, 5 April 1888.

46 Paul O'Donnell, *The GAA in Mullagh 1884–1887* (n.d.), p. 5.

47 *Our Boys (1982/1983)*, p. 9.

48 P. D. Mehigan, 'Carbery', *Carbery's Annual 1948–9* (1948), p. 21; P. D. Mehigan, ed. Sean Kilfeather, *Vintage Carbery* (1984), pp. 59–62.

49 *Midland Tribune*, 5 April 1888.

50 Meelick GAA Club, *Centenary 1888–1988: First All-Ireland Hurling Final* (1988), p. 18.

51 *Evening Herald*, 8 March 1965.

52 Raymond Smith, *A Complete Handbook of Gaelic Games* (2006).

53 *Sport*, 7 April 1888.

54 *King's County Chronicle*, 19 April 1888.

55 *King's County Chronicle*, 19 April 1888.

56 *Midland Tribune*, 19 April 1888.

57 *King's County Chronicle*, 5 April 1888. Three weeks after the All-Ireland final, St Brendan's Hurling club wrote to the *Midland Tribune* to express their thanks to Johnny Farrell for

the gift of his field for the All-Ireland championship final and the King's County championship matches, 'knowing such was in compliment to the members of this club and for the furtherance of the Gaelic movement'. It does not appear that the field was used much after that for hurling, and later it became known locally as Hoare's Field. It is now the site of a branch of Tesco.

13. The Future

1 *Sport*, 7 April 1888.
2 *Sport*, 29 October 1887.
3 *Sport*, 5 May 1888.
4 *Sport*, 5 May 1888.
5 Ollie Byrnes, *Around the Square: The Story of Ennis Hurling* (2003), p. 11; *Sport*, 14 January 1888.
6 See, for example, *Sport*, 22 January 1887.
7 *Celtic Times*, 30 April 1887.
8 *Sport*, 5 May 1888. In the years immediately after the founding of the GAA, Irish cricket, lacrosse and athletics teams had travelled to America and Canada. See, for example, *Sport*, 18 November 1885, 11 April 1886 and 11 February 1888.
9 *Sport*, 5 May 1888.
10 Pat Davin, *Recollections of a Veteran Irish Athlete* (1938), p. 27.
11 Pat Davin, *Recollections of a Veteran Irish Athlete* (1938), p. 24
12 Faugh-a-Ballaghs GAA Club Minute Book, 1885–9.
13 Pat Davin, *Recollections of a Veteran Irish Athlete* (1938), p. 26.
14 Pat Davin, *Recollections of a Veteran Irish Athlete* (1938), pp. 23–34.
15 Séamus Ó Riain, *Maurice Davin (1842–1927): First President of the GAA* (1993), p. 60.
16 *Irish Times*, 26 June 1889.

17 W. F. Mandle, *The Gaelic Athletic Association and Irish Nationalist Politics* (1987), pp. 77–9; NAI CBS DCIS, Monthly Report Western Division, May 1891.

18 See Séamus de Vál, 'Patrick Prendergast Sutton (1865–1901)', *Uí Cinsealaigh Historical Society*, No. 16 (1988), pp. 53–8, p. 56.

19 *United Ireland*, 25 July 1891.

20 *Limerick Leader*, 7 April 1890.

21 See W. F. Mandle, *The Gaelic Athletic Association and Irish Nationalist Politics, 1884–1924* (1987).

22 *Irish Sportsman*, 7 April 1888.

23 Marcus de Búrca, *Michael Cusack and the GAA* (1989), p. 173.

24 John Cusack undated notes on Cusack family history, NUIG Archives, Michael Cusack File; Seán McNamara, *The Man from Carron* (2005), pp. 72–3; Marcus de Búrca, *Michael Cusack and the GAA* (1989), p. 173.

25 *Irish Times*, 13 June 1903.

26 *Irish Weekly Independent and Nation*, 13 December 1902. See also *United Ireland*, 4, 11, 18 and 25 March and 29 April 1899.

27 *Irish Weekly Independent and Nation*, 13 December 1902.

28 *Irish Weekly Independent and Nation*, 13 December 1902; *United Ireland*, 4 March 1899.

29 P. D. Mehigan, 'Carbery', *Gaelic Football* (1941), p. 121.

30 Seán McNamara, *The Man from Carron* (2005), p. 43.

31 Seán McNamara, *The Man from Carron* (2005), p. 16.

32 NAI census returns, 1911. The return for 11 Goldsmith Street, Dublin, shows the presence of the only Frank Cusack then living in Dublin.

33 James Hardiman Library, NUIG, Special Collections, Michael Cusack Papers, note, n.d.

34 See Séamus de Vál, 'Patrick Prendergast Sutton (1865–1901)', *Uí Cinsealaigh Historical Society*, No. 16 (1988), pp. 53–8, p. 56.

35 *Sport*, 25 June 1887.

36 *Celtic Times*, 24 December 1887.

37 'Sceilg', '*An Camán*', in Séamus Ó Ceallaigh, *Gaelic Athletic Memories* (1946), p. 11.

38 *Sport*, 24 September 1887.

39 *Sport*, 30 July 1887.

40 See Séamus de Vál, 'Patrick Prendergast Sutton (1865–1901)', *Uí Cinsealaigh Historical Society*, No. 16 (1988), pp. 53–8, p. 56.

41 *Sport*, 30 July 1887.

42 NAI CBS DICS, Western Division Monthly Reports, August 1890.

43 NAI CBS DICS, Western Division Monthly Reports, January 1894.

44 Meelick GAA Club, *Centenary 1888–1988: First All-Ireland Hurling Final* (1988), pp. 15–16.

45 *Freeman's Journal*, 2 February 1998.

46 *Evening Herald*, 8 March 1965. The Meelick club was revived around 1920 and lasted a couple of years before folding again. It was revived a second time in the early 1930s and reached an East Galway junior final, where it was beaten by Portumna. It lapsed again and was re-formed once more in 1939, only to be beaten in that year's East Galway junior final by Loughrea.

47 Later, in the 1930s, the hurlers from Smith O'Briens who remained living in East Clare were gathered for a photograph.

48 The GAA's annual convention in 1911 had passed a resolution agreeing that medals should finally be provided for the 1887 Thurles team, as well as for Limerick Commercials as 1887 All-Ireland football champions.

49 *Tipperary Star*, 25 January 1913.

50 See P. D. Mehigan, 'Carbery', *Carbery's Annual 1948–9* (1948), p. 21; P. D. Mehigan, ed. Sean Kilfeather, *Vintage Carbery* (1984), pp. 59–62.

51 *Irish Times*, 22 December 1882.

Acknowledgements

I owe a huge debt to many people who have helped with this project over the years. Without that help, it would never have been completed. I would like to thank everybody who read part or all of this book and gave such time and consideration to their comments: Seán Kearns, Rónán O'Brien, Cathal Billings, Caitríona Lally, Cian Ferriter, Mark Duncan, Pat Bracken, Tom Hunt, Leanne Blaney, Tom Butler, Brian Casey, William Murphy and Kevin Lee.

By a fine stroke of luck I discovered that the eminent Irish-American historian the late Professor Emmet Larkin was a grandson of a man who played in the first All-Ireland final, and he was also extremely generous with his comments on the text.

I would like to thank the following for their help with the research: Liam and Ann-Marie Fleury, the late Mícheál Maher (Thurles), Mike Lynch (Meelick), the late Dónal Curtin, Clodagh Doyle, Mike Cronin, the late Séamus Ó Riain, Pádraig Rooney, the late Ann Coughlan, Liam Ó Donnchú, Willie Nolan, Mary Daly, Seamus Leahy, Pat Leahy, Seamus Kelly, Dónal McAnallen and Nancy Murphy.

I am extremely grateful for the assistance of the staff of the following institutions: Offaly County Library in Tullamore, Birr Library, Thurles Library, Kilkenny County Library, Wexford County Library, Limerick County Library, Clare County Library, Cork City Libraries, the Dublin City Archive and Public Library, the National Library of Ireland, University College Dublin Library, the National Folklore Collection at University College

Dublin, the James Hardiman Library at NUIG, the British Library, Offaly Historical and Archaeological Society, Trinity College Dublin Archives, the GAA Museum and Archives, the IRFU Archives, the *Irish Examiner* and Boston College.

Thank you to everybody at Penguin Ireland, particularly Brendan Barrington.

Thank you to my colleagues and students in the School of History and in the College of Arts and Humanities in University College Dublin.

Thank you to my teachers at Durrow National School and Tullamore CBS (now Coláiste Choilm, Tullamore), and to everyone at Tullamore GAA Club, St Oliver Plunkett Eoghan Ruadh GAA Club in Dublin and UCD GAA Club.

Finally, this book is dedicated with love to my children Cáit, Éilis and Joe. I thank them for everything they have given me. For that, too, I would like also to thank Nuala. And I would like to thank my parents, my brothers and my extended family.

Select Bibliography

Primary Sources

i. Manuscripts

GAA Museum and Archives
Central Council Minutes, 1899–
Maurice Davin Collection

Irish Rugby Football Union Archives
Council Minute Books, 1874–
Irish Champion Athletic Club minute book

Limerick County Library
Séamus Ó Ceallaigh papers

National Archives of Ireland
Census Returns, 1901–1911
Crime Special Branch Papers
Fenian Papers

National Folklore Collection, University College Dublin
Iml. 629, Iml. 888–91, Iml. 921 and Iml. 1747

National Library of Ireland
Ms. 5605: Gaelic Union Papers
Ms. 8723: P. D. Mehigan Papers
Ms. 15385, T. F. O'Sullivan Papers

National University of Ireland, Galway
Michael Cusack Papers

Private Ownership
Faughs GAA Club Minute Books
Seamus King Notes and Manuscript on Hurling in South-
East Galway

Trinity College Dublin Archives
Dublin University Boat Club Collection
Ms. 2639: Charles Barrington Letter
Ms. 2255–7: Minute Book of the University Foot-Races

ii. Newspapers, Magazines and Periodicals

Advocate (Melbourne)
Age (Melbourne)
Boston Globe
Celtic Times
Clare Examiner
Clare Journal
Cork Constitution
Cork Examiner
Cork Herald
County Tipperary Independent
Enniscorthy News
Evening Herald
Evening Telegraph
Freeman's Journal
Gael
Galway Express
Galway Vindicator
Gorey Correspondent
Independent (Ennis and Limerick)
Irish Press Golden Jubilee Supplement

Irish Sportsman
Irish Times
Irish Weekly Independent and Nation
Kildare Observer
Kilkenny Journal
Kilkenny Moderator
King's County Chronicle
Limerick Chronicle
Limerick Reporter
Midland Counties Advertiser
Midland Tribune
Munster Express
Munster News
Nenagh Guardian
Our Boys
Shamrock
Shan Van Vocht
Sport
The Times (London)
Tipperary Advocate
Tipperary Leader
Tipperary People
Tipperary Star
Tuam Herald
Tuam News
United Ireland
United Irishman
Watchman
Waterford Citizen
Waterford Mail
Western News and Star
Wexford Independent
Wexford and Kilkenny Express
Wexford People
Wichita Daily Eagle (Kansas)

iii. Official Publications

Hansard, House of Commons Reports

iv. Theses

Cathal Billings, *Athbheochan na Gaeilge agus an Spórt in Éirinn, 1884–1934* (UCD: PhD Thesis, 2015)

Patrick Bracken, *The Growth and Development of Sport in Co. Tipperary, 1840–1880* (De Montfort University Leicester: PhD Thesis, 2014)

Paul Rouse, *Sport and the Politics of Culture: A History of the GAA Ban, 1884–1971* (UCD: MA Thesis, 1992)

Eoin Ryan, *Blaming Parnell: Accounting for the Decline of the GAA, 1889–1894* (UCD: MA Thesis, 2013)

Secondary Sources

i. Journal Articles and Book Chapters

Patrick Bracken, 'The Emergence of Hurling in Australia, 1877–1917', *Sport in Society*, Vol. 19, No. 1 (2016), pp. 62–73

'Celt' (P. J. Devlin), 'The Founder of the GAA', *An Gaedheal Óg* (1923), pp. 7–9

R. V. Comerford, 'Patriotism as Pastime: The Appeal of Fenianism in the Mid-1860s', in Alan O'Day (ed.), *Reactions to Irish Nationalism, 1865–1914* (1987), pp. 21–32

Mike Cronin, 'Fighting for Ireland, playing for England? The nationalist history of the Gaelic Athletic Association and the English influence on Irish sport', *International Journal of the History of Sport*, Vol. 15, No. 3 (1998), pp. 36–56

L. P. Curtis, Jr, 'Stopping the Hunt, 1881–1882: An Aspect of the Irish Land War', in C. E. Philpin (ed.), *Nationalism and Popular Protest in Ireland* (1987), pp. 349–402

Michael Cusack, 'The Rise of the Gaelic Athletic Association', *Shan Van Vocht*, Vol. 2 (1897), pp. 147–8

Éarnan P. de Blaghad, 'Cold War in Dublin GAA, 1887', *Dublin Historical Record*, Vol. 22, No. 3 (Oct 1968), pp. 252–62

Séamus de Vál, 'Patrick Prendergast Sutton (1865–1901)', *Uí Cinsealaigh Historical Society*, No. 16 (1988), pp. 53–8

Paddy Dolan and John Connolly, 'The Civilizing of Hurling in Ireland', *Sport in Society*, Vol. 12, No. 2 (2009), pp. 196–211

Neal Garnham, 'Accounting for the Early Success of the Gaelic Athletic Association', *Irish Historical Studies*, Vol. 34 (2004), pp. 65–78

S. L. Gwynn, 'Canning, Hubert George de Burgh, Second Marquess of Clanricarde (1832–1916)', in *Oxford Dictionary of National Biography* (2004)

Larry Larkin, 'The Early Days', in Anon. (ed.), *Comóradh an Chéid: Centenary Tribute to the GAA in Wexford* (1984), pp. 11–15

A. T. Lucas, 'Hair Hurling Balls from Limerick and Tipperary', *Journal of the Cork Archaeological and Historical Society* (1971), p. 70

R. B. McDowell, 'Burgh, Ulick John de, First Marquess of Clanricarde (1802–1874)', in *Oxford Dictionary of National Biography* (2004)

W. F. Mandle, 'The IRB and the Beginnings of the Gaelic Athletic Association', *Irish Historical Studies*, Vol. 20, No. 80 (1977), pp. 418–38

Denis G. Marnane, 'Land and Violence in Nineteenth-Century Tipperary', *Tipperary Historical Journal* (1988), pp. 53–89

Gerard Moran, 'The Fenians and Tipperary Politics', *Tipperary Historical Journal* (1994), pp. 73–90

Nancy Murphy, 'Frank R. Maloney – Nenagh's GAA Pioneer', *Tipperary Historical Journal* (1997), pp. 74–82

Nancy Murphy, 'Joseph K. Bracken: GAA Founder, Fenian and Politician', in William Nolan (ed.), *Tipperary: History and Society* (1985), pp. 379–93

Liam Ó Donnchú, 'Hurling in Mid-Tipperary Pre-1884', *Tipperary Historical Journal* (2001), pp. 43–51

Donal O'Gorman, 'The Game of Hurling', in William Nolan and William Corbett (eds), *Thurles: The Cathedral Town: Essays in Honour of Archbishop Thomas Morris* (1989), pp. 141–64

Art Ó Maolfabhail, 'Hurling: An Old Game in a New World', in Grant Jarvie (ed.), *Sport in the Making of Celtic Cultures* (1999), pp. 149–65

Art Ó Maolfabhail, Roddy Hegarty and Dónal McAnallen, 'From Cú Chulainn to Cusack: Ball-playing, camán, shinny and hurling in Ulster before the GAA', in Dónal McAnallen, David Hassan and Roddy Hegarty (eds), *The Evolution of the GAA: Ulaidh, Éire and Eile* (2009), pp. 62–78

Paul Rouse, 'The Politics of Culture and Sport in Ireland: A History of the GAA Ban on Foreign Games 1884–1971. Part One: 1884–1924', *International Journal of the History of Sport*, Vol. 10, No. 3 (1990), pp. 333–60

—'Michael Cusack: Sportsman and Journalist', in Mike Cronin, William Murphy and Paul Rouse (eds), *The Gaelic Athletic Association, 1884–2009* (2009), pp. 47–61

J. M. Tobin, 'Who was Present at the Founding Meeting of the GAA at Thurles in 1884?', *History Ireland*, Vol. 23, No. 5 (Sept/Oct 2015), pp. 32–4

ii. Books

Anon., *Gaelic Union for the Preservation and Cultivation of the Irish Language* (1882)

Anon., *Sixty Glorious Years: The Authentic Story of the GAA* (1946)

Alan Bairner (ed.), *Sport and the Irish* (2005)

John Boyle O'Reilly, *Athletics and Manly Sport* (1890)

Patrick Bracken, *'Foreign and Fantastic Field Sports': Cricket in County Tipperary* (2004)

Thomas Brett, *Life of the Most Reverend Dr Patrick Duggan, Bishop of Clonfert* (1921)

Ollie Byrnes, *Around the Square: The Story of Ennis Hurling* (2003)

R. V. Comerford, *Charles J. Kickham: A Study in Irish Nationalism and Literature* (1979)

Mike Cronin, *Sport and Nationalism in Ireland* (1999)

Conor Curran, *Sport in Donegal: A History* (2010)

—*The Development of Sport in Donegal, 1880–1935* (2015)

L. Perry Curtis, *The Depiction of Eviction in Ireland, 1845–1910* (2011)

T. S. C. Dagg, *Hockey in Ireland* (1944)

Pat Davin, *Recollections of a Veteran Irish Athlete* (1938)

Marcus de Búrca, *Michael Cusack and the GAA* (1989)

—*The GAA: A History* (1999)

Philip Fogarty, *Tipperary's GAA Story* (1960)

Laurence M. Geary, *The Plan of Campaign, 1886–1891* (1986)

Daniel Grace, *Portrait of a Parish: Monsea and Killodiernan, Co. Tipperary* (1996)

Christy and Maeve Kearns, *The History of the GAA in Meelick–Eyrecourt–Clonfert: 1884–2007* (2007)

Charles Kickham, *Knocknagow* (1873)

Seán Kierse, *History of Smith O'Brien GAA Club, Killaloe, 1886–1987* (1991)

Seamus King, *A History of Hurling* (1996)

Seamus King, *A History of the GAA in the North Tipperary Division* (2000)

Denis Kinsella, *The Mooncoin Story* (1990)

John Lawrence, *Handbook of Cricket in Ireland* (1877–8)

Peter Lovesey, *The Official Centenary History of the Amateur Athletic Association* (1981)

F. S. L. Lyons, *Culture and Anarchy, 1890–1939* (1979)

Catherine McCullough and W. H. Crawford, *Irish Historic Towns Atlas No. 18, Armagh* (2007)

Owen McGee, *The IRB* (2005)

Seán McNamara, *The Man from Carron* (2005)

Elizabeth Malcolm, *'Ireland Sober, Ireland Free': Drink and Temperance in Nineteenth-century Ireland* (1986)

W. F. Mandle, *The Gaelic Athletic Association and Irish Nationalist Politics, 1884–1924* (1987)

Meelick GAA Club, *Centenary 1888–1988: First All-Ireland Hurling Final* (1988)

P. D. Mehigan, 'Carbery', *Carbery's Annual 1948–9* (1948)

—*Gaelic Football* (1941)

—*Hurling: Ireland's National Game* (1946)

—(ed. Sean Kilfeather), *Vintage Carbery* (1984)

William Nolan (ed.), *The Gaelic Athletic Association in Dublin 1884–2000*, Vols 1–3 (2005)

Liam Ó Caithnia, *Báirí Cos in Éirinn* (1984)

—*Scéal na hIomána: ó Thosach Ama go dtí 1884* (1980)
—*Mícheál Cíosóg* (1982)
Séamus Ó Ceallaigh, *Gaelic Athletic Memories* (1946)
—*History of the Limerick GAA* (1937)
—*The Mackey Story* (1982)
Liam Ó Donnchú, *Thurles Sarsfields GAA Story Volume 1* (2017)
Paul O'Donnell, *The GAA in Mullagh 1884–1887* (n.d.)
Tony O'Donoghue, *Irish Championship Athletics 1873–1914* (2005)
—*The Arravale Rovers Story: The GAA in the Parish of Tipperary* (1995)
Antóin Ó Dúill, *Famous Tullaroan* (n.d.)
Michael O'Dwyer, *The History of Cricket in County Kilkenny: The Forgotten Game* (2006)
T. K. O'Dwyer and Jimmy Fogarty (eds), *The Moycarkey–Borris GAA Story* (n.d.)
Padraic Ó Laoi, *Annals of the GAA in Galway,* Vol. 1, *1884–1901* (1983)
Art Ó Maolfabhail, *Camán: 2,000 Years of Irish Hurling* (1973)
Séamus Ó Riain, *Maurice Davin (1842–1927): First President of the GAA* (1993)
—*Moneygall* (n.d.)
Seán Ó Riain, *Killimor Hurling Club, 1884–1984* (1984)
Donal O'Sullivan, *Sport in Cork: A History* (2010)
T. F. O'Sullivan, *Story of the GAA* (1916)
R. M. Peter (ed.), *The Irish Football Annual* (1880)
John P. Power, *A Story of Champions* (1941)
Pádraig Puirséal, *The GAA in its Time* (1982)
Paul Rouse, *Sport and Ireland: A History* (2015)
Paul Rouse, Mike Cronin and Mark Duncan, *The GAA: A People's History* (2009)
Tom Ryall, *Kilkenny: The GAA Story 1884–1984* (1984)
Donal Shanahan, *Toomevara GAA* (n.d.)
Raymond Smith, *A Complete Handbook of Gaelic Games* (2006)
Jimmy Smyth, *In Praise of Heroes: Ballads and Poems of the GAA* (2007)
Sean Spellissy, *The History of Galway* (1999)
Mark Tierney, *Murroe and Boher* (1966)
Sean Whelan, *The Ghosts of Bygone Days: An Enniscorthy GAA History* (1998)

Picture Credits

1   a. National University of Ireland, Galway
    b. National University of Ireland, Galway

2   a. Dublin University Archives

3   a. National Library of Ireland
    b. National Library of Ireland

4   a. GAA Museum

5   a. National University of Ireland, Galway

6   a. National Library of Ireland
    b. National Library of Ireland

7   a. Open source
    b. National Archives of Ireland

8   a. Liam and Anne Marie Fleury, private collection
    b. National Archives of Ireland
    c. Courtesy of the late Seamus Ó Riain

Index